MEASURE OF A LIFE

MEMOIRS, INSIGHTS AND PHILOSOPHIES OF

LEROY E. HOFFBERGER

DEDICATION

My father, Jacob (of blessed memory), whose commitment and devotion to our Family, his work and his friends instilled in me a drive to follow in his footsteps.

My mother, Mildred (of blessed memory), whose love and guidance were the foundation for my desire to learn and my ability to enjoy things academic and cultural.

Rabbi David Fohrman, whose unique method of teaching Scripture gave rise to my faith in G-d and my belief in the Torah (Pentateuch).

This work is a memoir. It reflects
my present recollections of
my experiences and interaction
with people over a period of years.
Dialogue and events have been
recreated from memory and, in
some cases, have been compressed
to convey the substance of
what I recall was said or occurred.
The views and opinions
expressed are mine alone.

Roy

CONTENTS

PROLOGUE

It is fair to state that my initial reason for writing these memoirs was merely to test my long-term memory – to find out how well I, at age 83, could remember those people, events and decisions that have shaped my life. With my short-term memory getting progressively worse, I wanted to discover if my long-term memory was still intact and to what extent I could jog it to unearth facts and names that I had not thought about for over half a century.

I have done this with more success than I anticipated. However, perhaps like the life I am recalling, this is still a work in progress. Names I've not spoken for years have clicked into consciousness as I've been driving, showering or using the old method of going through the alphabet. I have not sought to obtain information by actually going to my legal or personal files; that would have undermined my memory-testing experiment.

However, what I did do on occasion, to establish the chronology of an event in my life, was to relate it to some public occurrence that took place at about the same time. By "googling" the public occurrence, I could approximate the date I was searching for.

After I began writing these memoirs, I thought that if I completed this task I would put these pages into a book with photos for my grandchildren and great-grandchildren, who one day might want to know a little about me and their Hoffberger roots. This possibility caused me to think about what such a book would really tell them about myself. It would set forth what had happened to me and what I had accomplished, but would it really tell them who I was?

Pondering this, and since for some time I have asked myself what my life has been all about, I decided that, in addition to testing my memory, this could be an opportunity to record my thoughts about why I believe I was put on earth by G-d. In the beginning of the morning prayers we religious Jews recite the following blessing:

Blessed art thou Lord our G-d, King of the Universe, who guides us on our path.

I understand this to mean that we are asking G-d to assist us in the fulfillment of the divine purpose for which we were born. I hope that when I am finished with this book, I will have an insight into my "raison d'être."

"Tree of Life," working drawing by Gustav Klimt for the mosaic of the Palais Stoclet Frieze in Brussels. It has been given numerous interpretations, one of which is its fruit-laden branches depict a source of life. In Hebrew Scripture (Proverb 3:18) The Torah (Hebrew Bible) is referred to as "...a tree of life for those who grasp it and all who uphold it are blessed."

© MAK-Austrian Museum of Applied Arts/ Contemporary Art

If I receive this insight, then I would like to, subjectively of course, determine how well I did at fulfilling my purpose here. I believe that G-d bestowed upon each of us certain capabilities and the ability to exercise "free will" in using our talents to pursue our destiny. Rabbi Fohrman, my friend and religious teacher, likens our G-d-given abilities and limitations to a hand of cards. Some hands are good and some are problematic. We can do little about the cards we are dealt, but, according to Rabbi Fohrman, with whom I agree, it is how we play the cards we are given that really counts. Using that as a measure, I must ask myself how well I played my hand to fulfill the purpose G-d intended.

Fortunately, I was born physically healthy, capable of performing most tasks required to live a full and productive life. I also believe that I was endowed with sufficient "gray matter" to succeed at most tasks that I desired to undertake. While I acknowledge having one card that impeded my ability to fully realize my potential, I believe that I was dealt a "pretty good hand" and, on the whole, played my cards as well as possible.

I realize that evaluating oneself gets a bit complex. Since none of us really knows why we were put on earth, how can we know whether or not we have made the right or wrong choices to achieve our potential? While I do not profess to have the answer, I hope that by reflecting on my life, I can express an opinion that satisfies both me and the reader.

For the most part, I have no regrets as to how I have lived and I like who I am. After reading these memoirs, I hope you will know me more fully and like me too.

At eighty years of age in my office in the Exchange Building, Baltimore, 2005. Photo courtesy of the *Baltimore Jewish Times*

ACKNOWLEDGMENTS

Since in the prologue to these memoirs, I state that the sole initial reason for my embarking on the task of trying to recall the story of my life was to test my long-term memory (my loss of short-term memory then already being of concern), I want to thank G-d for having kept my hippocampus (i.e., gray matter) sufficiently intact that I could accomplish that objective. When I began eight years ago, I had no idea that I would be able to remember so many of the events in my life which would enable me to write a 336-page book depicting my major accomplishments (and setbacks), as well as revealing a path that I believe I have traveled to become the person I am today. Along the way, I was able to expand my mission to include an opinion as to why G-d put me on earth in the first place and how I should measure the extent to which I felt I had achieved that purpose.

Since I believe G-d works in many unknown ways, I want to give thanks to him/her for having kept me safe from harm's way, particularly where life threatening events were beyond my control, as I describe in these memoirs. Not described in this book is my recent challenge from critical cardiovascular and renal disease. I want to thank G-d for having endowed my team of Johns Hopkins doctors with the skills and compassion that it took to get me through some dark days. My primary care doctor, Dr. Samuel "Chris" Durso, Chief of Gerontology at the Johns Hopkins Bayview Medical Center, not only provided me with his ongoing, exceptional care, but organized a team of exceptional specialists who included: Dr. David Meyerson, Director of Cardiology Consultation Services at Bayview; Dr. Jeffrey Brinker, Professor of the Medicine, Heart and Vascular Institute, who put seven stents in my heart via a series of catheterization procedures; Drs. Steven P. Shulman and Sheldon H. Gotlieb, Chiefs, respectively, of the critical care units of the "downtown" and Bayview Campuses of Johns Hopkins; Dr. Valeriu Cebotaru, Department of Nephrology, Bayview; Dr. Kapil Parakh, now a White House Fellow; and Dr. Sammy Zakaria, my cardiologist, for his extraordinary judgment and compassionate care. I also want to thank Dr. Constantine Lyketsos, Chief of Psychiatry at Bayview, for his advice and counseling. Not to be overlooked were the fabulous PAs and RNs who so skillfully and caringly applied their talents to my recovery and rehabilitation.

Next, I want to thank my mother for having kept just about every letter, report card, diploma, newspaper article and photograph appearing in these memoirs.

Next, I want to thank my mother for having kept just about every letter, report card, diploma, newspaper article and photograph appearing in these memoirs (particularly those from my youth) and without which I could not have tested the validity of my memory. While I know that my father was proud of my accomplishments, his delight was verbalized and shown in different ways. Mother was the record keeper, more for my purposes (it appears) than hers. It also turned out that my younger brother, Stanley, whose memory of certain matters in which he was involved is very good, remembered names and events more accurately than I, for which I am deeply appreciative.

My first editor, Betty Ann Howard, whom I did not know when I began this project (but who was highly recommended to me by a mutual friend), was an unexpected gift who not only greatly enhanced my memoirs in their initial stages, but also my life. We met weekly for about one year, after I had done my own editing, to fine-tune what I thought was a product worthy of someone else, far more professional at composition than I, turning it into a work that I would be proud to have published. During those months of weekly meetings, I had the privilege of getting to know a talented human being with a big heart in a petite body. Betty Ann actually became my confidant and probably knows almost as much about me as my wife, Paula.

Paula recommended that I turn to a long-time friend, Ann Holcomb, to bring a fresh set of eyes to the project. I am grateful to Ann for her thorough copy editing of the text and her great suggestions for fleshing out certain events and eliminating others. She played an important role and her dedication and contribution have been invaluable to this undertaking. Knowing that I was still struggling with the graphic design of the book, Ann reminded Paula that the Maryland Institute College of Art – with which (as these memoirs note) I have had almost a lifetime relationship – has one of the best graphic design departments of any school in the country. Armed with this information, I met and engaged Jennifer Cole Phillips, director of MICA's Graphic Design MFA Program, as the designer. She, together with Emily Goldstein, principal of M Design, have worked diligently to design this book, much to my satisfaction.

Jennifer and Emily literally worked magic with the concept and layout of the book. They also worked closely with Paula and me, bringing to their task the utmost attention to detail. They were patient and meticulous, even as the text continued to be revised. I cannot praise them enough for bringing my story to such vivid life on the page.

I desire to make the helping hand of my dear wife, Paula, apparent. Throughout the long process of producing this book, Paula has not only been emotionally supportive but hands-on, working tirelessly to help me to produce the best manuscript I am capable of writing. Her advice has been deeply appreciated. Calling upon her background as a fine art photographer, she has guided me in the selection of images and illustrations, as well as contributed her own photographs. Paula's colleagues Nancy and Alan Gilbert of DOC Artist Services rephotographed, scanned and retouched, with the support of their talented staff, the photographs and documents – many quite faded and old – included in this book.

Kudos are also due Paula and Ann for having brought to the table the fine-honed skills of a young woman named Marianne Amoss, a freelance writer, editor, and proofreader who is currently the Communications Officer at Notre Dame of Maryland University, to do the proofreading of the completed book including the scrutinizing of the index produced by Diana Witt, a 25-year veteran in indexing beginning with *The New York Times.*

Not to be accused by my law firm, Gordon Feinblatt LLC, of having overlooked their essential legal advice concerning copyright issues and sensitive matters better left unsaid, I want to thank its members and staff for their astute guidance, particularly input from Mary Rose Cook Esq. and Ned Himmelrich Esq. While I feel that what I have written is an accurate recollection of the events included in my memoirs, they convinced me to protect myself by disclaiming any liability for unintentional misstatements of fact and by prohibiting the unauthorized use of any material herein.

Finally, a little confession! The most difficult part of writing these memoirs was trying to recall names and dates to maximize the accuracy of my manuscript. It was a personal challenge, perhaps more meaningful to me than to the reader. With respect to persons whom I knew and events that occurred over fifty years or more ago, I no longer had any familiarity, so I had to rely on the slow process of retrieving the information from my long-term memory, what I call my hard drive. The process was tedious, as explained in the book, but I hope it lends credibility to the text and enjoyment to the reader.

> I desire to make the helping hand of my dear wife, Paula, apparent. Throughout the long process of producing this book, Paula has been emotionally supportive.

CHILDHOOD AND
FORMATIVE YEARS

SPOILED AND PRIVILEGED ON THE ONE HAND BUT TAUGHT TO BE RESPONSIBLE AND CARING ON THE OTHER

My baby picture, 1927[1]

My birth certificate reads that I was born in Baltimore at Women's Hospital[2] on June 8, 1925, and was given the name of LeRoy Edward Hoffberger. My Hebrew name was intended to be the male version of my maternal grandmother's name, which was Leah, the Biblical name of the first wife of Jacob.[3] I was the second son, and my brother Charles, known later as Bert, had been named after my paternal grandfather.[4] He was three when I was born.

Grandmother Hoffberger, Sarah, was the matriarch of the Hoffberger Family (consisting of my father, Jack, and his six brothers). Grandfather Hoffberger, Charles, had died in 1907. As a result, my grandmother had to withdraw her sons (except my Uncle Sam who graduated from high school and then went to law school) from public school to go to work. With Grandmother's help, each son acquired a horse and wagon that was used by each of them to sell ice in the summer, and coal and wood in the winter to Baltimore restaurants, bars and individual homeowners. At the end of each working day, all of the monies were given to my grandmother, who decided how they were to be spent and divided.

Grandmother Sarah Hoffberger emigrated from the Austro-Hungarian Empire and arrived in Baltimore with her husband Charles and their son Abe in 1881.

Mom and Dad in Hawaii
on a worldwide trip via a
Pan American turboprop
aircraft, c. early 1950s

Me in a quiet mood,
Ocean City, age four,
1929

By the time I arrived, the Hoffberger Families had moved out of East Baltimore to Forest Park, a new neighborhood in northwest Baltimore on the west side of Liberty Heights Avenue where the land deeds did not have a restriction against ownership by Jews, Blacks or "Orientals." My Uncle Harry had built four similar houses for himself, Abe, Saul and my father, Jack, on Springdale Avenue. There was one large garage for four cars, but there were four separate clothes lines. Our back yards were adjoining, and the sidewalk beside them was designed to connect our houses for convenience, constant reminders that the Hoffbergers were in many ways one big Family. With two of the other three brothers around the corner, this was especially true.

According to my mother and the older female cousins of my generation (of whom there were six in the block in which I lived as an infant), I was a "beautiful chubby baby with curly hair" and was treated like a showpiece. My girl cousins evidently lined up to push my baby carriage around our neighborhood. As a result of all this attention, I must have been a spoiled brat. Why do I suspect that?

"One time," Mother told me, "I took you to Ocean City, Maryland. I will never forget the tantrum you had on the boardwalk. It was bad enough for me to simply pack up and take you home the next day."

This behavior was an unacceptable means of getting my way with my mother then and was the forerunner of the tremendous sibling rivalry that evolved between Bert and me that lasted almost to the time of his demise.

Our household included two African-American women, probably in their mid-fifties, who worked for my parents. Carey, our cook, was pleasant and had an air of dignity about her. She also made great lamb chops. The other woman, who cleaned the house and did the laundry, was named Lillabelle Gloster Scott. Lilla had a very likeable personality; she was warm and loving.[5]

Once a week when Mom and Dad would go out to dinner, most often to a nearby Chinese restaurant, Lilla would babysit for us. Bert and I would sit at a creamy-white, round children's table and play some sort of card game that we all loved (I believe it was called "Whist"). She also told us stories that captured our imaginations and enthralled us.

However, sometimes Mother's unmarried sister who lived with us would assume the babysitting responsibilities and this, on the occasions when I was too "rambunctious," was not good. Aunt Leonore was a strict disciplinarian who unfortunately used scare tactics to control me. She would tell me that if I didn't behave, the "boogieman" would come and take me away. One day, when she was babysitting, a Scissor-Grinder sauntered down the alley behind our house, hawking his trade of sharpening scissors and knives. Perhaps I was being naughty, so she said, "Better go run and hide so the boogieman won't take you away!" I was terrified and ran inside, up the stairs and hid in the attic.

As I looked out the attic window, I could no doubt see the "boogieman" getting closer, and I moved deeper into the darkness, ending up in the crawl space. I was terrified that I would be found. This memory has haunted me in dreams for my entire life and I attribute periodic nightmares to the indelible impression her scare tactics must have left. I suspect my mother knew about her threats; why didn't she put a stop to this? I am sure that neither my mother nor my aunt realized what a lasting effect her method of dealing with my misbehavior would have on me, so I have forgiven them in my heart. I knew my Aunt Leonore loved me, and at times she would show her affection by making the most delicious fudge for us, giving me first dibs on scraping the pot of the remnants of chocolate.[6]

As I write, the smell of that fudge comes back to me. I was very aware of smells and asked, "What I smell?" so often that my mother and Aunt Leonore would refer to me by saying, for example, "Here comes What I Smell." If a new food was put in front of me, before I would accept a spoonful, I would bend over in my chair and stick my nose in it to determine if the odor was pleasing.

Our Family at home on Springdale Avenue, 1932

One of my favorite smells was that of cigars. When someone who smoked them came to the house, I would stay close to him so that I could secondarily inhale the fragrance. Later, in my early adulthood, I tried smoking cigars after dinner and some drinks. However, that did not last long, for the pleasantness of the bouquet while smoking was always offset by the wretchedness of the taste in my mouth the next morning. While smoking is not "de rigueur" today, I still like the smell of a good cigar, lit or not. One last substance that I will mention and that I liked nearly as much as cigar smoke was the leather on a pair of newly soled shoes. Whenever my mother brought home a pair of old shoes that had been resoled, I could hardly wait until they were unwrapped so that I could stick my nose close to the sole and take in the aroma of the leather. Most people like the feel of new leather, but I liked its smell.

In addition to Carey and Lilla, my parents also employed an African-American janitor who did the heavier chores around the house and worked on our lawn and shrubbery. His name was Jacob Wheeler, and he was a slightly built man, perhaps in his fifties, with a most pleasant demeanor. He was always humming or whistling spirituals as he worked. What really fascinated me about Jacob was his ability to whistle two harmonious notes at the same time. Only once can I recall hearing on the radio someone who could do the same.[7]

I believe my behavior, in general, was normal. However, there were too many times when that was not the case when I was with Bert in the presence of my mother. The interaction between Mother and me was not the problem. Rather, it was the friction between Bert and me that gave rise to my stubborn disobedience. When Mother tried to intervene in the arguing, teasing and sometimes fighting between us, I refused to obey.

There was, for sure, a tremendous sibling rivalry between Bert and me. I, of course, was unaware of this term. All I knew was that when I felt he was belittling me, I could "get his goat." We would tease and taunt one another to the point where one of us would lose it and chase the other (once with a knife) around the house. To the best of my knowledge, no blows were struck, but a wrestling match would sometimes ensue.

When Mother's patience was exhausted, she would threaten that she was going to tell Dad about us when he came home from work. That was always sufficient to bring a prompt halt to our fighting, and we would then anxiously wait to see if she would, in fact, tell him. If so, we would await whatever punishment my father was going to mete out. In those days, physical punishment was not considered child abuse, so I remember too many times when my behind was mighty sore from being whacked with my father's pants belt, and sometimes with his razor strop.

One aspect of my childhood that now puzzles me was my propensity to be the victim of numerous injuries. Some were clearly due to my foolishly taking risks (perhaps to get attention), but some were just bad luck. They all resulted in wounds (not broken bones) serious enough to require stitching. Whenever I sustained such a deep cut, I would run or be carried home to Mother who would then summon Dr. Harry Goldberg, our pediatrician, to come to the house to sew me up. She would next call Dad to come home to assist him.

I would be laid on the formal dining room table (otherwise used only on family holidays) and held down by my father and probably Jacob and another African-American man, Carroll, who worked next door for my Uncle Saul. Dr. Goldberg would then proceed to do the stitching without any anesthetic being given me. In one instance, the stitching was in an area under my right eyelid, next to my eye. You can imagine the pain and the fear that I underwent. I can hear my screaming as I write this. After the operation, I was rewarded with a lollipop.

There was one instance where I could have suffered a severe injury but was, fortunately, savvy enough to avoid it. On a cold winter day, I decided to see what would happen if I put my tongue on the iron railing that adjoined the outside steps to the basement. Lo and behold,

> One aspect of my childhood that now puzzles me was my propensity to be the victim of numerous injuries.

Dad, Bert and me in Asheville, NC, early 1930s

my tongue froze tight to the railing! I was really frightened, but I did not panic by trying to pull it off. Instead, I let my warm breath and saliva melt the thin layer of ice that held my tongue to the railing, releasing it undamaged.

No doubt my conduct as a child justified Mother referring to me as "Peck's bad boy." The term is defined in Webster's dictionary as a "mischievous or recalcitrant person," and it was probably an accurate description of me. However, having said that and having attributed much of my misbehavior to the rivalry between Bert and me, I think it is interesting that neither Bert nor I had such feelings of competitiveness with our younger brother, Stanley. He was born when Bert was seven years old and I was four, never challenging either of us as he grew up. Both Bert and I had a loving relationship with him, and in later life as an adult Stanley stepped in on occasion as a peacemaker.

Although I was mischievous and difficult for my mother to control, I dearly loved and respected her. Mother loved and nurtured me in every way possible, encouraging me to excel academically and to pursue whatever other interests and talents I had. It was, for instance, because of her willingness to schlep me to hundreds of music lessons and orchestra practices that I not only became a pretty good drummer, but developed a lifelong appreciation of both classical and modern music. When I was about ten years old, she would faithfully drive me to drum lessons with Mr. Soistman on Bentlow Street. A little later in my musical career, she would take me to the C.G. Kahn building on Howard Street where I played with an accordion orchestra on Friday nights.

> Although I was mischievous and difficult for my mother to control, I dearly loved and respected her.

Mother also took me to the Maryland Institute College of Art for art lessons every Saturday. Little did I realize that my introduction to this school as a child would culminate years later with my being chairman of its board. On many Saturday afternoons, she was also my chauffeur for innumerable trips to the movies. Most weeks, after synagogue, she would give me fifty cents and drop me off at Wagner's Drugstore which had a soda fountain and counter. There, I could get two coddies on crackers (codfish cakes) with mustard and a Coke for 25 cents. After this, I would go to the movies with the remaining quarter. Sometimes I desperately wanted to re-watch a part of the film, so I would stay beyond the time Mother expected me to be outside the theater. Then she would come into the theater with the usher shining his flashlight to find me.

Being a housewife, Mother was always present when I needed her. Although she had her own friends, with whom she enjoyed playing cards and mahjong, her main delight was her children. She dressed modestly and, apart from her diamond engagement ring and wedding band, did not wear much jewelry. Also, in spite of being a beautiful woman, she could be self-deprecating, and would, for example, complain that her legs looked like "piano legs."

I never remember my parents entertaining their friends except on my father's seventieth birthday. Mother's philosophy, based on an old Jewish superstition, was – "For every joy you have, you're going to shed a tear." She felt that by celebrating Dad's big birthday, G-d had some tragedy in store for her. She therefore blamed herself for Dad's illness and death just a few years after she gave him the party.

I am sorry to say this, but Mother taught me fear. To this day, if I say something positive, such as "I'm in good health," I follow it with *"Baruch Ha Shem,"* which means "Blessed is the Name" and which supposedly, according to tradition, takes away the "evil eye." This is not an uncommon custom among Jews, but I believe that much of Mother's fearfulness (that she passed along to me) came from the horror of growing up in a home with an abusive stepmother.

Fortunately, her father was a kind man. We called him "Pop," and often on Sundays, he would come and visit, bringing us a bag of bagels. He did not drive, so he would take the streetcar from the Gwynns Falls area, where he lived, to our house. What was most memorable about Pop was his little mustache which I liked to touch; and when I put my finger on it, he'd go – "Whuff!"– as if to try to bite my finger.

Although Mother actually raised me, as indicated, my father was my one and only real hero, not only during my childhood and adolescence, but throughout my adult life. It has been in his footsteps that I have tried to walk. Since he was what is now called a workaholic, devoting seven days a week to managing the Hoffberger Family's ice company, he did not have a great deal of time to spend with my brothers or me. He never took us to a baseball game, nor did he ever even chuck a baseball to us. But what he would do, when I begged him in the presence of other adults, was to tear a thick telephone book in two or knock the glass bottom out of a beer bottle filled with water by hitting it on the small opening at the top! Having done physical labor all his life, even in his early forties, he was quite strong. I was so proud of his physical prowess that I asked him to show it off whenever he was willing.

Of much greater importance, though, is that Dad gave me the opportunity, at an early age, to sense the pride and gratification that comes from accomplishment. During the summers when I was 15 and 16, he allowed me to work on the platform at his Gay Street plant. There I learned to push a three-hundred-pound cake of ice from the

Mother in her American Red Cross uniform, 1943

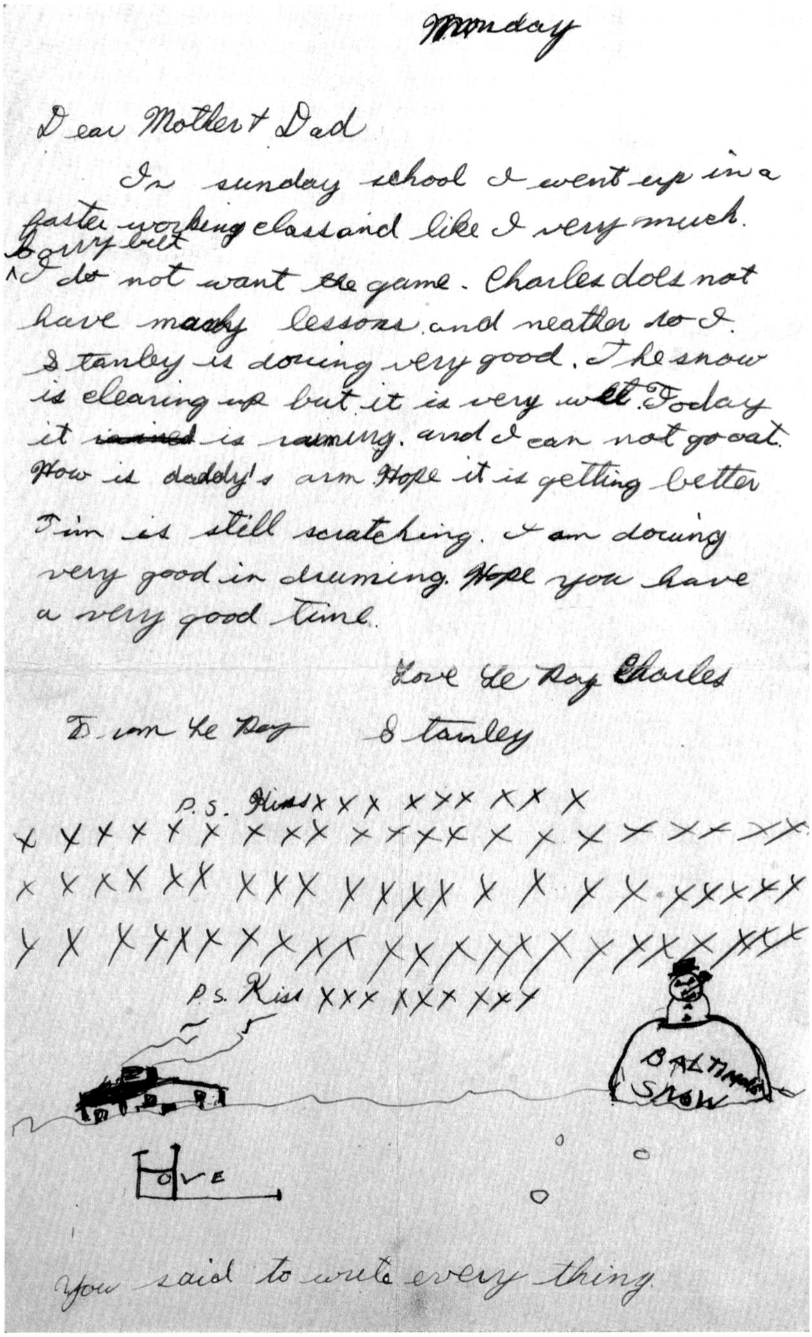

Monday

Dear Mother & Dad

In sunday school I went up in a faster working class and like I very much. I do not want the game. Charles does not have many lessons. and neather so I. Stanley is doing very good. The snow is clearing up but it is very well. Today it is raining. and I can not go out. How is daddy's arm Hope it is getting better Tim is still scratching. I am doing very good in druming. Hope you have a very good time.

Love Le Roy Charles

D. von Le Roy   Stanley

P.S. Kiss X X X X X X X X X
X Y X X X Y X X X X X Y X X X X X Y X Y X X
X X X X X X X X X X X X Y X X X X X X X X X X X X Y
Y X X Y X X X X X X X X X X X X X X X X X X X X X X
P.S. Kiss X X X X X X X X Y

Love

You said to write every thing

I report on life at home to my mother and father vacationing in Florida, 1936

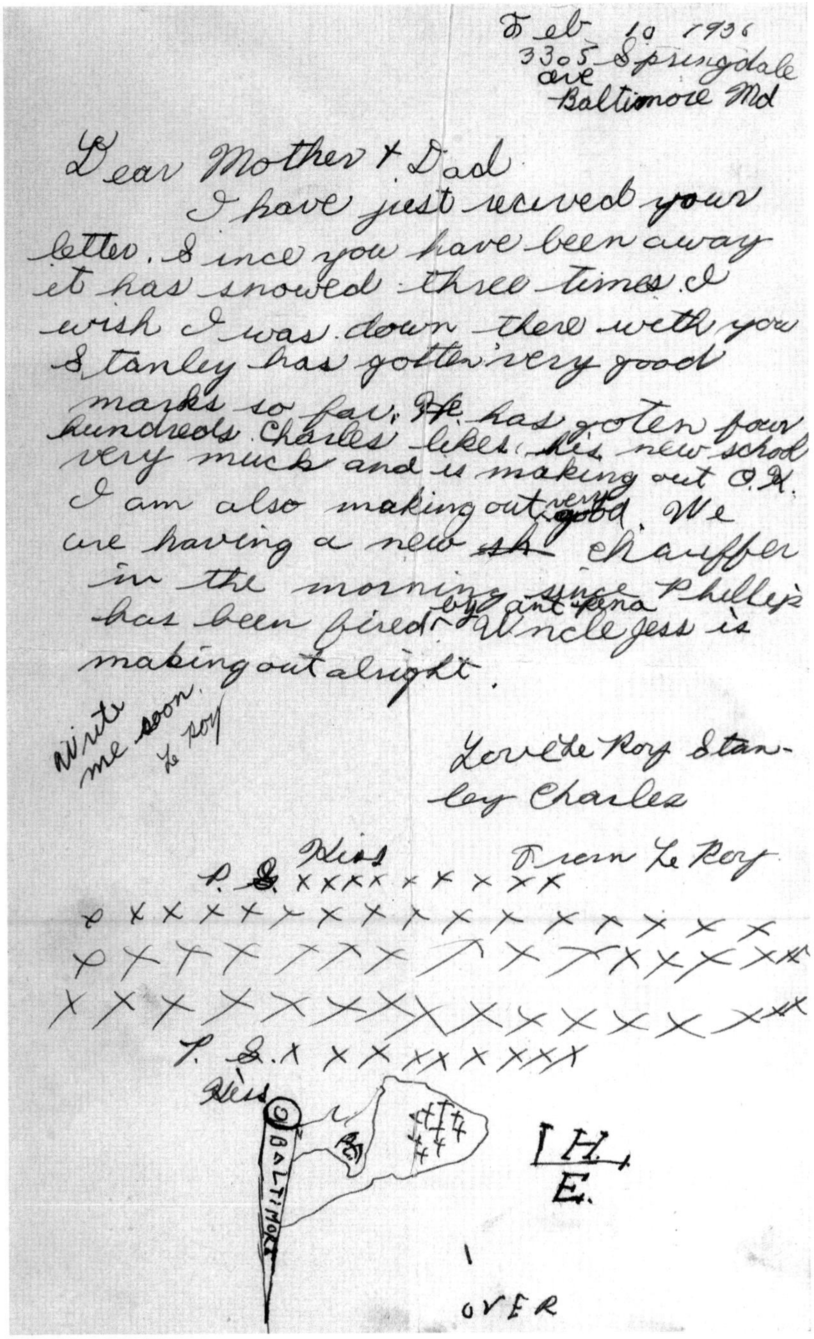

Feb 10 1936
3305 Springdale
ave
Baltimore Md

Dear Mother & Dad,
    I have just recived your
letter. Since you have been away
it has snowed three times. I
wish I was down there with you
Stanley has gotten very good
marks so far. He has goten four
hundreds. Charles likes his new school
very much and is making out O.K.
I am also making out very good. We
are having a new chauffer
in the morning since Phellex
has been fired. Uncle Jess is
making out alright.

Write
me soon.
Le Roy

Love Le Roy Stan-
ley Charles

P.S. Kiss
X X X X X X X X   From Le Roy
X X X X X X X X X X X X X X X X X X X
X X X X X X X   X X X X X X X X X
X X X X X X X X X X X X X X X X X X X
P.S. X X X XX X X X X
Kiss

BALTIMORE

H.
E.

OVER

Mom, Dad and Aunt Mollie, in the back yard on Springdale Avenue, 1934

storage house across the platform, turn it on its side, visually score it to determine the size of the piece a customer wanted and then chop it into variously sized pieces with a razor-sharp ice axe. I would then take a long pair of ice tongs and lower the piece from the platform to the customer. My sales were modest, ranging from a ten-cent piece of ice to a fifty-cent piece (half of a cake); but I felt proud that I was doing my job to the satisfaction of the men with whom I worked and that I was accepted by them as a fellow worker and not because I was the boss' son.

My father had a profound wisdom, and even in my youth I appreciated his homespun philosophy. Some of his favorite adages were:

It is better to be in the rear and discovered, than up front and found out.
To be successful, you have to learn to look around corners.
Once ever, twice never.

These have been lifelong guidelines for me. The first expression taught me to be modest. The second taught me to think out of the box and be creative. The third taught me to give someone the benefit of the doubt, but once only.

Often in the evening, after dinner, my father would visit with one of his six brothers. I assumed they were talking business. Dad usually went to their houses, and I began to realize that he must have been some sort of a messenger among his brothers. As I later learned, he was actually a peacemaker. Whenever there were issues or territorial battles that pitted one brother against another, it was my father who, having the respect of all of the brothers, mediated the problem until a compromise was reached.

While as a youth I did not know what was really going on, I saw by my father's example of closeness to his brothers that the greater Hoffberger Family was very important to him. Therefore, I concluded that it should likewise be important to me. I felt a deep obligation to foster the well-being of the Family as a whole, and this has motivated me throughout my entire professional and business career.

Apart from having a close relationship with his brothers, Dad had few social friends. However, he considered his employees, regardless of their station in life, to be his friends. No matter how menial their jobs, if they worked hard and were loyal to the company (to him), he would do just about anything for them. That included getting up at 2 AM to go bail an employee out of jail for drunken and disorderly conduct.

In one case I considered one of Dad's employees to be part of our Family. Dad had a lifelong friendship with an African American, Luke Downs, his "right hand." He relied on Luke to do all sorts of special tasks which had to get done correctly and expeditiously. Luke never let him down. The wonderful thing that I was privileged to observe was that Luke was not treated by my father as an employee, but as a trusted friend. When my father died, Luke mourned his passing like a member of our Family. He continued to work for my brother Stanley, until his retirement and even afterwards. Until his death, Luke would regularly help my mother.

Although he belonged to a country club, Dad never went there to play golf or swim or play cards, preferring to do chores around the house, tend his vegetable garden and take care of his bees. He had sixty thousand! My friends used to say, "If you go over to Roy's, you'll leave with four tomatoes, a cucumber and a jar of honey."

Luke Downs, Dad's right-hand man, 1962

He considered his employees, regardless of their station in life, to be his friends.

Dad at a food convention, 1950

Dad, in his office at
Pompeian Olive Oil
Company, 1950

Dad and his six brothers.
From left to right: Joe,
Saul, Sam, Harry, Jack,
Mike, Abe, 1935

PRIMARY AND SECONDARY PUBLIC
SCHOOL DAYS

Through grade 11, I received my education in the Public School System of Baltimore City. I started out at Public School #64, walking the six blocks with six or eight other boys who were in my class.

School started at 9 AM and the morning session ended at noon. At 12 o'clock, Mother was waiting in her large four-door Packard to pick me up and take me home for lunch. Since the afternoon session started at 1 PM, it was important to get home quickly, eat and return within an hour. This being the case, all of my friends with whom I walked in the morning wanted to hitch a ride with Mom and be dropped off along the way back to our house. Every day, Mother faithfully did this. However, she did not drive us back to school, and while I don't know why, I suspect she had a good reason.

Including kindergarten (which was in an old frame house adjacent to the brick school), I spent seven years at Public School #64.[8] My class of thirty or so kids was made up of about the same number of boys and girls – a pretty close-knit, highly competitive group. While most of my classmates were smart, I managed to consistently stay among the top five or so of the best academically. Your rank was indicated by where you sat (i.e., if you had the highest marks overall during a term, you sat in

My PS #64 Elementary School report card, grade six, June 1937

RECORD OF ACHIEVEMENT	First Report	Second Report	Third Report	Fourth Report	Fifth Report
Reading	E	E	E	E	
Spelling	E	E	E	E	
Handwriting	G	G	V·G·	E	
Oral English	VG	VG	V·G·	E	
Written English	E	E	E	E	
Literature	E	VG	E	E	
Arithmetic Computation	VG	VG	E	E	
Arithmetic Problem-Solving	G	E	E	E	
Geography	E	E	E	E	
History	G	VG	E	E	
Health Education	E	E	E	E	
Physical Education	E	E	E	E	
Elementary Science	VG	VG	E	E	
Art	E	E	E	E	
Music	E	E	E	E	

Report of Hoffberger, LeRoy

EXPLANATION OF MARKS IN SUBJECTS OF STUDY

E	Excellent:	95 - 100		M	Moderate:	70 - 79
V G	Very Good:	90 - 94		P	Poor:	60 - 69
G	Good:	80 - 89		D	Deficient:	below 60

the first row, first seat and so on). As I recall, I usually sat somewhere in the first row of seven or eight desks.

I recently went to see a movie called *The King's Speech* which was about the second son of King George V, nicknamed "Bertie," and his sudden ascension to the throne following the abdication of his older brother, Edward. The horrendous problem confronting Bertie was that he had a very serious stutter, particularly when he had to speak in public. The film portrayed how Bertie's wife, the future Queen Elizabeth, engaged a little-known actor with no professional credentials in speech therapy, to help her husband. In his first public radio broadcast as King of the British Empire, aired at the beginning of World War II, Bertie managed to get through a stirring speech with the therapist in the broadcasting room coaching him.

While watching this film I found myself strongly identifying with the King. I remembered that while in elementary school, I had been diagnosed with a speech impediment called "lisping." I could not pronounce "s" properly; I said "th." I was therefore sent to a speech therapist who visited the school once a week. I don't lisp now, so somehow I got rid of it. However, since that memory was awakened by this recent movie, I have had an uncomfortable feeling that leads me to believe that being singled out for this impediment must have bothered me as a child.

After PS #64, my next educational stop was at Garrison Junior High School, grades seven through nine. While it was about twice as far away, it was nevertheless within walking distance, and my same gang of friends still walked together. Now, however, we did not come home for lunch. While lunch could be bought at school, most of us brought our lunch. Mine consisted of a peanut butter and jelly, corned beef or chicken salad sandwich, a pickle and some potato chips.

Now, there was an art to carrying a lunch to school. To begin with, it was almost mandatory that it be packed in a brown bag. I usually had my large notebook and several textbooks that I needed for my homework. The masculine way to carry these and your brown bag was all under your right arm, with the lunch bag on top of the textbooks. The art of "brown-bagging it" was to do this without crushing the contents of your lunch bag. It was humiliating to be seen carrying your lunch bag in your left hand, which at all times had to be free. The girls had their own way of carrying all of their wares, cradling them against their chests.

My Garrison Junior High School report card, grade nine, June 1940

At Garrison, I again did well academically and delighted in playing the drums in the school orchestra. Although I do not recall her name, I feel especially indebted to my music teacher. She liked me and, while I was not yet in high school, she recommended that I be accepted as a member in the All-Maryland High School Orchestra, which contained the best young musicians from around the state. This experience gave me a chance to play with talented young musicians (one of whom even had a Stradivarius violin) and heightened my interest in music, making it a lifelong pursuit.

My Garrison Junior High School eighth grade class, 1940

While I was in elementary and junior high school, classes ended at 2:30 or 3 PM, after which I walked home. Once home, I would have a glass of milk and some cookies and change to clothes suited to the sport I was about to engage in with my friends. I then headed to nearby Hanlon Park. By about 4 o'clock each weekday, at least fifteen to twenty of us had gathered on a sloping plot to choose sides for either softball or football, depending on the season. The field on which we gathered was far from ideal. It was located in a rather remote corner, away from a much larger, grassier main playing area. That section, however, was usually taken over by a group of slightly older Christian boys who lived on the east side of Liberty Heights Avenue and who were overtly anti-Semitic, there being no Jews allowed to live in their neighborhoods. So up until the time I was 14 – 15 years old, my group of mostly Jewish playmates chose to play some distance away from this threatening enclave.

Then, one fall, my adult cousin "Chick" Hoffberger (Charles II), who had played football at Hopkins, became our coach. He was fearless and saw no reason why we should be willing to play on a sloping, bare little plot, when we could play up on the level, grass-covered public field adjacent to where this bullying gang of anti-Semites played. So, up we went with him to the much nicer field.

It was not long before the Christian group challenged us to a football game. Chick welcomed this and said we would be ready in a week. Needless to say, we were scared, but my cousin was determined to instill in us a sense of confidence and, more importantly, a will to fight (literally) the threat of anti-Semitism. We practiced all week and then, not too convinced we were ready, played our daunting opponents. Needless to say, we were badly beaten, but we hung in there. After that game, the Christian bullies were less bullying, and we continued to play up on the better field. This was my first encounter with anti-Semitism but, sorry to say, not my last.

To prepare me for my bar mitzvah, my parents arranged for me to be tutored twice a week by Rabbi Neuhausen. An older man with a heavy Yiddish accent, he would come to our house to teach me my Torah and my *Haftarah* portions as well as the prayers that related to both. He always wore a black fedora and, in greeting my mother, would tip his hat from the back, rather than from the front. I can't say that I was his best student or that I liked giving up my after-school time dedicated to playing ball with the guys.

Nevertheless, I did quite well when it came time for me to be a bar mitzvah. The ceremony took place on a hot summer day in June at Beth Tfiloh Synagogue, an Orthodox synagogue that my Family helped to found. Afterwards, my parents had a luncheon for all of my pals and the Family. The kosher food was prepared by a well-known caterer and included one of my favorite appetizers, chopped chicken liver.

Unfortunately, it had not been properly refrigerated, and many of the guests were struck with ptomaine poisoning.

My brother Stanley, my mother and I ended up in Sinai Hospital – as did several of my friends – for about a week. No one ever forgot my bar mitzvah! Although I have long forgotten my *Maftir* (Torah portion) and my *Haftarah*, I can still remember how sick I was, and, to this day, I seldom have the nerve to order chopped chicken liver when the weather is hot.

While, much to my regret, I did not continue to study with Rabbi Neuhausen after my bar mitzvah, I did still go to Sunday School at Baltimore Hebrew Congregation, a Reform synagogue, until I was confirmed several years later. That was the last of my formal Jewish education until I was in my late sixties. Then, I once again began to study Torah, at first on my own, and then with a rabbi who gave me an unbelievable insight into the meaning of Hebrew Scripture and helped me become a religious Jew.

No one ever
forgot my
bar mitzvah!

A proposal from the Southern Hotel for my formal bar mitzvah dinner, which was held for our Family and my parents' friends, 1938

Prior to my entering high school, our Family compound had begun to break up. With more Family wealth, there were more choices. Dad found a place for us in upper Park Heights on Bancroft Road, where he would have more land to garden. The house, Tudor in style, had formerly been owned by the Hechts, but had been destroyed by a fire. Dad restored it for us, and it was our happy homestead well into my adulthood.

Our home at 3404 Bancroft Road, where we moved in about 1940

When it came time for me to select a high school, I had the opportunity to choose one of three: Forest Park Senior High School, which was co-educational; City College, all male; or Polytechnic High School, also all male and specializing in mathematics and science. Because Forest Park had been the school that Bert had attended and liked, and since it was closer to my new home, I chose to attend it.

I don't think the fact that Forest Park was the only co-ed school entered into the equation, but I remember that, once there, I saw that there were some very good-looking girls who, unfortunately, were in the upper classes and older than I. While I was becoming increasingly aware of them, I was quite shy. It was not until I was 16 or 17 years old that I got the nerve to date. I had a crush on a beautiful blonde girl, Elaine Farbman. I recall holding her hand in the movies and considering this quite a sexual conquest. It was not until I was 18 years old and had just graduated from preparatory school that I first kissed a girl (whom I nicknamed "Blue Eyes") and not until I was in the Navy that I lost my virginity.

In 1941 and 1942, I attended Forest Park in the tenth and eleventh grades. Again, I did well academically. I also continued to pursue my interest in music as a percussionist, playing with the Forest Park marching band and orchestra and continuing with the All-Maryland High School Orchestra. In 1943, at the beginning of my senior year, I left Forest Park to go to the Peddie School in New Jersey. As I will relate later in these memoirs, I had my rationale for doing so and, unbeknownst to me, my father had his rationale for encouraging me to do so.

My mother saved everything!

SUMMERS WERE A TIME TO PLAY AND LEARN

Most of my childhood summers were spent on the Bush River in Harford County, Maryland, where my father bought a large frame summer home for the entire family to get away and enjoy summer together in the country. [9]

Today, with its large suburban developments and multiple shopping centers, Harford County is no longer the rural haven it was in 1932. In those days, it took us at least one and a half hours to drive to our shore home. The only so-called highway was U.S. I, a winding single-lane road with no median strip. If we got stuck behind a slow truck, passing it could be a harrowing experience. I can remember that to make the trip go faster my brothers and I would play a game we invented that involved spotting certain out-of-state license plates, or numbers on Maryland plates. But, as arduous as traveling on U.S. I was, it did not take us right to our doorstep.

Mom, Dad, Stanley and me with Duke, our Boston bull terrier whom we had for many years, at our summer home on the Bush River, 1938

After exiting off of Route I, we had to travel the last two or three more miles on a dirt road. While we might have been only thirty or so miles from Baltimore, going to the Bush River was quite a trek and it brought us to a world apart from life in the city.

My Uncle Sam had bought a house next door to ours. His family included Aunt Gertrude and my three cousins – Jerry (Charles IV), Lois and Rosel. Except for Saturdays, when they would drive to Baltimore to buy groceries, both Mother and my Aunt Gertrude spent the week with us. They were assisted by Carey, Lilla, my aunt's housekeeper and a handyman who took care of the grounds and our two ponies. Dad and my Uncle Sam commuted to Baltimore every weekday, as did my cousin Jerry. On the weekends my father spent most of his time tending his vegetable garden and working with the handyman on things that had to get done.

One of our ponies was called "Brownie" and the other "Blackie," obviously because of their colors. Brownie was a pretty old little pony that was tame and easy to hook up to the cart that Dad had made by someone in his truck repair shop. It was painted green, of course, like all of the C. Hoffberger ice and oil trucks. Blackie was a large stallion, almost the size of a horse, who was "wild." No one tried to actually ride him, but with difficulty he could be hitched up to the cart. A ride with

The Bush River Gang,
August 7, 1939

Teddy Schwartzman
and me at Bush River, 1935

Blackie was an adventure as there were times when he would start to gallop until he decided to slow down and, like it or not, we could not control him.

Dad, as a teenager, had handled work horses that pulled his ice wagons before the automobile was a common means of transportation. He knew everything there was to know about horses. He could tell if a horse was sick and knew just what to do to make it well. He also knew that castrating a stallion would "calm it down" and had performed this procedure a number of times as a youth on his work horses. So, believing that Blackie would be more manageable if castrated, he proceeded to do so. I remember watching.

First, he had several workmen hold Blackie still. Then, he put his hand up into Blackie's scrotum and extracted his testicles. It sounds awfully cruel, but I am sure that my father knew what he was doing. Blackie was rendered less strident, but he was still difficult to handle.

The eight or nine summers spent on the Bush River were, perhaps, the most carefree times of my life. Once there, I wore only a pair of shorts – no shirt, no shoes, no underwear. By the end of the summer, my skin was dark brown from the sun and the bottoms of my feet were like leather. My friends were an older boy named Eddie Freeberger and the two Tigh brothers, Leonard and Michael, one older than I and one younger. They all lived on the Bush River the year round. Although their backgrounds were different from mine (i.e., they were not Jewish and they were from blue-collar, working-class families), we got along extremely well. I cannot recall ever having a fight or even an argument with any of them.

From time to time, I would have a friend from Baltimore come to visit. Sylvan Offit was one whom I invited. Mother picked him up on one of her weekly trips to Baltimore and took him back the following Saturday. Sylvan, who is now 84 and still working as the managing partner in his well-known local accounting firm, told me of the unforgettable time he had with us and was particularly effusive about how kind and welcoming my parents were.[10] Teddy Schwartzman, another friend, also came down for a week as well as others whose families' economic circumstances during the Depression of the 1930s did not enable them to go to camp.

One of my favorite activities as a six- or seven-year-old was to dig in the dirt around the roots of a grove of oak trees near the riverbank to carve out make-believe garages and highways for my little toy cars. My friends and I would then guide our cars along the dirt roads we had made and crash them, now and then, to simulate what happens in the real world. This game occupied me for hours; perhaps, building imaginary roads and garages was a harbinger of my fascination with real estate later in life.

Twice a day like clockwork, once in the morning and again in the afternoon, Mother and Aunt Gertrude would appear at the top of the wooden stairs that led down the bank to a small stony beach in front of our property. They would chat, knit and watch while I, together with my brothers, cousins and friends, would swim. On the weekends, we had lots of visitors consisting of Hoffberger Family members and business associates of my Uncle Sam's who swam with us.

Three things about my swimming experiences stand out in my mind. First, I learned to swim quite well. Secondly, had I or anyone else begun to drown, it is highly doubtful that either Mother or my Aunt Gertrude could have done more than scream; yet, we all felt secure and safe. And thirdly, we swam right next to the cesspools that served our two homes; the sewage often overflowed into the river. Why our parents were not concerned about that, I shall never know, particularly since, one summer, my cousin Rosel got typhoid fever, no doubt from the effluence that came from the cesspools.

> Not knowing what we would find when the net was dragged up on the beach was thrilling!

In addition to swimming twice a day, Stanley and I would often go seining along the shoreline for a mile or more and bring ashore in our net all sorts of little fish, crabs, eels and, once, even a water snake. Not knowing what we would find when the net was dragged up on the beach was thrilling! I also would walk along the shore by myself with a dip net looking for soft crabs in the seaweed where, defenseless until they stopped molting, they would hide from the hard crabs that would eat them if found. One day, I came upon a very large hard shell that had been sloughed off, so I suspected that not far away I would find a soft crab hiding in the seaweed. Sure enough, I did. The crab was huge! With great pride, I brought it into the kitchen to be cleaned, fried and eaten.

We had an "outboard" motor-boat which, when I was ten or eleven, I was permitted to operate as long as someone else was along. I remember that one day I decided to go fishing with one of my friends in the "outboard." When we got to where we wanted to cast anchor, I threw the anchor overboard, but somehow my fishing line got tangled in the anchor line and was pulled down with it. Unfortunately, as the line was being dragged down into the water, the fishing hook at the end of my line got caught in my thumb. The further down the anchor line went, the further into my thumb the fishing hook went. Somehow, I was able to grab the anchor line and begin to haul it back up into the boat. This relieved the pressure on the line and kept the hook from continuing to dig into my thumb. Once the anchor was in the boat, I was able to extract the hook. Fortunately, not much damage was done to my thumb, but it was a horror that I never forgot.

I spent each summer at our Bush River home until I was 15. Then, as previously mentioned, I went up to Baltimore with my father each weekday to work on his Gay Street ice plant. Bert was by then getting ready to go to Duke University, and Stanley had become an avid camper at Camp Wigwam in Maine. For each of us, the carefree days of our youth on the Bush River were coming to an end, and in 1940 or 1941, my father sold our Bush River home, as did my uncle.

Sadly, I lost track of my friends who had been my close companions for those many summers of my childhood. Years later, I learned that Eddie Freeburger had joined the Canadian Air Force in about 1940 and had been killed in the "Battle of Britain." One of the Tigh brothers (I think it was Leonard) was drafted into the Army and was also killed in action in Europe. As I recall, the younger brother, Michael, died of some illness while I was still going to the Bush River. All of these young men were fine, caring human beings for whom I had genuine affection.

Newspaper article from *The Evening Sun,* revealing the death of Lieut. Edward Freeburger in the European war theater, 1943

WORLD WAR II

MY SENIOR YEAR AT THE PEDDIE SCHOOL

The United States entered World War II on December 8, 1941. Bert was then 19 and a junior at Duke University. When he graduated the next year, he entered the Coast Guard Academy; and by 1943, he was at sea as an ensign on a cutter that accompanied convoys of Liberty ships on their way to England and Russia across the North Atlantic. It was his ship's job to protect these largely defenseless vessels from German U-boats intent on sinking them.

In the fall of 1942, I was about to enter the 12th grade at Forest Park and was 17 years of age. Believing that I would be drafted into the military when I became 18 the following June, I thought it would be a good idea to transfer to a private military school (the Staunton Military Academy in Virginia was the school that I had in mind) where, upon graduation, I would be an officer in the Army. This seemed to me to be much preferable to being drafted as a private. I told this to my father who (for a reason not then known to me) was receptive to my going to a preparatory school, although he did not think that going to a military school for the reason I had given him was a good idea.

Bert in his Coast Guard uniform with Lady, our mastiff, 1944

What I now believe motivated Dad to immediately agree to my going to a private school was the disappointment he and Bert had suffered three years previously when Bert, having graduated from Forest Park with honors, was turned down by Dartmouth College. I believe my father felt that the reasons Bert had not been accepted were that he was Jewish (and it was known that Ivy League schools had a small quota for Jewish students) and that he was a graduate of a public school (it likewise being known that 90% of the students at Ivy League colleges were from preparatory schools). While I never discussed this with my father, I am certain that he saw in my wish to attend a military preparatory school an opportunity to start me on a path toward admission to an Ivy League college.

The next thing that I remember was my father telling me that we had an appointment to meet the assistant headmaster of a school called "The Peddie School for Boys" in Hightstown, New Jersey.[11] I had never heard of the school and had no idea that it was affiliated with the Baptist Church and that attendance every Sunday at church services was mandatory. I'm certain that my father didn't know these facts either. However, he (not I) probably knew that it was a "feeder" school for Princeton and other Ivy League schools.

Dad drove me to The Peddie School and, as arranged, we met with the assistant headmaster who was a little baldheaded man whose office floor was strewn with papers. After greeting us, he left his office for a moment. For some reason, my father thought that the papers on the floor had blown off of the assistant headmaster's desk so he asked me to pick them up. I began doing this when the assistant headmaster returned and shouted that I should stop immediately since he had a reason for having placed these papers on the floor in piles! Though this was not an auspicious beginning, he nevertheless said that there were two openings and that my grades qualified me to be admitted.

The school term had actually started so I don't remember whether we went home to pack and return or whether I had already packed and upon being formally accepted, stayed at Peddie. I was taken to the fifth floor, south, of Wilson Hall, an old five-story Victorian brick building, and introduced to the Hall Proctor, William Boyd, more affectionately known as "Wild Bill." I was shown to my room which contained two single iron-framed beds, two tables that served as desks and two plain bureaus. Sometime later my roommate arrived. I don't remember his name, but he was from Afghanistan and the son of an important official.

About a week into the term, he unfortunately began having seizures and for some reason, he went to room with someone else. As I think about it, the seizures probably had nothing to do with the room change. I believe that because he was a Muslim and I a Jew, someone decided that we were unlikely to become fast friends.

Unquestionably, his departure was fortuitous, for my new roommate, William Horridge, became one of my best friends at Peddie and is someone with whom I continue to maintain contact. Bill, who had the nickname "Horrible," was from the small rural community of Netcong, New Jersey. He had a laid-back demeanor and a dry sense of humor. I immediately took a liking to him and he to me. We never argued or had a serious disagreement.[12]

My roommate, William Horridge, Netcong, NJ, and my classmate, Charles Fredericks Jr., Red Bank, NJ, 1943

My senior year at Peddie was the most formative year of my youth. Bill was typical of the kind of young men that Peddie attracted – the friendships that I formed, particularly with the fellows on my floor, were among the most memorable relationships of my life, though for the most part of short duration. However, one more enduring relationship was with a very funny and extremely savvy young man named Charlie Fredericks. I had the good fortune to catch up with him again after the war ended and to room with him at Princeton. Thereafter, we saw each other at Peddie as well as Princeton reunions. I have singled out Charlie as, unknowingly, he played an important role in redirecting my thinking about where I should go to college. For this I am very grateful.

Perhaps the reason for my strong feelings about my friendships at Peddie was because for nine months I lived, ate, studied, played and, yes, prayed with these young men. Having had the bad experience with the Christian boys that I have previously described, I did not know what to expect of the primarily Christian students I was going to be living with. How pleased I was to find that my friends at Peddie did not have an ounce of prejudice in them! They were decent, caring human beings.

In particular, I was privileged to be close to two young men on my hall who were "the salt of the earth." One, Willet Chinery, was from St. Joseph, Michigan, and the other, Ian Fraser, was from Waverly, New York. Both were bright and great fun to be around. I brought both of them home to meet my parents and stay with me over a weekend, an experience which I know (through our correspondence) neither one of them ever forgot. Tragically, both of them were killed, one during World War II and the other sometime after, trying to land his plane on an aircraft carrier. Sixty-nine years later, I still think of them and miss them.

My classmates Ian Fraser, Waverly, NY, and Willet Chinery, St. Joseph, MI, both of whom were killed while serving in the military

Recently, in looking through my Peddie class book, I found two letters from Will Chinery written when he was waiting to be shipped out to the Pacific. They were filled with stories about his amorous experiences with girls he had met on leave and with questions concerning girls with whom I had had amorous interludes that I evidently had written to him about. Now, when I think of those letters, I believe we (then still two virgins) were communicating superficially about what seemed to be all-important – i.e., our manhood – while, in truth, we were both unable to discuss our fears about what might be in store for us in the war.

Another significant recollection of my senior year experiences at Peddie (although not realized then) was the required attendance at Vespers every Sunday evening. Reverend Wilber Saunders, our Baptist Minister Headmaster (referred to by the students as the "Black Doctor" because of his dark complexion), would briefly set the mood by saying a few spiritual words concerning, very often, the "fellowship of man." He remarked one time that while we probably did not appreciate the importance of the entire school getting together on Sunday evening just before the beginning of each week, we would, one day, look back and remember those moments of communion as the most meaningful experiences we had at Peddie.

Print the complete address in plain letters in the panel below, and your return address in the space provided on the right. Use typewriter, dark ink, or dark pencil. Faint or small writing is not suitable for photographing.

TO: L. HOFFBERGER V-12 USNR
BROOKS HALL RM. 308
UNIV. OF PENN.
PHILA. 4, PA.

FROM
PFC. W. CHINERY
Co. A 381ST INF. APO 96
c/o PM, SAN FRANCISCO

PASSED BY U.S. ARMY EXAMINER

(CENSOR'S STAMP) SEE INSTRUCTION NO. 2 (Sender's complete address above)

Philippines Mar. 10

Dear Roy – I'm determined to get that letter I owe you off tonight, so if I can finish it before my gas torch explodes I'll be able to sleep tonight. — Had a swell letter from 'Horrible' and it is evident that he hasn't changed any. He said he runs into you now and then at school. So you are a 'drummer boy' once more? I can remember all the racket you made one Thanks-giving in Baltimore. Horrible said he too had enjoyed a weekend at the Hoffberger home, and I can realize that he too had a swell time. I would stand some of your hospitality right now.

I wish we could make a date for our 'Fifth Hall' reunion, but we'll just have to sweat it out. I'll spend a couple of drunks in New York (strictly on your uncles, National Premium) and then take a trip down to Philly and gang Jeanne (Scotch permit-ting.) Have you been after that? Did you ever have another date with 'Blue Eyes' from Forest Hills?

I imagine that I can start plans for a welcoming celebration out here. Your welcome, but we don't have much to offer. Best of luck – your pal

Roscoe

HAVE YOU FILLED IN COMPLETE ADDRESS AT TOP?

REPLY BY V···–MAIL

HAVE YOU FILLED IN COMPLETE ADDRESS AT TOP?

18

U. S. GOVERNMENT PRINTING OFFICE : 1943 16—28143-5

Of course, we chuckled, but the truth is, I do remember Vespers with great fondness. Although the hymns were Christian, many of the verses were expressions of love and fellowship that resonated with me, particularly when hearing them sung by five hundred young men. To this day, if I happen to attend the church funeral or wedding of a Christian friend, the words of many of the hymns come back to me.[13] When my Christian friends see me singing right along with them, they are puzzled, knowing that I am a religious Jew, by my familiarity with the words. However, my recalling of the hymns brings back the beautiful memories I still have of those Sunday evening convocations.

Toward the end of the school year, we were asked to select the two or three colleges we wanted to apply to, even though practically all of us realized that we would be going into the armed services upon graduation. For some unknown reason, my first choice was Cornell University. While in the process of finalizing my application form, Charlie Fredericks came to my room and asked me which college was my first choice. I told him "Cornell" (located in Ithaca, New York) to which he replied: "What are you, an Eskimo?"

> To this day, if I happen to attend the church funeral or wedding of a Christian friend, the words of many of the hymns come back to me.

The Peddie School
Hightstown, N. J.

May 12, 1943

My dear Mr. and Mrs. Hoffberger:

    It gives me great pleasure to inform you of the election of your son to the Cum Laude society. He richly deserves this award and we are proud to welcome him into our membership. I know you too will be glad to know of Roy's achievement.

    Since the society has no means of support, it is necessary to charge its members a fee to defray the expenses of the certificate and key. This charge amounts to $3.50.

    The initiation will take place at Commencement. I know you will be present if possible and I shall look forward to seeing you at that time.

               Very cordially yours,

               W. S. Litterick

               W.S.Litterick
               Sec. Peddie Chapter of Cum Laude

Mr. and Mrs. Jack H. Hoffberger
3404 Bancroft Rd.
Baltimore, Maryland

WSL:DT

He then asked me why I had not applied to Princeton, since I was a national honor student and likely to be accepted. I told him that I had not thought about Princeton. Frankly, although Princeton was only 15 miles from Hightstown, I had never visited the Princeton campus and knew only that it was a renowned Ivy League school. Nevertheless, I respected Charlie's opinion and having no strong feeling about Cornell, I switched my first choice to Princeton. To my surprise, I was accepted into the Class of 1947.

Me in the Peddie yearbook, Class of 1943

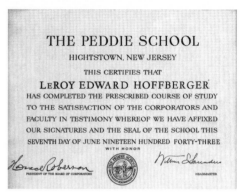

THE PEDDIE SCHOOL

HIGHTSTOWN, NEW JERSEY

THIS CERTIFIES THAT

LeROY EDWARD HOFFBERGER

HAS COMPLETED THE PRESCRIBED COURSE OF STUDY TO THE SATISFACTION OF THE CORPORATORS AND FACULTY IN TESTIMONY WHEREOF WE HAVE AFFIXED OUR SIGNATURES AND THE SEAL OF THE SCHOOL THIS SEVENTH DAY OF JUNE NINETEEN HUNDRED FORTY-THREE

WITH HONOR

One more thought to end this story: My experience at Peddie must have pleased my parents, particularly my father. When Stanley finished Junior High School, he also went to Peddie; in fact, the year I graduated, Stanley entered Peddie in the ninth grade.

Then, my son Douglas decided to follow in my footsteps when he graduated from the Middle School at Gilman. This, of course, pleased me greatly, and only later did I come to realize that going away to school was perhaps his way of escaping from an unhappy home. His mother and I were not getting along, and this disturbed him terribly, to the point where he was having frequent migraine headaches. Getting away cured that. Douglas' career at Peddie was filled with fun, mischief and a little studying. By then, the school had become co-educational, and I can remember him telling me that, as much as I enjoyed Peddie, he had enjoyed Peddie even more since there were girls on campus.

My experience at Peddie must have pleased my parents, particularly my father.

Paula and me at my
65th Peddie reunion,
2008. Photograph by
classmate Bob Risch

The Peddie School
for Boys graduating
class of 1943

EXPERIENCES (GOOD AND BAD) IN THE NAVY V-12 OFFICER TRAINING PROGRAM

I received my draft notice shortly after graduating from Peddie. However, instead of going into the Army, I qualified (after having a brace painfully put in my mouth to correct my malocclusion and after having cheated to pass the eye test by memorizing the 20/20 line on the eye chart) for a Naval officers training program known as the "Navy V-12 Officer Training Program." Unfortunately, I was not sent to Princeton, but to Columbia University where I spent one of the most horrific years of my youth.

Unlike the young men with whom I had lived at Peddie, those who were on my floor in the dormitory building where I was quartered at Columbia were the most anti-Semitic and bigoted human beings I had ever met. They were a good match for the group of Christian kids in Hanlon Park. However, in this instance, I had to live with them. What puzzled me at first was that these young men were educated and middle class, but I soon realized many were from New York City, where anti-Semitism was rampant.

I really was unprepared to deal with such hatred and, when confronted with their bigoted remarks, was therefore evasive about being Jewish. They would say, "Hoffberger – isn't that a Jewish name?" or "You know, you look Jewish." To these and other baited questions, I would give ambiguous answers. "Hoffberger is an Austrian name," or "Is that right?" There was no doubt that they suspected that I was Jewish, but I just wasn't going to take the additional verbal abuse that I felt would come if I admitted it.

Me as an apprentice seaman in the Navy V-12 Officer Training Program, 1943

Needless to say, I was not proud of the fact that I was afraid to be forthright, but, at age 18, I did not have the moral fortitude to do battle; and I simply saw no way out of continuing to endure the humiliation of hiding my Jewish faith. I even considered dropping out of the program and risking whatever might be in store for me as a regular seaman. Fortunately, toward the end of the year, we were all given a choice of either continuing our training to become "Deck Officers" by going to Harvard for ninety days or of becoming "Supply Corp Officers" by going to the Wharton School of Finance at the University of Pennsylvania for 18 months, and then going to Harvard to finish our training. The choice was a no-brainer for me, so I did not hesitate to switch to the Supply Corp.

My experiences at Columbia and those at the University of Pennsylvania were like night and day. Fortunately, the men in my class at Penn were not from New York City or any other place where there was an ingrained hatred of Jews. Rather, my class was made up of young men who were more like the Christians whom I had met at Peddie. A number of the men with whom I chose to associate were a few years older than I and had seen active sea duty in major battles in the Pacific. Maybe their terrible experiences had something to do with making them caring human beings; whatever, it was a great relief!

At Wharton, I not only appreciated my new friends, but I thoroughly enjoyed the courses that we were offered. Statistics, economics and finance all interested me, and I was quite prepared to return to the Wharton School for my senior year after the war ended. Since the school was in Philadelphia, I was able to get home many weekends and would often take some of my new buddies with me. One such friend was Broadus King. Perhaps I remember him because he left his after-shave lotion at my home, and I never returned it to him. I kept it in my bathroom cabinet for years – I assume for nostalgic reasons.

In March 1945, we completed our courses at the Wharton School and were sent to the Bayonne Naval Supply Depot to wait for our final

> Fortunately, the men in my class at Penn were not from New York City or any other place where there was an ingrained hatred of Jews.

Me as an Ensign in the U.S. Navy Reserve, 1945

ninety days of training at Harvard. Two months later, the war in Europe ended! I can remember being given leave to go to New York where I celebrated on Broadway with thousands of other servicemen and women and civilians. I was still scheduled to go to Harvard to train for duty in the Pacific, but the atomic bomb was dropped on Hiroshima and Nagasaki in August and the war with Japan ended. As a result, the Navy decided to immediately commission us as ensigns and discharge us, with the understanding that we would serve in the Naval Reserve until being recalled for active duty or retired.[14]

THE

Pŕesident of the United States of America.

To all who shall see these presents, greeting:

Know Ye, that reposing special Trust and Confidence in the Patriotism, Valor, Fidelity and Abilities of _____ LEROY EDWARD HOFFBERGER _____ I do appoint him

_____ ASSISTANT PAYMASTER WITH THE RANK OF ENSIGN _____

in the Naval Reserve of The United States Navy to rank from the _____ TWENTIETH _____ day of SEPTEMBER 1945. He is therefore carefully and diligently to discharge the duties of such office by doing and performing all manner of things thereunto belonging.

And I do strictly charge and require all Officers, Seamen and Marines under his Command to be obedient to his orders. And he is to observe and follow such orders and directions from time to time as he shall receive from me, or the future President of The United States of America, or his Superior Officer set over him, according to the Rules and Discipline of the Navy.

This Commission to continue in force during the pleasure of the President of the United States, for the time being.

Done at the City of Washington this _____ TWENTIETH _____ day of SEPTEMBER in the year of our Lord One Thousand Nine Hundred and _____ FORTY-FIVE _____ and of the Independence of The United States of America the One Hundred and _____ SEVENTIETH. _____

By the President:

James Forrestal
Secretary of the Navy

329209

Needless to say, I was happy to be out of the Navy and back to civilian life. On the other hand, I felt somewhat guilty that, although not having any "points" for overseas duty (which was the regular basis for determining the order of discharge), I was nevertheless given my "ruptured duck," the pin issued to discharged servicemen to be worn in the lapel of your civilian jacket to indicate you were a veteran. I wore it, but not with a great deal of pride, since I felt that I had not really earned it.

I came back to my home on Bancroft Road to live with my mother and father until returning to the Wharton School for my senior year in the fall of 1945. I mentioned to Dad what my plans were and indicated that I wanted to finish college at Penn as quickly as possible, and then go to work in whatever Hoffberger business he and my uncles felt would be appropriate. I remember my father's response: "Would you do me a favor and contact some of your friends from Peddie, who may be at Princeton, just to see if you might find Princeton more to your liking?" My reaction was twofold. First, I told him, as vehemently as possible, that I liked the University of Pennsylvania, that the Wharton School was a good school and that I had friends there. Secondly, since my father's requests were like commands to me, I knew I had to do what he had suggested.

I am not sure how I found out that my Peddie friend Charlie Fredericks was still at Princeton, but I did. I contacted him by phone and told him that I was out of the Navy and that I would like to meet with him to learn more about Princeton since I was thinking about matriculating there for my senior year. He was happy to hear from me, and we arranged to meet one day during the next week in his dormitory room.

With reluctance, I drove to Princeton, found Charlie's dormitory room in Holder Hall and was let into his room by one of the janitors. The room was pitch black and reeked of beer. As my eyes adjusted to the darkness, I began to see my surroundings. On the far side of the living room was a bar on top of which was a keg of beer. Mostly empty glasses of beer were all over the place.

Soon Charlie returned from class. We embraced and exchanged stories about what we had been doing in the two and a half years since we left Peddie. I then admitted that the only reason I was there was because my father had asked me to visit Princeton in the hope that I would find some reason to change my mind about going back to Penn to get a degree in one year from the Wharton School. Typical of Charlie, the first thing out of his mouth was: "Why the hell do you want to get a degree from that trade school?" He then proceeded to tell me what life at Princeton was like: great professors in all the departments, but more importantly, great campus life consisting of nightly beer drinking in the dorms or at the Nassau Tavern and girls from New York and New England women's colleges arriving for weekend parties.

While the University of Pennsylvania had a famous bar called Smokey Joe's that I was quite familiar with as a result of having frequently sneaked out after lights-out with some of my V-12 buddies, it did not seem to compare to Charlie's description of available watering spots at Princeton. My interest in attending Princeton began to heighten. I then asked Charlie what department he thought I should major in based on my background at the Wharton School.

Charlie said that there was a school founded in the 1920s by Woodrow Wilson to carry out his ideal of educating college youth for government service. It was called "The Woodrow Wilson School of Public and International Affairs" (known in my day as the "SPIA") that offered an array of courses in economics, political science, sociology and history mixed with courses that dealt with current national and international issues. That sounded interesting so I asked if he would take me to the SPIA building to meet someone with whom I could talk about applying.

I remember we walked across the campus to a relatively small two-story white brick building that looked like a cottage. That charming but somewhat insignificant building was the humble home of what is, today, the famous Woodrow Wilson School, now housed in a magnificent modern building with a beautiful reflective pool at the entrance. [15]

As luck would have it, the then-Dean of the School was in, and I was immediately ushered into his office. I told him that I was interested in attending the Woodrow Wilson School in the Class of 1947 and showed him a transcript of my grades at both Columbia and the Wharton School. I suspect that it was not my grades alone that impressed him. Since the war had just ended and there were so few civilian students returning for classes in the fall of 1945, I believe the Dean was anxious to fill the slots still available and that I was one of the few civilian students interested in applying. There was one catch, however, and that was that I had to enter Princeton as a junior.

When I returned home, I told my father that I appreciated his encouraging me to take a look at Princeton and that I found its academic programs quite interesting. I explained that I would have to spend an extra year to get my BA degree, but that I felt it would be worth it. Of course, I did not mention the fact that the extracurricular activities (i.e., the parties) had strongly motivated my decision. I know my decision

When I returned home, I told my father that I appreciated his encouraging me to take a look at Princeton and that I found its academic programs quite interesting.

pleased him, for although he had only a sixth-grade education, he was convinced that having a degree from a university as prestigious as Princeton would have a major impact on my life. I believe that he was right and that I have benefited in many ways from having graduated from Princeton (with honors).

TWO GREAT YEARS AT PRINCETON

Charlie, who was to complete his senior-year courses and submit his thesis in mid-year, arranged for seven of us, some of whom were returning veterans, to room together at 111 Little Hall. This was an entire section of the dormitory complex of two-story walk-up stone Gothic buildings. Our space contained four individual bedrooms and a living room on each of two floors and a single bathroom on the second floor. In those days, we even had a janitor who cleaned our quarters and made our beds. What sheer luxury, particularly compared to what I had just experienced in the Navy!

Besides myself and Charlie, our group consisted of John Kennedy (the freshman son of a New York congressman), Jack Barry (who I think had been in the Navy V-12 Program), Pete Garvin (who had been a tail gunner on a B-17 in Europe), Joe Lackey (who I don't think was in the service) and Bill Foster (a fellow Peddie boy, who had been in combat in the infantry in Europe, and was from Charlie's hometown of Red Bank, New Jersey). John and Bill were freshmen, and the rest of us were juniors, except for Charlie, who was a senior.

Since there was one more bedroom than there were occupants, we turned one of the downstairs bedrooms into a bar and painted the entire room black (not to the university's liking). On a recessed window ledge behind the bar we stood two bookcases which were used to store glasses. Usually, on the weekends, we had a half keg of beer on the bar. There was an upright piano and my set of drums outside the bar in the hall. Bill Bryan (a six-foot-four-inch New Yorker) played a mean piano and I did my best to provide the rhythm. During the fall football season of 1945, 111 Little was the place to be.

Although we did not all hang out together, we got along pretty well. (There was only one occasion when an anti-Semitic remark was made by Jack Barry in the heat of an argument, but this was quickly followed by an apology.) I became most friendly with Pete Garvin who was easygoing and intelligent and whose sense of humor and personality matched mine. I cannot remember ever having an argument with him during the two years we roomed together, even though by no means

Party at the Tower Club on a football weekend, 1949

did we always agree – he tending to be conservative and I liberal when it came to social/political issues.

One traditional ritual at Princeton threatened to split up our group, and that was "bickering," a process whereby juniors were interviewed by the various "eating clubs" for admission. Since John Kennedy and Bill Foster were only freshmen, they were not eligible to join a club. That left Charlie Fredericks, Jack Barry, Joe Lackey, Pete Garvin and me. After being interviewed by several clubs we liked, Jack Barry decided he wanted to join Cannon Club, and the remaining four of us set our sights on Tower Club. Not being sure that Tower's selection committee wanted all of us, we decided to form what was known as an "Ironbound." This meant that none of us would join Tower, if invited, unless all of the others in our "Ironbound" were also accepted.

I told the group that I was not sure they should include me in the "Ironbound" since I was the only Jew in the group and that perhaps Tower did not accept Jews. Several of the very socially prominent clubs did not. My friends were surprised that I would even think of such a thing, but by then I knew too much about discrimination not to raise the issue. The question was asked of Tower, and the answer was "Yes, Jews are welcomed," so all four of us joined Tower Club which was then (and still is) one of the finest.

Once you join a club, it becomes the focus of your social activities and its members become your new friends. While our "Ironbound" group remained my closest friends, I was fortunate to befriend a group of young men who were formerly at Princeton in the Marine V-12 Program. They were "Whitey" Meyers, Rocco Annese, Bud Hinse, Bob Bauer and Rodney Cathcart – all of the Class of 1948. Now, when we partied on the weekend, they (and their girlfriends, most of whom they ultimately married) were a part of my social set.

I became quite fond of hanging out with them and on occasion went up to Cranford, New Jersey, where most of them lived. I also went with Pete to Ridgewood, New Jersey, to visit his mother, who was a widow. Pete's deceased father had been a lawyer and had also been twice elected Mayor of Bayonne, New Jersey.[16] At the end of the 1945 school year, we all rented a cottage at the beach resort of Point Pleasant, New Jersey, and the partying continued throughout the summer as groups of us would come and go. Those were my second (and last) set of carefree days.

For our senior year (1946 – 1947), Pete and I decided to room together. The rest of our roommates had dispersed, but we found another first-floor suite with two bedrooms and a living room. We had our group at Tower with whom to socialize, but we became more serious about our studies and spent more time in our suite, poring over our books. Now, that did not mean every night. As I can clearly remember, we would

> Once you join a club, it becomes the focus of your social activities and its members become your new friends.

Members of Tower Club, Princeton, 1949, with Pete Garvin, circled at left, and me, circled at right

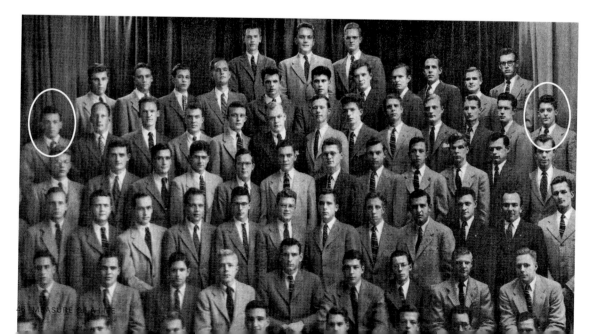

often shoot wads of paper into the wastepaper basket, with the winner deciding whether we should study or go to the movies. Quite often, the movies won out.

Toward midterms, I began to get concerned about writing my senior thesis as I was still struggling to find a topic related to what I was studying at the SPIA. As I recall, we were analyzing the pros and cons of the federal government continuing to control prices and wages after the war. There were shortages of all kinds, which necessitated consideration of the extension of price controls, and there were pressures by labor to increase wages. Industrialists were obviously arguing against it and labor unions were for it. I therefore decided to write my thesis on: "The Influence of the NAM (National Association of Manufacturers) vs. the CIO (Congress of Industrial Organizations) on the Extension of the 1946 Price Control Act."

Having never written a thesis, I found it quite a challenge to do the research required and to interview the people on the "firing line." I had to thoroughly analyze the techniques used by these two organizations to influence public opinion and Congress. Many years later I came across my thesis so I sat down and read it. It seems that I referred to those lobbying organizations as "pressure groups," a term that I don't think would be politically correct today. It also appears that I concluded that each side had some cogent ideas that appealed to Congress. The Bill to Extend the Office of Price Administration was vetoed by President Truman and was then rewritten by Congress to keep controls on, but also to establish a more lenient procedure for granting exemptions allowing selective price increases. I believe my thesis was purely an objective exercise and that I was not emotionally concerned about the outcome. Perhaps I should have been (i.e., sided with the NAM) because, not known to me, the Family businesses had applied for exemptions to price control which, I believe, were granted.

In June of 1947, on a beautiful sunny day on the lawn of Nassau Hall, I received my BA with honors. My mother and father attended the ceremony and I know they were proud of me, particularly Dad. Happily, it was not the last Princeton graduation that he witnessed, as my brother Stanley graduated in the Class of 1951.[17]

> Toward midterms, I began to get concerned about writing my senior thesis as I was still struggling to find a topic related to what I was studying at the SPIA.

Two of my five original roommates, Joe Lackey and Jack Barry, with me at our fiftieth Princeton reunion, 1997

My generation of Hoffbergers had been raised to understand that we were to work in one of the Family's businesses.

After another summer of primarily hanging out with my Princeton friends at Point Pleasant, I returned home ready to go to work wherever the "powers that be" (i.e., my father, Uncle Sam and Uncle Saul) decided I was needed. While I am writing this as though it is quite normal for family elders to decide on the career path of the next generation, I fully realized then that such a practice was unusual, to say the least. However, that is simply the way things were done in my Family.

My generation of Hoffbergers had been raised to understand that we were to work in one of the Family's businesses. Therefore, it was not a great leap to expect to be told in which business I would work. At this time, there were a number of Family businesses, and this practice worked; but in later generations, it would result in some costly mistakes and some hurt feelings.

Upon being discharged from the service, Bert had been designated to run the Family's freight transportation company, Motor Freight Express, and my cousin Jerold had been selected to run the National Brewing Company. Thus, I was waiting for a decision as to where I would fit in. Being tired of "book learning" and anxious to put my education to work, I awaited their decision.

What I did not expect was for my father to ask once again, "Would you do me a favor?" I knew that I was in for a surprise. He said that the increasing amount of legal work in my Uncle Sam's law firm necessitated the addition of a lawyer and that it was decided that it would be ideal for me to fill that position. Furthermore, he said, my Uncle Sam was getting older and the Family should have a Hoffberger to take over when he retired.

Well, it was obvious I could not fulfill this mandate unless I went to law school. Believe me, going to law school and becoming a lawyer were not matters that I had given any previous thought to, so I was really caught off guard when my father asked me to once again do him a "favor." I told him that I would have to think about it.

The next day, when Dad and I had a chance to talk, I told him that I was willing to go to law school. Nevertheless, I said that I would not apply to Harvard or Yale; that I had had enough of dormitory life and that I would live at home and apply to the University of Maryland Law School located in downtown Baltimore. I had decided that I wanted the comforts of home (have my meals at home, have my laundry done), but be able to come and go as I pleased. He and Mother agreed, and I went to the University of Maryland Law School to apply for admission to the Class of 1950. I met with the then-Dean of the School (Dean Howell) and was immediately accepted.

Bert, who was assigned to be president of Motor Freight Express upon discharge from the Coast Guard

Jerold, who was assigned to be president of the National Brewing Co. upon discharge from the Army

Stanley, who was assigned to Pompeian Olive Oil Corp. upon leaving the Army

Upon discharge from the Navy, I was slated to join Uncle Sam's law firm after graduating from law school.

The day class of 1950 consisted of about fifty or so students, mostly men, who were residents of Maryland and many of whom were veterans.[18] Of the few women in the class, one was from a prominent African-American family in Baltimore and the first black woman to be admitted to the Law School. Most of the lectures were given in an amphitheater where we were seated alphabetically. On my right was Dutch Hoffmeister and on my left was Bill Higgins. Dutch was at least three or four years older than I was and had seen action as a Marine in the Pacific. Bill was from the Eastern Shore and had seen active duty in the Navy as a pilot. Both became good friends.

Law School required a great deal more daily preparation than did Princeton. The method of teaching was called the "case system" where, in addition to lectures on a particular aspect of the law, you were required to read and make notes on numerous cases that supported the doctrine of the law being discussed, or in some instances differed from the prevailing "weight of the law." I was a copious note taker, so when it came time for exams, several students (including Dutch and Bill) would spend all night at my house, studying from my notes.

Me as student representative for the class of 1950 at the University of Maryland School of Law

Often, Dutch and I went out on the town. Bill joined us sometimes, but he had a girlfriend and spent most of his spare time with her. Dutch was a heavy drinker and not a pleasant drunk. I suspect that his experiences in the war had something to do with his propensity to become intoxicated. Still, he was very intellectual and I enjoyed his company. Unfortunately, several years after we graduated, Dutch got drunk at a bar and got involved in a fight with someone on the parking lot. His opponent hit him one time, knocking him down on the gravel. Whoever told me the story said that Dutch's head struck a hard object and went "pop" and he died. Thus, I lost another good friend.

If you were a veteran, you were permitted to take the bar exam at the end of your second year of school. The rationale for this was that many men in law school were older and married and needed to make a living as quickly as possible. Although neither old nor married, I qualified to take the exam.

Since none of us had had certain courses that were included in the exam, we took a "cram course" conducted by the Caplan Brothers. They were not only good teachers but walking case books, familiar with all of the Maryland cases asked on the bar exam for the past ten years or so. More than likely, a number of the cases on which they prepped us would be on the exam, and they were. I forget the minimum score required to pass, but I recall that I exceeded it by 19 points!

Although I had one more year of law school to go, I was now qualified to practice law in the State of Maryland. This meant that I could be a part-time member of Uncle Sam's law firm. He was determined that I should get some trial experience and, knowing all of the Circuit Court judges, he arranged to have Judge Sherbow appoint me to defend an indigent man accused of participating in an armed robbery. Fortunately, the other defendants' lawyers involved in the case were experienced and did most of the defense work.

I was scared to death as I did not feel adept at recognizing and objecting to inadmissible evidence called "hearsay," but Judge Sherbow helped me by doing so himself. I recall that I was so nervous that, to keep from shaking, I hung one of my legs over the arm of the chair I was sitting in. When the trial ended and my client was sentenced to forty years in prison, Judge Sherbow called me into his chambers. He said some nice things (obviously not true) about my participation in the case, but proceeded to chastise me for having hung my leg over the chair arm, saying it was not appropriate for a lawyer to sit that way in court. I said that I was sorry, but I did not reveal to him that I had done this to keep from shaking.

On the brighter side, Sig Kallins, the only trial lawyer in my uncle's firm, asked me to write a brief for the Maryland Court of Appeals in connection with a case he had tried and won in the Maryland District Court (then known as the People's Court). The case was docketed as "Vane v. C. Hoffberger Company."

As I recall, Vane was sued by the C. Hoffberger Company for its failure to pay for some minor work done in the repair of an oil-fired furnace. Evidently, Vane failed to show up to defend the suit in the District Court and a judgment was rendered against him for a relatively minor amount, probably less than $500. Vane was notified of the judgment and decided to appeal the decision to the Circuit Court.

In response to Vane's suit that he did not owe the money for which the C. Hoffberger Company had obtained a judgment, the C. Hoffberger Company pleaded "res judicata," that is, that the matter had already been decided by the lower court and could not be raised again. The judge in the Circuit Court agreed and dismissed Vane's suit. Surprisingly (because the amount did not warrant it), Vane appealed the decision to the Maryland Court of Appeals, Maryland's highest court.

I had never written a brief, so I turned to another lawyer in the office for assistance, Morton Hollander. Morton, who had a law degree from Harvard, was my uncle's right hand in legal matters and had taken on the job of mentoring me. Thus he helped me organize my approach, but I did all of the research and wrote the brief. I was confident that I had the "weight of the law" in my favor and that I had a good chance of winning. However, very late in this research process, I came across a Pennsylvania case that seemed to support an opposing view (i.e., that a judgment in a court of lower jurisdiction did not preclude the defendant from a new trial in a court of higher jurisdiction).

I was now in a quandary. Was I required to reveal this contrary case and try to distinguish it from my case or was it the responsibility of the appellant's lawyer to find and cite it? If he hadn't found it in his research, was it the appellant's tough luck? On the other hand, did I have a responsibility, as an officer of the court, to reveal it to the judges? With some advice from Morton, I decided that my client did not owe the court that duty. The Court of Appeals in 1950 decided that the rule of "res judicata" applied. Vane v. C. Hoffberger Company (196 Md. 450) is the law of Maryland today, as far as I know.

Morton, who had a law degree from Harvard, was my uncle's right hand in legal matters and had taken on the job of mentoring me.

Again, when arguing before the judges in the Court of Appeals, I was very anxious, and having won my first case in the highest court of the state while still in law school, I decided to cease appearing in any court while I was ahead. It was clear to me that litigation was not going to be my forte, and I never tried another case. What I should have realized was that litigation was not my nemesis, but that my extreme anxiety was. My fear of not performing up to my own expectations (and what I perceived to be those of Uncle Sam) would ultimately overcome me and send me into a deep depression.

My last year of law school was somewhat anticlimactic since I had already passed the bar. However, I did well in my courses and graduated in 1950 in the upper part of my class. Thus, I became a full-time member of my uncle's law firm. The other lawyers who worked for him at the time, in addition to Morton and Sig, were my Uncle Jesse Rose, who was my mother's brother; Emanuel Gorfine, who was a former Speaker of the House of the Maryland Legislature; and Harry Suls, who was a lawyer and a CPA in charge of the accounting office.

PROFESSIONAL AND BUSINESS LIFE

At the time I began working full-time for Uncle Sam, he was counsel for all of the Hoffberger enterprises. The Family was involved in a number of diverse businesses, many of which were owned wholly or in part by the Family's holding company, called Merchants Terminal Corporation. Merchants was established in 1928 as the entity for providing executive management and capital for the original businesses of the Family. These included the refrigerated warehousing enterprise and all of the operating facilities of the C. Hoffberger Company engaged in the manufacturing and distribution of ice, coal and fuel oil. As other businesses were acquired, Merchants became the sole or major shareholder. These additional businesses included the Baltimore Transfer Company (ultimately, Motor Freight Express), the Pompeian Olive Oil Company and the National Brewing Company. My Uncle Saul was the president of Merchants at the time I became a member of Uncle Sam's firm.

Initially, my work consisted primarily of drafting leases for the Real Estate Holding Company and Keystone Realty Company Inc., both Family-owned enterprises created and run by Uncle Sam. I also prepared wills and trusts for Family members. My first office was on the third floor. I mention this because, as my uncle thought that I was progressing, he moved me to the second floor with most of the other lawyers and so that I could be nearer to him. Since his office was in the rear, by a gradual series of moves from the front to the middle of this floor I ended up with only the waiting room between us. Such proximity made it easier for Uncle Sam to walk into my office or to ask me to come into his. While I am sure that being more accessible to him was intended to indicate his increasing confidence in me, from my point of view it put me more under his scrutiny and heightened my anxiety.

My Uncle Sam, who had become a lawyer when it was not necessary to have an undergraduate degree to go to law school, was not known for his great knowledge of the law, but for his intuitive sense (known as "street smarts") of how to apply the law to the many business endeavors in which the Family was engaged. He knew what was essential in a legal document (be it a lease, a deed, a mortgage or a business contract) to achieve his objectives and to protect against possible, but not obvious, pitfalls.

Uncle Sam, Dad's brother and my mentor, 1959

As my father would have described him, Uncle Sam could "think around corners." He had been both opportunistic and successful in acquiring a number of local businesses (including the National Brewing Company, Pompeian Olive Oil Company, the Solarine Company, Abbotts Bitters Inc.) and was highly respected in the business and financial communities of Baltimore. He knew all of the important "players," so I was systematically introduced to all of the bank presidents and other executives with whom he did business.

He was also tied into the political life of the city, state and country through his ability to raise significant funds for the candidates (exclusively Democrats) that he supported. These ranged from city councilmen to U.S. senators and even to presidential candidates. Since he assumed that I would follow suit, he started to introduce me to his political friends – Mayor Howard Jackson, Councilman Jack Edelman, Mayor Tommy D'Alessandro Sr., Governor William Preston Lane, Senator Millard Tydings, Ambassador Joseph Davies and Senator Herbert O'Conor among them.

I also met Senator Tydings' son, Joe, who was just entering law school and just beginning to be active in the Democratic Party. Joe and I became good friends over the years. When he married and had his first daughter, Mary, he asked me to be one of her two godfathers. When he ran for the Senate, he asked me to serve as his finance chairman for both of his runs. Having joined the Young Democrats of Maryland with

Me and other Young Democrats, *The Evening Sun*, 1973 (The paper misidentifies me as Uncle Sam's son.)

YOUNG DEMOCRATS—Sons and daughters of a number of Maryland party officials pitched in to help with the rally tonight for Senator Barkley (D., Ky.) at the Lyric. They are, (left to right) Paul Bishop, son of William H. Bishop, Jr., party secretary; Walter Dorsey, son of Philip H. Dorsey, People's Counsel to the Public Service Commission; Herbert R. O'Conor, Jr., son of Senator O'Conor; LeRoy Hoffberger, son of Samuel H. Hoffberger, campaign executive director; Thomas D'Alesandro, Jr., son of Mayor D'Alesandro, and Wilbur Dorsey. (Seated) Miss Dorothy Lane, daughter of Governor Lane; LeRoy W. Preston, vice chairman of the Democratic State Central Committee, and Miss Joyce Fallon, daughter of Representative George H. Fallon.

Joe, I met other Democratic activists and office holders from around the state. Among them was Daniel Brewster, who subsequently became both a member of the U.S. House of Representatives and a U.S. senator. Another was Congressman Steny Hoyer, who became the majority leader of the U.S. House of Representatives when the Democrats controlled the House.

Like my uncle, I, too, gained a reputation as a successful fundraiser and, a number of years later, was selected by Barbara Mikulski as Finance Committee Co-Chair in her first run for the U.S. Senate. Barbara, a long-time community activist, became the first woman Democrat to be elected to the Senate in her own right, not a successor as the spouse of a deceased senator.[19]

Politics was an avocation for my uncle and me but was also considered important to the Family's interests. Although we never sought to use political influence in support of an unjust cause, there were occasions when our political connections gave us the opportunity to present our viewpoint to the powers that be.

Hoffberger Gets Party Club Post

Joseph D. Tydings, president of the Young Democratic Clubs of Maryland, announced today the appointment of Leroy E. Hoffberger, of Baltimore, as his assistant.

David J. Preller was named Baltimore city chairman and James B. McCloskey, vice chairman, for the city. Miss Mary Anne Estey, of Montgomery county, was appointed executive secretary of the organization.

The appointments were made at an executive committee meeting held in Easton.

Regional Directors

Regional directors named were Elroy G. Boyer, Kent county, for the First Congressional district; Walter Tabler, Jr., Baltimore county, Second district; Edward S. Digges, Charles county, Fifth district, and Charles B. Buscher, Sixth district.

Chairman of committees are C. Audry Thompson, Dorchester county, legislative; Dan Brewster, Baltimore county, speakers; Charles Keehne, Frederick county, constitution and by-laws; Frank Wright, the University of Maryland, students; Miss Gene H. Miller, Anne Arundel county, publicity.

The Evening Sun,
Baltimore, n.d.

Senator Joseph Tydings
and me on the occasion
of his 85th birthday, 2013.
Photograph by
Paula Gately Tillman

In a way, the highlight of my career in politics occurred not when Joe or Barbara won seats in the Senate, but when I was named on President Nixon's "second enemies list" in December 1973. This meant that I, along with 574 other Americans, was to be harassed by the IRS for having played an active role in Senator George McGovern's unsuccessful run for president. My Democrat friends and I considered this a "badge of honor"!

Senator Barbara Mikulski and me in her DC office. I was her Finance Committee Co-Chair for her successful first campaign in 1986. She is now the senior woman in the U.S. Senate.

As much as he liked politics, Uncle Sam's true love was real estate. In the 1940s, he had accumulated in the Real Estate Holding Company Inc. and Keystone Realty Company Inc. a portfolio of Class B and C office and storefront buildings, mostly in downtown Baltimore.[20] More significantly, he sensed that the growth of the Baltimore Jewish community, following World War II, would take place in northwest Baltimore, where he had acquired large parcels of developable residential land. He had first bought land within the city in the upper Pimlico area, and later he purchased a large land holding just beyond the city line in the vicinity of Smith Avenue, formally known as the Curtiss-Wright Air Field.

Barbara A. Mikulski
United States Senator
Washington, D.C. 20510

November 4, 1992

Mr. and Mrs. LeRoy Hoffberger
233 East Redwood Street, Suite 800
Baltimore, MD 21202

Dear Roy and Rebecca:

You made it happen! It was the support of friends like you that enabled me to put together a winning campaign organization. On election night, the voters of Maryland overwhelmingly re-elected me to the United States Senate.

I am especially honored to have their support and proud to be able to return to the U. S. Senate to welcome in a new era of leadership and to work hand in hand with a Clinton-Gore administration, a new Congress and my new women colleagues.

When I was first elected to the United States Senate in 1986, I pledged to be a full time advocate for the people of Maryland and the people of this nation. I promised to be a fighter for our country and the concerns of its most valuable asset -- its people.

I pledged to stand with you to fight for the issues we care so deeply about and to see that our nation was ready for the 21st Century. You can continue to count on me. I still go to work each day with you in mind and those promises in my heart.

I cannot thank you enough for the friendship and support you have shown me. You have truly been the bridge that brought me over. I look forward to serving as your Senator and to enjoying your friendship in the years to come.

Sincerely,

Barbara

Barbara A. Mikulski
United States Senator

You're really just special

Not Printed at Government Expense

2d enemies list appears in IRS probe

'They're insane,' cries Marylander, 1 of 17 on latest White House list

By GORDON W. CHAPLIN

"They are insane," said David H. Tucker, of Columbia, yesterday on learning he was on the latest White House enemies list.

Mr. Tucker is among 17 Marylanders on the list, along with James W. Rouse, the developer of Columbia, two members of the Meyerhoff family and Leroy Hoffberger, a relative of Jerrold C. Hoffberger, chairman of the Baltimore Orioles board of directors.

The list, containing 575 names, was made public yesterday by the Joint Committee on Internal Revenue Taxation. Most persons on it were involved in some way with the McGovern presidential campaign.

"You're kidding, I just can't believe it," Mr. Tucker said. "It is absolutely beyond my comprehension how I could have been included, a citizen in exercise of his political rights. If that makes me an enemy of the White House, that makes their understanding of the political process even less than their understanding of government."

Mr. Tucker said that he and another person on the enemies list, Malcolm Sherman, also of Columbia, had between them taken out a bank loan of $1,000 for the McGovern campaign fund and had done some fund raising in the Columbia area and campaigning in Howard county. Mr. Tucker had also staged a rally for Senator McGovern in Columbia a few days before the primary. Mr. Tucker is director of performing arts for the town of Columbia.

Mr. Sherman thought being on the list was "great news. It's the best thing I have to tell my son about myself. I feel better about this than any kind of honor that could come to me."

In addition to helping arrange the $1,000 bank loan, he said, he had also done some campaigning around Columbia and was a member of Business Executives for Vietnam Peace.

David L. Hollander, of 2518 Talbot road, in Baltimore, called his inclusion on the list "far out."

"Judging from the people on the first enemies list, I am in good company," he said.

Mr. Hollander said he had contributed about $3,000 to the McGovern campaign and was campaign chairman in the Fifth district for the New Democratic Coalition.

P. McEvoy Cromwell, of 710 Circle road, Ruxton, allowed that "they are certainly correct in including me on the second list. But I haven't had enough opportunity to do as much damage as the Nixon administration deserves.

"I'm glad someone out there in the inner sanctum of the White House has correctly identified my sentiments," he said.

Mr. Cromwell, a tax lawyer, said he contributed "in the thousands" of dollars to the McGovern campaign, although he was not active in it.

The Sun, Baltimore,
December 21, 1973

To actually develop portions of the land Uncle Sam had acquired, he had employed an old family friend and distant relative by the name of Max Goodman. Max was more a maintenance man than a developer as his main job was maintaining the Class B and C buildings the Family owned downtown. Nevertheless, Max could, and did, build a modest number of houses for our real estate companies.

In order to finance the acquisition and development of the land he acquired for the Family, Uncle Sam had created a company called Merchants Mortgage Company Inc. Likewise, he founded Union Federal Savings and Loan Association in which he placed the surplus funds of our operating companies and some of the trust funds of members of my generation. Since Union Federal was also open to the general public, it became a convenient resource for residential mortgages needed to provide financing for the purchasers of the houses that Max (and later another developer by the name of Stanley Podger) had built.

> Uncle Sam saw to it that I involved myself in these real estate and financial enterprises.

Uncle Sam saw to it that I involved myself in these real estate and financial enterprises. I soon became a director, an officer and ultimately the head of Merchants Mortgage, Union Federal, Real Estate Holding Company and Keystone Realty Company. In addition, Uncle Sam felt it was essential for me to have a working knowledge of the Family operating businesses, so he made me a director of the National Brewing Company, Pompeian Olive Oil Company and the Solarine Company. Since putting me on the board of Merchants Terminal Corporation and Motor Freight Express would have required the approval of my Uncle Saul, he did not attempt to do so, not because he didn't think I would be an asset, but because it meant calling Uncle Saul for his okay. Although I had many telephone conversations and meetings with Uncle Saul about Merchants' business, my becoming a director of those entities did not occur until after Uncle Saul was bought out of all of our Family businesses.

Uncle Sam and Uncle Saul were cordial to one another but very territorial toward their business domains. That does not mean that my relationship with my Uncle Saul was not good; it was excellent, but it was as a lawyer that I related to him. As such, and because he liked me and thought that I was smart, he confided in me many of his concerns about how Bert and my cousin Jerry were running their respective businesses, Motor Freight Express and National Brewing. I concluded that his worries derived from the fact that both Bert and Jerry, contrary to the mentoring arrangement they had agreed upon, refused to report to him or to take his advice.

After my Uncle Sam was no longer alive, real estate also became my true "love" and avocation. Following in his footsteps, I would travel around Baltimore County looking for land that I felt had future development potential. However, while my intuitions were pretty good, I was less of a risk taker and less willing than my uncle to rely on my gut. Before buying, I would get extensive information from my engineer, Lester Matz, and from the County Planning Department as to approximately when the particular property that I was considering purchasing would be ready for development and what sort of zoning the county had in mind.

Over the years, I became quite adept at this and acquired a number of parcels that I ultimately disposed of at substantial profits for the Family. This experience and my relationship with Lester led to my most adventuresome and creative real estate endeavor – the acquisition in 1962–1963 of a number of parcels of farmland, totaling over 2,000 acres, in Germantown, Montgomery County. This accumulation resulted in the creation of the "New Town of Germantown," now home to over 80,000 people living 25 miles northwest of Washington, DC. My role in this project will be described later.

GEORGE ENGLAR: FIRST NON-FAMILY CLIENT, MENTOR AND INTIMATE FRIEND

Soon after I joined my uncle's law firm, he introduced me to George Englar. George was in his mid-fifties, was slight in build and had a marvelous twinkle in his eyes. There was a certain elegance about him, as his photo indicates. He lived with his family on Gibson Island and was from a prominent Maryland family (his father being a State Senator). George was well regarded in the business community as a successful real estate investor. How he and my Uncle Sam met I never knew, but they had a very good working relationship – thoroughly trusting and respecting one another.

George Englar, 1960

Together, our families owned two major office buildings (beaux arts in style) in downtown Baltimore. George managed these properties and was responsible for all operating decisions. Uncle Sam used the Family's funds to provide the equity capital. Both buildings had been rebuilt after the "Great Baltimore Fire" of 1904 and were considered to be Class A properties. The American Building had previously been owned by the *American News*, a daily newspaper of significance for well over a century. However, it was ultimately unable to compete with *The Baltimore Sun* and closed. The building that had housed the defunct *American News* was a 14-story structure then considered a high-rise building. The other building, known as the Equitable Building, was located on Calvert Street two blocks south of my office. It too was considered to be a Class A high-rise structure, although it was only ten stories high. However, it contained more gross footage than the American Building, and commanded more rent per square foot.

George soon put me on the boards of both of the companies owning these buildings, not only because I was their legal counsel (and as such would benefit from knowing what was going on), but also to educate me about the commercial real estate business. Knowing when to get in and out of a piece of real estate are keys to success. Avoiding overpaying for a property is an important part of making money, so George developed a simple formula: an improved commercial property was worth ten times its net cash flow unleveraged, that is, when you are buying it. This produced a more conservative, less speculative valuation. Sometime after we owned these two properties, professional appraisers began using projected cash flow (usually on a ten-year basis) to determine the value of improved commercial properties. Because this method was more speculative it produced higher values, on the assumption that rents continue to go up. That may be a good assumption when selling or mortgaging, but not when buying, so I tried to follow George's hard-and-fast rule during my real estate career.

Working with and learning from George was a delight, and so enlightening that I considered him to be my real estate mentor. During the twenty years or so that I had the privilege of knowing him, we developed a much more meaningful relationship; he had become my intimate friend and I his confidant. He trusted me as he had Uncle Sam, only, I believe, on a deeper level. The affection we felt for each other was like that of father and son.

THE ONSET OF DEPRESSION IMPEDES MY CAREER

Winston Churchill Called It His "Black Dog"

As more and more responsibilities were given to or assumed by me, I began to feel less and less able to fulfill them to the degree that I felt was expected not only by Uncle Sam but by my father and other senior members of the Family. After all, I had graduated from Princeton with honors, passed the bar in two years and was slated to fill my uncle's shoes. Yet, there were so many things that I did not know and it seemed that my uncle was often critical of my work, this being his way of teaching me. I was beginning to lose my confidence. I was very ill at ease and anxious during meetings with my uncle, which felt like I was on trial. When he called and told me to come to his office, I shuddered, and when I was in his office, I physically shook. Mostly my head would shake, which I was sure he noticed. Just as I had thrown my leg over the arm of the chair in court as a crutch, I likewise developed a way of tightly holding the arms on the chair I sat in, and somehow this stopped the shaking. When I went to board meetings and I was called on for a comment, I went through the same symptoms and agony. The worst part was that my anxiety distracted me from listening and being able to respond intelligently.

This state of anxiety continued to increase. I remember discussing it with Morton Hollander who had become my confidant. He concluded that because I was a perfectionist, I expected too much of myself.

"Don't take yourself so seriously," he would say. "We all make mistakes. You're doing fine." Coming from Morton, whom I admired and looked up to, such comments were comforting and somewhat reassuring, but only until the next time I was confronted by a challenging situation.

I realized that I was no longer able to cope with this situation so I decided that before I became totally dysfunctional the best thing for me to do was to stop working for a while. I told Uncle Sam of my decision, and he was, of course, shocked, as was my father. While there is no doubt that the physical symptoms of my illness were not as apparent to others as I thought, I was going through so much physical and mental pain that I felt that I could not continue to adequately fulfill my responsibilities.

Now, what to do? Since I did not think that by merely removing myself from the sources of stress I would, with the mere passage of time, be cured, I decided that I needed professional help. However, I had no idea from whom that should come. Someone, perhaps Bert, told me about a psychiatrist who had been highly recommended for treating patients with depression. I believe his last name was Wendell (or maybe Waddell). He was an older man, tall and stately. He was friendly, but I still found it difficult to confide in him all the intimate matters that were perhaps the underlying causes of my malaise. In those days, there were no antidepressant medications to relieve my anxieties or alter my somber mood, so through the process of psychoanalysis he would listen, week after week, to my fears and concerns, hoping to discover the underlying causes of why I had lost my confidence and become depressed. It was a difficult and arduous process.

I realized that I was no longer able to cope with this situation so I decided that before I became totally dysfunctional the best thing for me to do was to stop working for a while.

Finally, after several months of counseling, I decided that I was well enough to return to my office. Nevertheless, I tried to avoid having too much contact with my uncle and others in the presence of whom I still felt quite ill at ease. Thank God for Morty Hollander who kept bolstering my confidence! My parents, who really did not understand how this could have happened to me, were also very supportive, as were my brothers. It is interesting that I do not recall being anxious around my peers (although I confessed to a few of them the "hell" I was going through, much to their surprise). For better or worse, since a lot of my spare time with my friends was spent at bars drinking, I was able to self-medicate on alcohol, which put me, temporarily, in a more relaxed mood.

I continued to see Dr. Wendell for several years. At first I went several times a week and gradually, as I seemed to improve, on a less frequent basis. At some point, I stopped. While I managed to carry on my life, it was obvious to me that my "Black Dog" had not been permanently penned. I was outwardly coping, but, inwardly, I still had strong feelings of fear, worthlessness and insecurity. [21]

Little did I realize then that I had become clinically depressed. In writing these recollections, I googled "Causes of Clinical Depression." An article titled "Definition of Clinical Depression" by Marguerite Croft states that: "No absolute universally accepted cause of depression has been identified, [though] there are several theories of which two are the most popular… " One theory is "…based on biological, psychological and social causes." The other theory is that: "…people with clinical depression have a pre-existing vulnerability, either genetic or schematic, that has been triggered by a stressful life event." An element of both theories is the belief that "…brain chemistry and genetics appear to be components." Reflecting now on what had happened to me, the second hypothesis seems to fit my situation.

My father's death in 1963 intensified my awareness of my lingering depression. He had had a serious stroke while on vacation in Palm Beach. After he had spent several months in a local hospital, we decided to bring him back to Sinai Hospital in Baltimore. Although unable to talk, Dad was alert, and it became obvious that he was depressed. A young doctor by the name of Nathan Schnaper was brought in to treat him. That is when I first met Nate, to whom I owe my life.

Dr. Schnaper was a professor of psychiatry at the University of Maryland School of Medicine, but he also had a private practice on the second floor of an old, ornate, walk-up row house on St. Paul Street. He was slightly built and always wore a bowtie and red socks. His casual

Little did I realize then that I had become clinically depressed.

appearance and soft-spoken manner were much more to my liking than the somewhat formal and stern appearance of my previous psychiatrist. Since Nate was also Jewish, I felt more able to relate to him. And relate I did for more than ten years!

At first, I saw him several times a week. He was a wonderful listener who did not seem to be at all judgmental. He took few notes, but had a steel-trap memory. Now and then at crucial times when I was confiding some aspect of my youth or young adulthood, he would ask probing questions that would help me see some important aspect of my thinking that no doubt contributed to my underlying feelings of inadequacy.

Dr. Nathan Schnaper, 2000

More importantly, when I would indicate to him that I was fearful about having to speak in public and that I did not think I could do it, he would say: "What's the worst that can happen to you? You're not going to die! If you find you have to stop, so what?" and he would always conclude with: "Get off your ass and do it." Thank God he did, for while I was often quite anxious and fearful, I ultimately became a good speaker with little apprehension about appearing before large groups. Some have even told me that when I am particularly passionate about a cause, my speeches are both convincing and eloquent – something which I would never have imagined possible.

Somewhere along the line in the 1950s, antidepressant drugs began to be marketed, so Dr. Schnaper decided to put me on small dosages of Elavil for my depression and Stelazine for my anxieties. I was willing to try anything he recommended. Within about two weeks, there was a dramatic difference in the way I felt and I had no apparent side effects. This was a miracle as far as I was concerned. While I still continued to see Dr. Schnaper, the outward manifestations of my "Black Dog" had greatly subsided.

I continued on, decreasing amounts of these two medications for over 35 years. The only visible side effect were tremors of my head that I would get sometimes when speaking, sometimes when I was frightened by an unexpected noise and sometimes when I was getting a haircut when the barber would get close to my ears with the razor. However, because I was beginning to feel less overwhelmed by my responsibilities (which had actually increased substantially), I was coming to sense that I was fully capable of fulfilling everyone's expectations and, most importantly, my own.

What I did not know, then, was that my vulnerability to clinical depression meant that I would always need medication to counter the chemical imbalance in my brain. I am not sure that Dr. Schnaper realized this either, since one day, long after he had ceased seeing me professionally, while he and I were having a social lunch, he said, "Are you still taking Elavil and Stelazine?" I replied, "Yes." He then said: "You don't need those drugs any more. Besides, a recent study has revealed that long-term usage of Elavil could cause arrhythmia in older people." So I stopped.

Within about three weeks, I began to have such a nervous stomach that I had to see a Hopkins gastroenterologist. He prescribed some medications that helped a little but did not keep my stomach from jumping around, day and night. Suddenly it dawned on me that having stopped even the small amounts of Stelazine and Elavil that I was used to had resulted in my once again being anxious.

Since Dr. Schnaper was no longer seeing private patients, I had to find a new psychiatrist and the right medications to replace the ones I had been told to discontinue. I tried at least two different doctors and perhaps ten different medications, none of which worked. Believe me, it was "hell" coming off of one and going on another. Finally, I said: "Let's go back to the Elavil and Stelazine. I'll take my chances." Whoever was the doctor I was then seeing, agreed. So back on these two medications I went; but, unfortunately, they no longer worked.

For some reason that I do not recall, I mentioned to my cousin Lois Feinblatt, a very seasoned lay analyst at Hopkins, what I was going through. She said that there was a psychiatrist at Hopkins who was also expert at pharmacology and that perhaps he could help. His name was Dr. Constantine Lyketsos.

I was able to get an appointment with Dr. Lyketsos, who was the head of the Department of Geriatric Psychiatry and The Memory Center at the Bayview Campus of Hopkins. To my great relief he was able to prescribe the medicines I needed for both my anxiety and mood changes, and I have relied on him ever since for advice about my medications. Although I feel that my depression has remained under control, I suspect that my "Black Dog" will always be nipping at my heels.[22]

LIFE GOES ON

As I indicated in the previous section, even while I was still suffering from the anguishes of my depression, I resumed my professional business, communal and social life. Primarily, due to Dr. Schnaper's therapy, I was able to take up my responsibilities at the office, although, as previously indicated, I initially maintained a low profile and relied on Morton Hollander when I needed his help.

In the early fifties, I had not yet risen in my communal activities to positions of high visibility. However, as my responsibilities in the office increased (due in part to my uncle's illness) and as I worked my way up the ladder of leadership in the organizations with which I was involved, I was able to meet daily challenges, bolstered by Dr. Schnaper's support.

I can recall that one of the first public events at which I had to speak was an Associated Jewish Charities dinner at which Senator Daniel Brewster was the keynote speaker. Although my role was merely to introduce a good friend, I told Dr. Schnaper that I didn't think I could do it. He got annoyed and chastised me, but at the same time his reassurance gave me courage, so I decided to go through with it. I made the introduction, being very anxious while doing so; but, under the circumstances, this was quite a personal achievement for me.

As Uncle Sam's mental health declined, George Englar began to rely on me for not only legal matters, but for advice concerning the real estate ventures in which the Hoffberger and Englar families were partners. The more we worked together, the closer we became as colleagues and friends. In the summer, he would invite me to his home on Gibson Island to spend time with him, his wife, Elizabeth, and his two children, Brud and Betsy, who were about my age. George prided himself on his mint juleps which, while not my favorite beverage, I nevertheless enjoyed while socializing with his family on the front lawn of his home overlooking the Chesapeake Bay and the Magothy River. As our friendship grew, I was becoming George's closest confidant.

In about 1956, George decided that it was the right time to sell our downtown office buildings. Since I felt that George was far more knowledgeable about the downtown commercial real estate market than I was, I saw no reason to question his judgment. As the next story will reveal, I am not sure his decision to sell was motivated purely by market conditions. Nevertheless, I believe the prices we got were fair.

Fortunately, the only property George could not sell was the jointly owned garage in the same block as my uncle's office on Calvert Street because it had been financed by a city bond issue that required city approval before any sale. Subsequently, that property, along with the building where I worked, became part of the footprint for a large structure that I was to build and lease to the Maryland National Bank for its back-office operations center. That undertaking is described later.

Sometime in 1954, a few years before George decided to sell our jointly owned properties, he told me that he had been approached with a business proposition by his friend Julius Amoss, who also lived on Gibson Island. Amoss had been a colonel in the OSS – the Office of Strategic Services and the equivalent of today's CIA – during World War II and had been parachuted into Greece to obtain military information concerning Nazi operations.

While in Greece he developed an itchy scalp condition, so he went into a barber shop and asked if the barber had any remedy for this. The barber gave him a bottle of a clear liquid with sediment at the bottom which mixed with the liquid when shaken. Colonel Amoss used the product with success, but he also noticed that the product was turning his hair back to what he believed was its natural color. He considered this to be amazing and felt this potion had commercial potential.

So, after the war ended, Amoss and a Greek friend of his, Stavros Theofanidis, who was the former Minister of Shipping under King Paul, negotiated a contract with the barber for the worldwide rights to produce and sell the product, except in Greece and Crete.

Amoss showed George the English translation of the manufacturing and distribution contract and the formula and process for making the product and asked George whether he would be interested in going into business with him. The fact that Mr. Theofanidis had been involved was not disclosed by Amoss to George.

> He considered this to be amazing and felt this potion had commercial potential.

After trying the product, George was intrigued, but said that he had no experience whatsoever in making or marketing a consumer product such as this. However, he told Colonel Amoss that his real estate partners, the Hoffbergers, were also in the beer business as well as in the business of processing and bottling olive oil and other household products (Solarine Liquid Floor Wax and Solarine Brass Polish, as well as a little-known bitters called Abbotts Bitters). He then said that he would find out if the Hoffbergers were interested.

Knowing that Uncle Sam was ill, George came to me to see if I thought the Family would be interested in participating in this opportunity. I told him that I thought we would be, but that first I wanted to ask my father, who was then CEO of Pompeian Olive Oil Company, if he thought the company would be interested in producing and bottling the product. Dad thought that production of the product would probably not be a problem, but, like George, he wanted to be a "guinea pig" to satisfy himself that this so-called "secret potion" really worked.

He had the company's chemist, Daniel Savanuck, make up a small batch of the product, according to the translated formula, which he began applying religiously to his gray sideburns. Sure enough, after about three weeks his sideburns darkened as predicted. He also sent the formula and a sample of the product to a chemical lab to have it analyzed.

It turned out that the basic active ingredient of the product was lead sulfide mixed with glycerin which, when applied regularly, left increasing amounts of lead in the gray (colorless) hair shaft. Lead had been used to color hair going back to Roman times. Thus, it was by no means a "secret potion," and certainly not patentable. Nevertheless, it worked and by controlling the frequency and amount applied to the scalp, it added natural-looking color to gray hair.

> Thus, it was by no means a "secret potion," and certainly not patentable.

However, the lead in the product was felt to be problematic. While lead in hair products was not banned by the FDA as carcinogenic, it was a substance that the government was concerned about, particularly in paint. We, therefore, anticipated that the product might at some time in the future be banned. Our challenge would be to find a substitute for the lead.

Despite this possible problem, I informed George that we would participate. The amount we had to contribute was $5,000, a sum to be matched by the Englar family. Amoss was to contribute the formula and the process together with the worldwide license from the Greek barber. Thus, World Wide Rights Inc. was formed in 1954.

George became quite enamored with the sales potential of the product and began to travel to New York to meet with possible distributors. Several regional hair product distributors agreed to market the product. One, Aegean Products Inc., actually came up with its name: Grecian Formula 16.

Among the people that George met in New York was Bob Smallwood, the head of Lipton Tea, a subsidiary of Lever Brothers, the huge Dutch/English conglomerate. Affectionately referred to as "Big Tea" Smallwood, Bob himself became interested in investing in one of the distributorships as well as having Lever Brothers consider marketing the product.

Knowing a multitude of movers and shakers in New York, Bob made sure that George met all the right people who might be interested in distributing Grecian Formula 16. In addition, Bob introduced George to a beautiful, middle-aged Swedish actress and opera singer, Margot Forsgren, and in time George confided to me that he was seeing Margot frequently and had fallen in love with her. Later, he divulged that he was going to divorce his wife of fifty years and go to Switzerland to live with Margot in Lugano. This new bit of information shed light on why he had rather suddenly decided to sell our jointly owned real estate.

One day, probably in 1955, a distinguished looking older man and his wife came to my office and presented his card to Beulah Saltz, formerly my uncle's secretary, but then mine. Beulah took the card in to me, and I read the name "Stavros Theofanidis," a person totally unknown to me. Nevertheless, I had Beulah usher him and his wife into my office.

Mr. Theofanidis said that he had traveled to Baltimore from Athens, Greece, for the purpose of discussing with me his interest in the product now being produced under the trade name Grecian Formula 16. He said that he had been the Minister of Shipping under King Paul of Greece, and, as a friend of Amoss, he had been asked to help negotiate a contract with a Greek barber (who had developed a product that restored color to gray hair) for the worldwide rights to produce and sell his remarkable product. For his services he alleged that he and Amoss had an agreement (which he produced) to split any profits derived from this enterprise.

Needless to say, I was bowled over by his claim. I asked Mr. Theofanidis, who was staying with his wife at a downtown hotel, to give me time to study the documents he had given me and to talk to George. I told him that I would call him later in the day. After he left my office, I immediately got on the telephone and contacted George, who was in New York. George was as shocked as I had been and suggested that I try to reach Colonel Amoss right away.

When I confronted Colonel Amoss over the phone, he confessed that there was such an agreement and that he had failed to inform us. I called George and told him that Amoss had admitted the truth, confirming Mr. Theofanidis' story. George said he would return to Baltimore immediately and asked me to tell Amoss and Mr. Theofanidis to meet us in my office the next morning.

How a former OSS operative could have assumed that Mr. Theofanidis would never surface, I don't know. Now, what to do about it? George and I met in my office before our meeting with Amoss and Mr. Theofanidis to think of a solution. The solution that he and I decided to present to Amoss and Mr. Theofanidis would give Mr. Theofanidis the one-third interest that Colonel Amoss held in World Wide Rights Inc., and George and the Hoffberger interests would reimburse Colonel Amoss for the $10,000 he had paid the Greek barber. George's family and the Hoffbergers would retain their respective one-third interests.

Mr. Theofanidis was agreeable to our solution, and while George and I were somewhat concerned about how we would get along with our new partner, this did not turn out to be a problem. Over thirty or so years of ownership, during which Mr. Theofanidis' interest passed from him to his widow, Clipa, and then to her two nephews, there were never any serious disagreements. In the late 1980s, the nephews' interest was acquired by CPC Inc., a Hoffberger/Englar entity, and Combe Incorporated, the company with which World Wide ultimately contracted to produce and market Grecian Formula 16 in the U.S. and Canada.

In the beginning, sales of Grecian Formula were not impressive, primarily because the firms that were distributing it did not have the resources to adequately promote it. As luck would have it, through an introduction made by Bob Smallwood, George met a man named Ivan Combe whose company had just sold its leading acne product for teenagers, called "Clearasil," to a major pharmaceutical company. Ivan was therefore in the market for something that, like Clearasil, would produce visible results and have the same potential for mystique.

Ivan had heard about Grecian Formula and thought it might be just what his company was looking for. After further investigation and testing, he offered to become the U.S. and Canadian distributor. As I recall, I went to New York with George to meet Ivan and to discuss the terms of an exclusive long-term (fifty-year) royalty arrangement.

In the granting of an exclusive distributorship, there are generally two key clauses in the contract: one that requires the distributor to do his best to promote and sell the product and another that restricts the distributor from developing or acquiring a competitive product on which the licensor does not receive royalties. However, in our situation, both Combe and World Wide knew of the possibility that lead would be banned in the future and that it was in the interest of both parties to seek a substitute that did not contain this chemical. Since the second provision would prevent Combe from developing or acquiring a replacement for lead, we had to use another approach that would permit Combe to develop another product not containing lead but on which World Wide would still receive royalties.

Combe's Chicago lawyers crafted an agreement in 1957 that gave Combe the exclusive right to make and distribute Grecian Formula 16 in the United States and Canada for fifty years (subsequently extended an additional 15 years to June 2021) in consideration of the payment of a royalty based on sales. The second provision, of which I was the primary author, allowed Combe to develop a new product

In the beginning, sales of Grecian Formula were not impressive, primarily because the firms that were distributing it did not have the resources to adequately promote it.

of any sort, free of lead, but specified that our company would be entitled to royalties if such a product competed with Grecian Formula.

Once we had entered into the manufacturing and distribution agreement with Combe, George was eager to establish similar agreements in Europe. Our first effort to find a distributor was with a Swiss-German whose company was headquartered in Zurich. This gentleman turned out to be very dominating and inflexible so, in the beginning, our talks did not go well. Not having much time to spend in Zurich, we concluded that we were wasting our time and told the gentleman that either he must agree to our basic terms or the negotiations were over.

After we said that, I never saw such an about-face. I recall him saying, "Now gentlemen, tell me what you want." A contract was thereafter prepared which allowed him to analyze and test our product. When he did so, he discovered that it contained lead. Although this did not concern him, it did concern the Swiss government which had previously banned the presence of lead in cosmetic products.

Our second stop was in Munich, Germany, where we were met by a man named Putzi Hanfstaengl, who was to be our translator. He was a large, coarse-looking man who, I learned, had been Hitler's favorite concert pianist. Although this fact did not please me, Putzi was a dynamic character who was revered in Munich, his birthplace, for his wit and stage presence. He was also ready to perform at a moment's notice. I remember the evening we spent with him having wurst in a large beer hall. Putzi, with a little urging from the crowd, played old German lieder and led the festive beer-drinking Germans with his booming baritone.

The following day, with Putzi translating, George and I met with a burly Balkan gentleman who had a cosmetics business in Germany. I recall drinking lots of Slivovitz (plum brandy) after dinner, which was not to my liking. Neither were the next day's negotiations, so we moved on.

Our last stop was in London where we were picked up in a chauffeur-driven Rolls-Royce by Sir Lacey Vincent, chairman of L.E. Vincent & Partners Ltd. and the prototype of an English aristocrat. He was accompanied by his wife, Lady Helen Vincent, who likewise bore all the trappings of a fine, aristocratic English woman.[23]

To represent us in our negotiations with L.E. Vincent & Partners, George had hired Hyman Stone, a well-regarded solicitor from a prominent Jewish family.[24] Hyman was a rather dapper gentleman who, though small in stature, had a giant presence. The combination of his extensive knowledge of U.K. contract law and his quick grasp of what and how we wished to relate to L.E. Vincent made it quite enjoyable to work with him. But, as fate would have it, Hyman died, before the negotiations were concluded. In his place, his junior associate, Dennis Humm, stepped in.

Assisting Dennis was Hyman Stone's son, Victor, who had "read law at Cambridge," the British way of saying that he had graduated from Cambridge University Law School. These two gentlemen were, for me, the quintessential English solicitors in their attire, speech and manners. Most interesting to me was the fact that, unlike my experience in the U.S., solicitors in England leave the negotiating to their clients, their job being to produce the documents containing the terms that evolve.

Once the distribution agreement with L.E. Vincent was in place (sometime in the late 1950s), we had Dennis and Victor set up a manufacturing company to produce and bottle "Formula 16." We then identified a chemical company that did private-label business and contracted with it to produce and bottle our product which our manufacturing company then sold to L.E. Vincent at an agreed-upon price.

Formula 16's introduction to the U.K. market was reasonably successful. The product was sold by the huge Boots chain of drugstores as well as by Harrods and other leading retailers. Then, to my surprise, Combe (who, unbeknownst to George and me, had sought unsuccessfully to buy L.E Vincent) began marketing "Grecian 2000," a product similar to Formula 16. His experience in and resources for marketing hair colorants were far superior to that of Sir Lacey's small organization, so Grecian 2000 quickly dominated the market. Nevertheless, Formula 16, running a poor second, continued to eke out a small profit. That is, until Sir Lacey died in 1963, and his partner, Max Bumford, had to take over. The agony and ecstasy of that story I will recall later. Suffice it to say that Formula 16 survived in the U.K. until the government banned the use of lead in cosmetics soon after the European nations banned all cosmetics containing lead.

With George having died in March of 1970, I had become the sole decision-maker in Grecian Formula 16's national and international business. I welcomed the responsibility since it gave me a chance to develop relationships outside of the Family businesses as well as the opportunity to spend time abroad, particularly in London. It was on these visits that I got to know and work with Victor, enabling us to create a lasting friendship.

In the early days, Victor had his bachelor's flat over his law offices on Hertford Street. I would often meet him there to begin an evening out on the town. Victor had decorated his flat in splendid taste with primarily English antiques, very interesting art of all sorts and a large collection of antique wine glasses. He was a devotee of classical music so we often went to the Royal Albert Hall to hear the London Philharmonic Orchestra or to Covent Garden for an evening of opera. Then we would go on to dinner at some swank restaurant. The White Elephant on the embankment of the Thames, a private membership club to which I belonged, was one of his favorites.

Of course, when we were both bachelors, we sought to have female company. Victor had a few regular girlfriends, and I would have Hildegard Voss (my first wife-to-be) fly over from Frankfurt. There were so many enjoyable occasions of rides in the English countryside and wonderful lunches at old (16th and 17th century) country inns. Victor did the driving, as in the fifty or so years that I have been going to England I have never had the nerve to drive on the left side of the road.

> Of course, when we were both bachelors, we sought to have female company.

At some point in this long and pleasant relationship, Victor met Naomi, an Israeli woman born in South Africa, who was living in London and working for British Airways Travel Clinics. She became a participant in our social life, and pretty soon it was evident that she and Victor were in love. They were married at the New London Synagogue in London.

Victor and Naomi moved to a lovely row house in South Kensington near the tube station. It was a four-story walk-up that they completely restored. The neighborhood was a mixture of wealthy English professionals and foreigners living and working in London. Being near the station, the streets were a polyglot of nationalities, making the area vibrant but very crowded.

It was, I suspect, at Naomi's urging that the Stones moved to Canary Wharf, which was a well-planned "city" of high-rise buildings, shops, restaurants and pubs. They took up residence in the penthouse of an apartment building on the Thames. Their building was part of a complex that included other apartment buildings, a five star hotel (where Rebecca, my second wife, and I often stayed when we came to London to visit the Stones) and a separate athletic facility with a large indoor pool – all united by beautiful gardens.

While, as indicated, the international phase of the Grecian Formula saga ended many years ago, I have maintained my relationship with Victor and Naomi. Each trip I take to Europe ends or begins with a visit to London to be with them, and although these visits are infrequent and limited in duration, we continue to have a warm friendship. Victor has been such an integral part of Grecian Formula's U.K. history that this "saga" would not be complete without acknowledging his role.

I have used the word "saga" in titling this part of my memoirs because it is a story of many twists and turns. As mentioned earlier, when the U.S.-Canada agreement with Combe was drawn up, I carefully drafted a provision that, in effect, said that if Combe ever acquired or developed another product that was competitive with Grecian Formula 16, even though this product did not contain lead sulfide and was entirely different in its process for changing the color of gray hair and/or in its chemical composition, World Wide Rights would still be entitled to royalties from the sale of this new product. I worked hard on the drafting of this clause to make it airtight, and both Ivan and his Chicago lawyers clearly understood its intent.

Dr. Naomi Stone and her husband, Victor Stone, my long-time friend and lawyer. London, 2010. Photograph by Paula Gately Tillman

Nevertheless, twenty years later, Combe came out with a product called "Just For Men," which I felt was intended to compete with Grecian Formula. Ivan not only denied that the two products vied with each other, but said that because they were chemically different and did not impart color in the same manner (i.e., Just For Men applied color instantly and Grecian Formula over a period of one or two months), they did not compete for the same customers. Thus, he insisted, World Wide was not entitled to any royalties on the sale of Just For Men in the U.S. and Canada.

Accordingly, my provision became the basis on which World Wide Rights sued Combe for breach of contract. I was outraged that Ivan would have knowingly violated our clear understanding. I had had a long relationship with him and thought that he was a man of integrity. I felt that he planned to deceive me and I did not intend to let him get away with it. Giving him the benefit of the doubt was not an option for me. As previously mentioned, I had already been misled by Amoss, so I was not about to again be victimized by Combe's intentional misinterpretation of the contract, as I recalled my father's advice of "Once ever, twice never."

The suit was instituted by World Wide Rights in the Federal Court for the District of Maryland. I used Larry Greenwald of Gordon Feinblatt to represent us. Combe's Chicago lawyers answered by filing a motion for a summary judgment claiming that the clause, which I had crafted, did not really mean what I alleged. Lo and behold, to my utter disbelief, the judge granted Combe's motion. As a result, World Wide Rights took an appeal to the Fifth Circuit Federal Court of Appeals that reversed the trial judge's decision and ruled that we had presented enough evidence concerning our interpretation of the clause to warrant that the case be remanded to the Federal District Court for trial.

In preparation for the trial, Larry Greenwald filed a Request for Discovery of Documents that required that Combe produce all documents, letters, sales records, inter-office memos, etc., related to this matter. It was my hope that these documents would produce evidence that Just For Men did compete with Grecian Formula, although different in its chemical composition and in the way that it worked, and that the clause I had drafted in the Distribution Agreement was intended to entitle World Wide Rights to royalties on Just For Men sales.

Since I was most familiar with the evidence needed to prove our case and had developed a concept to show that the two products competed, Larry and I flew to Combe's offices in White Plains, New York. Thousands of documents had been assembled in a room. Our job was to examine each and every scrap of paper for clues that showed that the two products were intended to serve the same men's market and to compare sales of Grecian Formula before and after Just For Men was introduced. By doing the latter, I felt I could relate the increases and decreases in Grecian Formula sales to the annual advertising expenditures on each product. If I could show a direct relationship, I would have the evidence that I was looking for to establish that Combe was not using its best efforts to promote Grecian Formula 16, which New York case law clearly required.

At least twice we returned to examine this humongous pile of documents. While I was able to show a clear relationship between increases and decreases in the sales of the two products, depending on the amount spent by Combe in promoting them, I did not feel that we had yet found the "smoking gun" that I was hoping would clearly prove that Just For Men was intended by Combe to compete with Grecian Formula and even replace it.

Then, one day while we were searching through the in-house documents of Combe, Harvey Lebowitz (another lawyer whom I had brought in from Gordon Feinblatt to assist me) came to me with an inter-office memo that was just what I had been looking for. The memo, written about the time that Combe had developed an unnamed product that colored gray hair almost any color a man would want, asked Ivan what the new product should be named. In effect, it said that since the product was intended to replace Grecian Formula (should the use of lead be outlawed), shouldn't it be called Grecian Formula something? What more could I want?

After reading it several times, I asked to see Ivan and presented him with the memo. His face turned white. Then, I said that while I was prepared to go to trial, I recommended we consider a settlement. To make a long story short, we amended the Distribution Agreement to give World Wide Rights half the royalties on Just For Men to which World Wide was entitled under the existing arrangement on the sales in the U.S. and Canada, as well as half the royalties on any other new product developed by Combe that colored men's hair. This put an end to this contentious episode and, ever since, the relationship between World Wide Rights, now a partnership managed by my son Douglas, and Combe Incorporated, run by Ivan's son Chris, has been reasonably good.

The royalty contract with Combe has been operating for well over fifty years. Off the top of my head, I would conservatively estimate that the Englars and Hoffbergers have shared more than $10 million in royalties and additional payments of at least several million dollars (capital gains) from the sale of our trademarks in the U.S. and other countries on the names "Formula 16" and "Grecian Formula 16," as well as the formula. Under the Extension Agreement, which does not end until 2021, we can still expect to receive about $500,000 annually in royalties.

For World Wide's remaining rights, Combe made an offer (November 2010) to purchase all of the partners' interests (87.5%) in World Wide Rights Limited Partnership not owned by Combe (12.5%) for approximately $3.8 million. Douglas made an analysis of the estimated present value of the royalties (payable over the remaining ten years of the original amended contract) which indicated that Combe's offer was at a premium worthy of favorable consideration. Douglas then negotiated a significant increase in the premium, and a contract was signed on September 31, 2011. Thus ended the Grecian Formula Saga – one that turned an insignificant investment of about $20,000 by the Englar and Hoffberger families into a treasure trove.

> Then, I said that while I was prepared to go to trial, I recommended we consider a settlement.

One more comment about Grecian Formula 16: while it has not for some time produced the amount of royalties as Just For Men, it is Grecian that has become symbolic of man's quest for a youthful look.

Cartoons about Grecian's powers have appeared in U.S. and British newspapers and magazines. One in the *London Times* showed an oil truck with the name on its side being "Grecian Formula 16," and the caption under the drawing was, "Well, I guess Reagan is going to run again."

More recently, Garrison Keillor read a poem on his radio show titled "Grecian Temple." It was about an older man who was concerned about holding his job and finding a young woman, both of which problems were solved by his applying Grecian to his hair and also to the hair of his old dog so that both would appear to be young. Not only was it quite funny, but the fact that it was a poem that Keillor knew would resonate with his large radio audience made me feel that, in addition to having been a once-in-a-lifetime investment, Grecian Formula has become a household name.

I ASSUME MORE RESPONSIBILITY

Drawing by Nathan Glushakow showing my name at the bottom of the glass door to Uncle Sam's law offices

While it may seem that my involvement in the Family's real estate projects and in the Grecian Formula 16 venture were the primary focus of my professional life, they were by no means all-consuming. With my Uncle Sam becoming increasingly dysfunctional, Morton Hollander and I had to handle the potential problems he was creating.

Soon, I had assumed full responsibility for the operation of the law firm, the two real estate companies previously run by my uncle and the mortgage company called Merchants Mortgage Company, as well as the Savings and Loan Association known as Union Federal. Therefore, in keeping with the tradition of the firm (i.e., the more authority you had the more to the rear of the second floor you moved), I moved my office from the middle of the second floor to the rear into the former office of Uncle Sam. He would still come in occasionally, but he could no longer climb the stairs and took an office on the first floor where Merchants Mortgage Company was located. However, the list of lawyers, whose names appeared on the wooden and glass door at the entrance to the law office remained unchanged, with my name still at the bottom.

AN OPPORTUNITY FOR AN EXCITING
SABBATICAL ABROAD

From Ivy League to Savile Row

As a result of having accompanied George Englar on several trips to Europe to establish distributorships for Grecian Formula, I had acquired an insatiable desire to spend more time abroad, particularly in London. As luck would have it, in about 1959, I learned from Irv Blum that Fair Lanes, a publicly owned operator of bowling centers primarily in Maryland, wanted to develop bowling centers in England, where there had been a tradition of "bowling on the green." It was, therefore, looking for someone to explore the possibility of getting English investors to finance the start-up. I told Irv that I was very interested in applying for the position. Sidney Friedberg, founder and controlling shareholder of the company, knew me since the Hoffberger Family was a holder of a relatively large block of Fair Lanes' stock. While Sidney was somewhat paranoid about the Hoffbergers taking over his company, he agreed to hire me.

Alex. Brown and Sons, the oldest privately owned investment banking firm in the U.S., had handled the IPO for Fair Lanes, and Sidney turned to Ben Griswold Sr., the CEO of Alex. Brown, for help in finding someone in London who could put me in touch with individuals or companies that might be interested. Ben's firm had an office in London and he knew all the right people in "the City," as the financial district of London was called.

Evidently, Ben told Sidney that he had just the right person. He happened to be the film star Douglas Fairbanks Jr., who had been knighted by the Queen for his help in creating a favorable attitude in America toward supplying Great Britain with ships, planes and tanks needed to resist the Nazis in the Battle of Britain. Douglas and Ben had served in the U.S. Navy together in the Mediterranean war zone and were good friends.

Off I flew to London, leaving Morty in charge of the office, with the understanding that I would be back when needed, but at least every ninety days as my passport required. Since I was being paid by Fair Lanes, the British authorities had no problem with my working in England.

Douglas' office was located just off of St. James's Street, not far from St. James's Palace. He and several other men in the office were involved in the film business, but beyond that, Douglas seemed to be mainly a

> Since I was being paid by Fair Lanes, the British authorities had no problem with my working in England.

Lois Marriott, aka Miss Moneypenny, and me at her daughter's wedding near Bath, England, 1991

This was, after all, a business that had been quite successful in the U.S. over many years, particularly since the invention of automatic pin-setters.

contact person or broker for companies like Fair Lanes which wanted access to British money. One of the men in the office was Tommy Clyde, who was a film producer and then in the process of divorcing the daughter of the Duke of Norfolk. Another was Peter Marriott, former Adjutant to the Viceroy of India. He was a film distributor for NBC and was married to a Canadian actress, Lois Marriott, who was Miss Moneypenny in the original James Bond movies. In addition, there were several nice-looking English secretaries, all of whom were quite charming. I was given a desk and access to secretarial help.

As for living accommodations, Douglas had arranged for me to temporarily have a bedroom and bath in a turn-of-the-century townhouse on Chesterfield Gardens in the West End. The building had been converted to a night club on the first floor called the 21 Club, with apartments above it. While my quarters were a bit cramped, I spent little time in them, and more in the night club which had a pretty good menu. In the beginning I dined alone, but not for long.

Night clubs in London were a bit unique in that they had a bevy of hostesses who would dine and/or dance with you, while sipping the champagne that you bought for them. As Douglas' friend, I was considered a celebrity and was introduced to all of the lovely young ladies, who were available if I wanted company. For a 35-year-old bachelor, this was as close to paradise as one could get.

However, before too long, I moved into a duplex furnished flat at 12A Davies Street, about a block off of Berkeley Square, the landmark made famous in the World War II song "A Nightingale Sang in Berkeley Square." This was a lovely residential and retail area in the West End, within easy walking distance of Douglas' office. The office opened at 9 AM, when the secretaries and I arrived. The bosses, however, usually arrived just in time for tea at about 10:30.

After I had familiarized Douglas with the bowling business, explaining how it operated with leagues to provide steady customers during the day and night, he began to make appointments for us with people he thought might be interested in investing in Fair Lanes' English subsidiary. This was, after all, a business that had been quite successful in the U.S. over many years, particularly since the invention of automatic pin-setters. There were two companies that produced these automatic pin-setters and Fair Lanes had a good relationship with both.

One of the first persons Douglas introduced to me was a short, cigar-smoking, no-nonsense South African who represented the Schlesinger Family of South Africa. The Schlesinger Family owned a number of large insurance companies in South Africa and, I am sure, other interests there and in England. I explained to their representative that we were looking for seed capital to enable us to construct and operate several bowling centers in the new towns surrounding London. I said that our objective was to establish their viability as quickly as possible and then to do an IPO to raise public money to expand the operation. I walked him through the process as I saw it, detailing the cost of a typical center and then its revenues and expenses. We met on several occasions before he indicated interest.

I recall engaging a very bright English solicitor, whose name was Philip English, from a prestigious law firm – no doubt recommended by Douglas – to prepare the documents, which included giving the Schlesinger interest a seat on the board. I have forgotten the amount of money that the Schlesinger Group put up, but I believe it was enough to construct and equip two centers. With construction costs in England being about twice those of the U.S., this was no doubt a considerable sum.

Douglas Fairbanks Jr. and me at his Capital Hotel flat in London, 1965

When it appeared that the transaction was going to close, Fair Lanes sent over a savvy and experienced young man whose name was Stewart Arminger and whose expertise was construction. Stewart and I got along very well and our friendship lasted long after this episode in my career ended. As Stewart traveled around finding an appropriate site for our first center, he was also learning about building costs. Meanwhile, Fair Lanes was looking for a person to permanently head this venture. An Englishman by the name of Wally Hall was finally chosen for the job. He was bright, well-spoken and a quick learner.

In spite of the commitment of the Schlesinger Group, which I felt gave our project credibility, the need for raising sufficient capital was not over. I wanted to find at least one more major investor to enable Fair Lanes to build one or two additional centers. After we made a number of unsuccessful presentations, Douglas finally introduced me to two self-made businessmen who were brothers, Sidney and Cecil Bernstein. They had founded with great success Granada TV, the independent TV network in the north of England.[25]

The Bernstein Brothers, smart and tough, were not easy to deal with, to say the least; but, having established a standard with the Schlesingers, we at least had a basis on which to negotiate. An agreement was finally reached, and the Bernsteins put up the same amount of money as had the Schlesingers, basically with the same terms and conditions. They too wanted one or two seats on the board.

And so, my job was done. It had taken me about two years to land the two investor groups, and Fair Lanes was well on its way to starting a new leisure time industry in England. Although England had a centuries-old history of outdoor "bowling on the green," indoor bowling in a modern, comfortable, family-friendly environment was new. I helped bring that about.

I returned to Baltimore around 1960 or 1961 a much more cosmopolitan person. Having immersed myself in the privileged world of Douglas Fairbanks, I had absorbed a way of life that suited me to a tee. Along the way, with the help of Douglas and Peter, I had completely changed my style of dressing from three-button Ivy League suits to two-button "Savile Row" tailored suits ("bespoke," in fashion parlance). Likewise, I changed my shirts from button-down collars to spread collars (called "Prince of Wales" collars). I had become a full-fledged Anglophile to the point that Irv Blum nicknamed me "Reggie," referring, I believe, to the fictional character Reginald Jeeves, "the gentleman's gentleman" in the P.G. Wodehouse novels.

I returned
to Baltimore
around 1960
or 1961 a
much more
cosmopolitan
person.

This sojourn to London was very meaningful for me. I had met and befriended interesting, well-educated, upper-class English men and women, and in the process I had become much more worldly. Fortunately, being a member of the board of Fair Lanes' English Bowling Company, I was able to return to London with a degree of frequency to attend board meetings and to maintain these relationships.

Unfortunately, Fair Lanes found it more and more difficult to operate its English subsidiary from 3,000 miles away. Sites for new centers were difficult to find, due to the very strict zoning regulations in England, and the high cost of building made it hard to achieve the returns we had predicted. One of the reasons for this was Fair Lanes' inability to get British housewives to join leagues and bowl on a regular basis. Furthermore, bowling had not caught on with the younger generation. Finally, the growing dissatisfaction of our British investors led Fair Lanes to eventually sell out to its U.K. investors.[26]

Nevertheless, for years after this adventure with Fair Lanes, I maintained my friendship with Douglas Fairbanks and with Peter Marriott and his wife, Lois. The untimely death of Peter from heart failure and the departure of Lois to Canada, where she was born, ended these lovely relationships (although I did return to England to attend the wedding of Lois' oldest daughter). Douglas moved back to New York City where I visited him on occasion until his death in 2000.

UNION FEDERAL SAVINGS AND LOAN ASSOCIATION

My Loyalty to Its Employees Costs Me $500,000 and Three Years of Agony

Back in the 1940s Uncle Sam had formed a federal savings and loan association when the federal government wanted to encourage more savings by Americans and agreed to insure up to $100,000 of every depositor's deposits. The association was called Union Federal Savings and Loan Association. For many years, it was successfully run by Raymond DeFord and then by Tom Guidera. Both of these men were honest and hardworking.

In the early days, after the war, Union Federal made only residential permanent loans which were insured by the federal government. Most of the mortgages it financed were on residential developments by small builders who had acquired their land from Keystone Realty Company. Union Federal had only about $40 million in deposits and with such limited resources had difficulty competing with the much larger associations for deposits and loans.

When Ray DeFord died suddenly, I needed someone to take his place. Tom Guidera was a small builder with whom I had done business. One of our in-house real estate companies had invested in some of his residential projects. Tom was honest, smart and knowledgeable about all aspects of the home building business, so I thought he would make a perfect replacement for Ray. I asked him if he would consider taking the job and he said he would. He agreed with me that Union Federal had to grow in order to compete and took the job with this objective in mind.

For a number of years Tom worked hard to expand Union Federal. However, during that time, federal savings and loan associations were given the authority to make land loans and to lend on commercial and industrial properties. This meant that Union Federal, still being relatively small and unable therefore to risk making large loans in these areas, was no longer viable as a stand-alone institution. It became clear that we should seek to merge with a larger association.

Tom, who by then knew most of the top executives in this business, went about quietly finding out which of the larger ones might be interested in merging with Union Federal.

Tom, who by then knew most of the top executives in this business, went about quietly finding out which of the larger ones might be interested in merging with Union Federal. One of the most rapidly growing associations in the state was First Annapolis Federal Savings and Loan Association. Its net assets were about $400 million, and it was located where there was a great deal of both residential and commercial development taking place. Moreover, the residents in the area were upper-middle class and promised to be a continuing source of depositors.

Tom approached Tom Norris, president of First Annapolis Federal Savings and Loan Association, about a merger with Union Federal, and he expressed interest. Then began a process of due diligence on our part. There was no doubt that First Annapolis Federal was successful, but Tom Guidera had some uncertainty as to whether Union Federal's employees would be absorbed into the merged firm in the long run. Nevertheless, he was willing to take the risk and thought that he, as an executive vice president of First Annapolis, could protect himself and Union's employees.

I met with Tom Norris on several occasions and believed him to be quite capable and knowledgeable about mortgage lending. I also met with some of the board members, prominent local professional and business men, with limited real estate lending experience. Having been asked by Tom Norris to serve on the board of First Annapolis in order to maintain a Baltimore connection, I agreed to do so primarily to keep an eye on what was taking place and to maintain contact with Tom Guidera. Since the Hoffberger Family would have over $1 million in deposits transferred from Union Federal to First Annapolis, I felt this was prudent.

Unfortunately, that decision turned out to be a costly mistake! I was obliged to spend $500,000 in legal fees defending myself and the other directors (who soon ran out of money defending themselves) against the federal government's Resolutions Trust Corporation (RTC) suit, filed in the early 1990s under the Financial Institutions Reform Recovery Enforcement Act (FIRREA), claiming $20 million in damages for negligence in approving the First Annapolis Association's making of certain large land and development loans.

The Evening Sun,
Baltimore, n.d.

LEROY H. HOFFBERGER   *THOMAS J. NORRIS*

Union Federal To Merge Into First Federal Savings

The Federal Home Loan Bank Board has approved plans for the merger of Union Federal Savings and Loan Association of Baltimore into First Federal Savings and Loan Association of Annapolis.

Thomas J. Norris, president of First Federal, and Leroy H. Hoffberger, chairman of Union Federal, said the merger would become effective within the next) to 60 days.

The merger will boost First Federal's assets to just over 100 million, making it one of half-dozen largest savings and loan associations in Maryland. The larger ones are Loyola Federal, Baltimore Federal, American National, all with main offices in Baltimore;

Maryland State, of Hyattsville, and Citizens, of Silver Spring.

Union Federal, founded here in 1925, opened an office at Howard and Fayette streets about fifteen years ago and has a second office at Randallstown. It has assets of about $17.5 million.

First Federal of Annapolis, founded in 1903, has assets of about $83 million. As the surviving association in the prospective merger, it will have offices in Baltimore and Annapolis and four Maryland counties: Anne Arundel, Baltimore, Calvert and Prince Georges.

Under the terms of the merger, Mr. Hoffberger and Alvin Blum, also a director of Union Federal, will become members of First Federal's board.

At the time the law suit was actually instituted against me and the other directors and officers of First Annapolis, I was no longer serving as a director. I had resigned about three years previously in order to comply with a banking regulation that prohibited my continuing beyond a ten-year grandfathered term that enabled me to serve on both the board of a national bank and a national federal savings and loan. Since I was on the board of The Equitable Bank, a national bank, and since Tom Guidera had recently resigned as an officer of First Annapolis Federal, I much preferred to continue to serve on Equitable's board. Not only did it spare me an hour drive each way to and from Annapolis, but I had been getting nervous about the size and nature of the loans First Annapolis was making.

Fortunately, after three years of litigation, the Federal District Court for Maryland dismissed the government's suit on the Defendants' Motion (i.e., the officers and directors of First Annapolis) for a summary judgment. I had been defended by my old friend, Melvin Sykes Esq., who is a masterful litigator and appellate lawyer, and the other officer and director defendants were represented by Daniel Goldstein Esq., also a very competent trial attorney. They had skillfully gotten all of the government's expert witnesses to admit in one way or another that they were not testifying as to whether First Annapolis Federal had adhered to industry standards when making the mortgages that were in default. Lacking an expert witness to testify as to what those standards were, the government's case was dismissed.

At one point in the case, the RTC said it would settle the claim if I paid them $2 million. Not wanting to part with $2 million and, more

Union Federal Savings and Loan building, *The Evening Sun*, Baltimore, n.d.

NEW UNION FEDERAL SAVINGS AND LOAN BUILDING

importantly, feeling that my reputation in the business community would be jeopardized if *The Sun* paper headlines read: "Hoffberger Settles RTC Claim of Negligence," I preferred to take my chances in court.

No doubt, the $500,000 I paid in legal fees and expenses was a good economic decision, but I felt that I had suffered an injustice and sought to find out if the law enabled me to recover from the government if its suit was found to be legally frivolous. In searching the federal statutes, I discovered an obscure provision which said, in effect, that if a suit by the government was dismissed on summary judgment and the defendant had a net worth of less than $2.5 million, the defendant was entitled to get the government to reimburse him for his legal fees and expenses. Since my net worth exceeded $2.5 million, I was out of luck.

However, I felt that if this statute, which was old, were to be updated by inflation, I might then be able to recover my expenses. I went to see my Democrat friends in Congress who heard me out and sympathized with me but would not introduce a bill to accomplish what, in my opinion, was justified. Since the House was then controlled by the Republicans, I decided to get an appointment with one of the Republican members of the Maryland Congressional delegation by the name of Robert Ehrlich. I had never met him, but he was a Princeton graduate, so he was willing to see an old fellow Princetonian, even if he was a Democrat.

I met with Bob and he was sympathetic to my cause. While in his office, he left to talk to the Chairman of the House Ways and Means about a bill that would accomplish what I was suggesting. He came back and told me that the Chairman (also a Princetonian) was receptive to such a bill. Consequently, a bill was prepared and introduced in Committee; but since it unfortunately got attached as a rider to another bill that became quite politicized, it died in Committee.

While I was disappointed, I never forgot what Bob Ehrlich did for me when all of my Democrat friends refused to get involved. I supported Bob each time he ran for Congress and also gave him a contribution when he ran for governor against Don Schaefer (whom I did not like but supported). Thus ended my efforts to right what I considered a gross injustice. In the process, I came to realize that sometimes being a "good guy" by looking out for the well-being of others as an act of loyalty and friendship does not always leave you with a good feeling. Since I had gone through "hell" for three years and had spent $500,000 in doing so, it was hard to sense any satisfaction.

> While I was disappointed, I never forgot what Bob Ehrlich did for me when all of my Democrat friends refused to get involved.

THE PASSING OF MY FATHER AND UNCLE SAM ENDS THE REIGN OF THE FIRST GENERATION

My Father's Death Gives Rise to a Second Bout with My "Black Dog"

Dad next to an ice sculpture, c. 1960

The life of my Uncle Sam came to an end in 1962 when he was 71 years old. His death was probably due to some form of cardiovascular disease since that is the illness that has taken all of the male Hoffbergers. He had been the driving force behind the expansion of the Family's business interests within my memory, although I have been told that, until my Uncle Harry had a stroke, he was even more dynamic. My Uncle Sam ruled with an iron fist until his dementia rendered him dysfunctional. He had his favorites and I believe that I was one of them. In spite of my fear in the beginning that I would fail to meet his expectations, I think that if he were alive today, he would feel that I had not let him down.

Within a year after Uncle Sam died, my father, age 72, passed away. Dad was the last of the seven Hoffberger brothers. Although he had been in a state of aphasia because of a massive stroke six months earlier, I was still overcome by his passing. At the time of his death, I had been plagued with a chronic "bad back." The anxiety and depression that hit me when Dad died undoubtedly caused tremendous physical stress that greatly intensified my back pain. At Shiva services at my mother's apartment on the eve following his burial, my back went into such painful spasms that I had to be carried to a bed in the apartment. All that night, my back kept going into spasms that were so painful that when Dr. Bernstein arrived in the morning, he had to give me a shot of morphine so that I could be put in an ambulance to be taken to Johns Hopkins Hospital.

Dr. Otenasek, a renowned neurosurgeon, was brought in to determine the seriousness of the problem. After some x-rays, he diagnosed a ruptured disc between the fourth and fifth vertebrae of my spine and ordered that I be put in traction for two weeks to see if that would provide relief. When the weights on my legs were removed, after the two-week period, the traction had not worked. Surgery was therefore the only solution, so Dr. Otenasek operated on me.

When I was brought down from the operating room to the recovery room, there were three people waiting for me: Mother and Aunt Lenore, who were sitting together, and Hildegard Voss, seated several chairs away. She was the German woman whom I had been seeing (primarily when I went to Europe). I had just helped her to obtain a visa and a "green card" so that she could live and work in New York where we could be together more conveniently.

Hilde and I were in love, and she had taken off from her work in the garment district in New York City to come to Hopkins to be with me for a day or so. The only problem was that, although Mother had heard about my romance from her friends, she had never met Hilde. I knew that Mother objected to my marrying anyone who was not Jewish, and I had witnessed her reaction to Bert's marrying a Christian, even though his wife converted. Needless to say, I was overwhelmed with the awkwardness of this gathering.

Fortunately, Dr. Schnaper had just entered the recovery room, sensed the situation and asked everyone to leave to let me rest. For the next several days Hilde and Mother visited me, separately, and to my knowledge did not speak to one another. In those days, a laminectomy was considered serious enough to require a week or so of hospitalization during which time Hilde returned to New York. Mother continued to visit me daily, however, not one word was spoken concerning my relationship with Hilde.

By the time I returned to my home at 16 East Mt. Vernon Place, I was beginning to again feel depressed. I knew I was going to have to tell my mother that I loved Hilde and intended to marry her, but I was having a hard time coming to grips with this reality. Dr. Schnaper, who had visited me several times at Hopkins, was aware of my dilemma and was concerned that I might slip back into a serious depression if I didn't soon make a decision.

On one of Mother's visits, I finally broached the subject of my relationship with Hilde and of my intention to marry her. When I did, Mother's response was: "Well, what is going to happen to me?" While that may seem like a strange response, it did not surprise me at all. Since my father had just died, I suspected that Mother was counting on me to be the one who would look out for her well-being. I had already assumed that responsibility prior to my father's death since both of my brothers were married. Now, Mother must have thought that my marriage to a woman whom she did not like would bring that relationship to an end. Not much more was said between us about my decision.

Soon thereafter, I proposed to Hilde and preparations were made for a small wedding at Baltimore Hebrew Congregation. Hilde had agreed to convert to Judaism (according to Reform Halachah) and spent several months learning about the Jewish faith from Rabbi Morris Lieberman who was to perform the ceremony. And so, in 1964, Hilde and I were married, with Mother, my brothers and their wives and my friends Dr. and Mrs. Alvin Aisenberg attending the ceremony.

On one of Mother's visits, I finally broached the subject of my relationship with Hilde and of my intention to marry her.

All of the events that I have described in this chapter occurred in a very brief span of time. I lost my mentor, Uncle Sam; I lost my idol, my father; and at age 42, I had taken on the responsibilities of marriage as well as of caring for and comforting my mother. At the same time, I was deeply involved with my Family duties and my communal work and being asked to do more. The anxiety and depression, which again struck when my father died, intensified. Having gotten to know Dr. Schnaper during my father's long illness, I felt that further therapy was needed to control my "Black Dog" who was once again running wild. I have already described my many years of psychotherapy with Dr. Schnaper and my indebtedness to him for his help in getting my depression and anxiety under control.

CREATING A NEW TOWN

Germantown, Montgomery County, Maryland

Sometime in 1961–1962, I got a call from my cousin Jerry Hoffberger, who was a member of the board of directors of Fairchild Industries. He said that he would like to set up a date for him and Ed Uhl, president of Fairchild, to come see me. Apparently, Fairchild wanted to relocate its headquarters from Dulles, Virginia, to Montgomery County, Maryland, and Jerry felt that because of my extensive experience in land acquisition, I could be of assistance.

Jerry's call was amazingly coincidental as I had actually been looking for an opportunity to acquire land in Prince George's and/or Montgomery Counties. I had heard some unbelievable stories about the rapid development taking place there. However, except for having been on the DC Beltway, I had never been in either county. Now, I had the incentive to get involved. I said that I would be glad to try to help, and a meeting was set up.

Soon thereafter, Jerry, Ed and I met in my office at 215 North Calvert Street. Ed told me that the company was looking for between two hundred and three hundred acres of land in the I-270 corridor. Such a location would give the company's personnel much easier access to Washington than they now had from Dulles. He asked me if I thought I could find that much acreage at a reasonable price and I, of course, said I would give it my best shot.

Ed then asked what compensation I would want, and I said "none" except that I be allowed to acquire any adjacent acreage that Fairchild did not need. He agreed. From my experience in Baltimore County, my belief was that if the county officials knew that Fairchild desired to move its headquarters to Montgomery County, they would be willing to extend public sewer and water to service the Fairchild Campus, and that that would substantially enhance the value of all the surrounding land with access to those utilities.

My job was now to find the right site for Fairchild and then to quietly acquire as much relatively inexpensive farm land nearby as I could. So, off I started. I called Lester Matz, the civil engineer whom I had used to advise me when purchasing land in Baltimore County, to find out if he was familiar with Montgomery County. Not surprisingly, he was. I told him of my assignment for Fairchild Industries and asked him to send me as much information as he could about the planning and zoning process in the county and to survey the I-270 corridor for potential sites.

Lester immediately began to send me the information that I needed, including a thick brochure that had been recently published by the Maryland-National Capital Park and Planning Commission of Prince George's and Montgomery Counties (MNCPPC). For years, development in these counties had been taking place so rapidly that the commission had concluded that a master plan was needed to control and coordinate future development by determining the areas where it would permit the extension of public roads, sewer and water to service communities, which it called "New Towns." These New Towns were to consist of clusters of residential, commercial and industrial land as well as open space surrounding them. The concept was that these communities would provide living, working and shopping space for their residents and thereby reduce congestion caused by workers using highways leading to Washington. At the same time, the towns would be linked to Washington by a network of major federal highways, some of which already existed or were under construction.

The brochure indicated that future development in Montgomery County was to be primarily in the I-270 corridor. I-270 was a federal highway being built to run from Frederick, Maryland, to connect with I-495, the Beltway around Washington, DC.

I took a drive along I-270 to acquaint myself with what development had already taken place or was in progress. As I got about 15 miles outside of the Beltway, I saw that a well-known residential builder, Kettler Brothers, had begun building a very large mixed-use development around the Gaithersburg interchange where the Federal Bureau of Standards had been built. Driving about ten miles farther, I noted that in the southwestern quadrant of the intersection of I-270 and Maryland State Highway 118, the Atomic Energy Commission had a major research and headquarters facility. The other quadrants

The concept was that these communities would provide living, working and shopping space for their residents and thereby reduce congestion caused by workers using highways leading to Washington.

surrounding this interchange consisted primarily of farmland and a few modest residences. The Master Plan designated this general area as the future location for the "New Town of Germantown."

Within about six weeks, Lester presented me with a brochure showing about four potential sites for sale along or within the I-270 corridor located as far as thirty miles and as close as five miles from the District. The site that I preferred was a three-hundred-acre parcel located adjacent to the intersection of I-270 and Maryland Route 118 within the area designated on the Master Plan for the New Town of Germantown.

Lester's analysis of each potential site for Fairchild indicated whether public utilities were already available or, if not, if it was feasible to extend public utilities to the site. Concerning the Germantown site, utilities already existed in the southwestern quadrant that served the Atomic Energy Commission. Lester's study showed that these could readily be extended to the northwestern quadrant and that the presence of the Fairchild headquarters and other facilities would justify such extensions.

Concluding that the Germantown site was the logical one for the location of the Fairchild Industries facilities, I set up a meeting with Jerry and Ed Uhl. My recommendation was accepted, and the Fairchild board authorized me to acquire both the acreage it desired and any additional land that I might want. With this support, I immediately engaged a broker to acquire the parcel of land adjacent to I-270 and Maryland Route 118 in the northwestern quadrant. I also told Lester to reveal Fairchild's plans to relocate in Montgomery County to the MNCPPC and to get its agreement to extend sewer and water to serve the site for commercial and industrial use, subject to the preparation and adoption of a master plan for the New Town of Germantown.

Since the nature of such a master plan was yet to be conceived, I deemed it necessary to hire a well-regarded land planner to work with the MNCPPC on a comprehensive zoning map. This map had to allow Fairchild to utilize its site for its intended purposes, including an airstrip, as well as permit mixed residential, commercial and industrial uses for the adjacent land.

With Lester's help, we determined that the ideal person for this undertaking would be Edward Echeverria, who was world renowned in this field and who maintained an office in Washington. As one of the land planners for the New Town of New Delhi, India, he had impressive credentials. Upon meeting Ed, I liked him at once and sensed his creativity.

Upon meeting Ed, I liked him at once and sensed his creativity.

Ed's concept for the New Town was to create a self-sufficient community, much like the English New Towns after World War II.

Ed's concept for the New Town was to create a self-sufficient community, much like the English New Towns that had been built surrounding London after World War II. Thus, his plan defined the areas to be developed with mixed uses and called for a public "green belt" consisting of a largely forested area that already surrounded the developable areas. This design had proven to be an effective way of preventing urban sprawl in England and, with proper enforcement by the Montgomery County Zoning Board, should (and actually did) work well in the development of Germantown.[27]

Next came the hiring of a prominent law firm in Montgomery County to steer the master plan for Germantown through the various stages of approvals that hopefully would lead to its adoption by the MNCPPC and to also handle the settlements of the parcels purchased. The county government was quite progressive and layered with sophisticated and well-regulated agencies. The officials with whom I dealt were by and large intelligent and honest, but not all were committed to further growth in the I-270 corridor. Nevertheless, most had an appreciation for the fact that bringing in Fairchild Industries was an important factor in creating an industrial base for the county.

The final essential component needed to assure the viability of the plan was long-term financing for the acquisition of the farmland not required by Fairchild (i.e. 1,700 acres or 3.125 square miles) and for the cost of the infrastructure and all operating expenses. Based on our study, the amount needed to accomplish these objectives was estimated at $6 million.

Because the New Town plan rezoned what had been farmland into developable land, the appraised value of the 1,700 acres had increased to about $10 million. This added value was sufficient to support the $6 million standing loan we would need for ten years.

The ownership group consisted of my brothers and me, my male cousins, the Blum Family (Alvin and Irv) and the Eisen Family (David and Milton) from the Bethesda/Chevy Chase area. We formed Churchill General Partnership, since I had named our acreage the Churchill Town Sector, reflecting my admiration for one of England's great prime ministers, Winston Churchill. Each of us had an equal pro rata interest, and I was the managing partner. A portion of the acquired land was put in a corporation called Germantown Investment Corporation, a move that turned out to be quite fortuitous.

Irv Blum, who was married to my cousin Lois, was a close friend and business associate, as I have previously indicated. We had worked well together on other real estate transactions, and I sought his advice and assistance whenever necessary. Irv happened to be a founder and director of a public supermarket company called Supermarkets General. Also on the board of Supermarkets General was a man named Bob Puder whom Irv had befriended. Bob was the managing partner of Puder and Puder, a public accounting firm that was the auditor for Supermarkets General and a number of other major companies, one of which was Prudential Life Insurance Company.

At my request, Irv approached Bob to see if we could get an appointment with the top decision makers at Prudential's headquarters in Newark, New Jersey. Irv explained that we wanted to present to them a unique opportunity to be in on the ground floor of the creation of a New Town near Washington. The appointment was made, and Irv and I joined Bob Puder in Newark to meet with the president of Prudential and other top executives.

The reader might be wondering why a $6 million loan was such a "big deal" for a huge company like Prudential Life Insurance Company that it would require such a high-level meeting. At that time, a long-term standing land loan was an entirely new type of loan for Prudential or any other insurance company to consider.

In this instance, we were asking that Prudential make a long-term, interest-only land loan on a large holding of undeveloped acreage in order to acquire the acreage and prepare it for future development. Instead of being asked to rely on a stream of income to assure the repayment of the loan, as in the case of a permanent loan on a building, we were asking Prudential to rely on two intangibles as sources of repayment and security. We were promising, first, that during the ten-year period of the loan, sales of acreage would reduce or pay off the loan and, second, that, during the ten-year period, the value of the undeveloped land subject to Prudential's mortgages would continue to increase as adjacent land was sold and developed.

> The process of taking title to the land was full of surprises and aggravation.

After extensive underwriting by Prudential, Irv and I, with the help of Bob Puder, were successful in convincing the powers that be at Prudential to make the loan, provided, of course, that the owners' group would guarantee its repayment. Convincing the partners of the Churchill Partnership to put up equity funds and to guarantee the mortgage was, surprisingly, not all that difficult. I can recall my brother Bert saying, "Let's shoot the works!"

The process of taking title to the land was full of surprises and aggravation. In some instances, in order not to tip off the owners that we were accumulating a number of the farms in the Germantown area, I used local brokers to negotiate for us. In more than one instance, instead of the contract being executed by the broker on behalf of an entity to be formed, the broker decided to enter into the contract in his own name. In most instances, when it came time for the broker to assign the contract to Churchill Partnership, he would do so. However, in one case the broker balked, claiming he was entitled to more than just a commission; he wanted a piece of the action! I can assure you that I did not react too well to this. Out of frustration and anger, I made all kinds of threats and recall staying up until the wee hours of the morning getting the broker to finally agree to turn over the contract to the Churchill Partnership.

The next all-important task was to get the master plan adopted by the MNCPPC and Montgomery County Council, which meant going through a series of public hearings. This process took several years to accomplish and was quite tedious and stressful. But the final plan bore the masterful hand of Ed Echeverria, and the Churchill Town Sector was designated for a variety of residential, commercial and industrial uses. I must say that the intelligence and sophistication of the zoning personnel, particularly of a woman by the name of Rita Davison who was the Zoning Commissioner (and who later became a judge on the Maryland Court of Appeals), made a difficult task manageable.

The land in the Churchill Town Sector was now ready for the installation of infrastructure – sewer, water, roads and a large man-made lake. For this part of the project, I engaged Whiting-Turner Contracting Company. Fortunately, my brother Stanley was living in Montgomery County, and he agreed to oversee this work. Within about a year the infrastructure was completed, and the Churchill Town Sector of the New Town of Germantown was ready for development!

Since none of us had major development experience, we decided that we would put the now rezoned 1,400 acres owned by Churchill General Partnership up for sale. The timing seemed to be just right as the housing industry was booming countrywide and a large mixed-use land area was highly desirable.

A national conglomerate with a real estate subsidiary purchased the land for a substantial price, subject to the Prudential mortgage. However, the transaction was not an all-cash one (few of this type of sale are), and we took back a considerable portion of the purchase price in the form of an unsecured subordinate note that was not guaranteed by the parent company.

However, in one case the broker balked, claiming he was entitled to more than just a commission; he wanted a piece of the action!

The buyer proceeded to develop the property and was doing quite well. Unfortunately, though, the economy was beginning to slow down, and other developments that our buyer owned were doing poorly – so poorly, in fact, that the real estate subsidiary filed for Chapter II. Having an unsecured note with no guaranty from the parent company did not auger well for Churchill. Upon default, Prudential promptly decided to foreclose not only on the parcel Churchill had sold, but on the three hundred acres that were titled in the name of Germantown Investment Company on which there was a separate mortgage for a proportionate part of the $6 million loan.

Understandably, our group was quite upset, knowing that if the properties did not sell at foreclosure for the amount of the mortgages, the partners would be personally liable for the shortfall. I canvassed the partners to see what they wanted to do. I assured them that in the long run all of the acreage we had acquired would be worth a great deal of money. The problem was did the group have the financial wherewithal (which it did) and the risk tolerance (which it didn't) to carry the mortgages and pay the real estate taxes until the economy turned around and development in Germantown was again feasible?

It was decided that the group was too uncomfortable to purchase both mortgages, so we decided we would not try to buy-in the larger portion of the mortgage on the 1,400 acres we had sold, but that we would try to do so on the smaller mortgage on the three hundred acres owned by Germantown Investment Company. At the auction, Prudential bought-in its own mortgage on the larger parcel, and we were successful in buying-in the small mortgage at its face value.

Ironically, Bert, who was originally quite cavalier about risking his wealth, expressed concern about his ability to pay his share of the carrying costs of the Prudential mortgage and real estate taxes on the land owned by Germantown Investment Corporation. To my surprise, he announced that he would no longer put up his share. This was quite upsetting to me and the group, not only because it meant we had to pick up Bert's share, but because we now had a dissident shareholder in our midst, whose only interest was in selling Germantown's land as soon as possible.

There was no interest among the other partners in buying Bert out and little desire to fight with him. Therefore, we decided to sell the acreage rather than hold it. This decision concerned me since I feared that the IRS might then consider the corporation to be in the business of buying and selling land and, thus, consider the proceeds of each

I assured them that in the long run all of the acreage we had acquired would be worth a great deal of money.

A map showing the New Town of Germantown, containing 10.8 square miles, surrounded by a "green belt" of public parks

Google Maps
http://www.city-data.com/city/
Germantown-Maryland.html
This image is licensed under a
Creative Commons Attribution
2.0 Generic License.

sale to be ordinary income rather than capital gain. And that is just what happened.

Realizing that we now had a major tax problem, I asked Thor Halverson of the law firm Covington & Burling to request a private ruling from the IRS explaining the unfortunate situation that had arisen (i.e., the impact of a dissident shareholder's action that had forced Germantown to subdivide and sell its land holdings). Thor had become aware of an IRS letter ruling in a similar situation where the act of a dissident shareholder had caused the corporation to involuntarily subdivide a large tract of land into smaller parcels in order to dispose of it. In that ruling the IRS said that the sales were in effect involuntary and that therefore the subdividing and sale of the tract in small parcels did not amount to being in the business of buying and selling land. Thor used this same approach in his request for a ruling, and we were successful in likewise convincing the IRS to treat the various sales of land by Germantown Investment Company as capital gains. This was a tremendous achievement that saved the shareholders of Germantown Investment Company a great deal of money.

There was one other hurdle to overcome in the successful development of Germantown that I do not want to overlook. At the time I assembled the acreage, the practice of the Maryland Department of Assessments was to promptly increase the assessment on former farmland that had been rezoned to categories that permitted various types of development. In our case, this would have meant that as soon as the entire Churchill Town Sector was reclassified, our ownership group would have been faced with an enormous real estate tax bill. Carrying 1,700 acres for a long period of time during its development would have not been economically feasible.

Churchill was not the only one confronted with this reality. Jim Rouse in the development of Columbia, Maryland, and the Kettler Brothers in the development of Gaithersburg were facing the same dilemma. It was obvious that new legislation was needed to enable New Town developers to hold land for extended periods of time while development was taking place, yet not have the undeveloped land taxed at appreciated values pending future development.

To accomplish this would require a revision in the state's assessment and taxation laws. So, the three of us and our legal representatives went to work drafting a piece of legislation for the state legislature's consideration. In essence, it proposed that for very large parcels (1,500 acres or more) undergoing long-term development for a New Town, the state would defer any increase in real estate taxes for dormant parcels that would continue to be taxed by the state as farmland, while parcels around such dormant land that had been reclassified in higher zoning categories would receive increased assessments as plats were recorded. As the dormant land was ultimately developed, there would be a formula by which some of the lost tax revenue would be recaptured.

Along the way it became evident that someone in the legislative committees dealing with this amendment was holding it up. That person turned out to be Dale Hess, a representative from Harford County, whom I previously knew from the Young Democrats. Dale owned a large holding of farmland in Harford County, but no parcel was large enough to have qualified for this special treatment. So what started out as a bill to apply only to holdings of 1,500 acres or more ended up being applicable to holdings of five hundred acres or more.

With this change in the proposed bill, the legislature approved it and sent it to the governor for his signature. It happened that Spiro Agnew had just been elected Governor of Maryland. Spiro was an old friend whom I had supported when he was County Executive for Baltimore County. I also knew his new Director of Public Works, Jerry Wolf, who had served in a similar capacity in Baltimore County. Meetings were arranged to fully acquaint the governor and his staff, including Jerry, with the merits of what we were trying to accomplish. The governor was

Location of Germantown in Montgomery County and the U.S. state of Maryland:
Coordinates: 39°11´0 N 77°16´0 W

Country	United States
State	Maryland
County	Montgomery
Total Area	10.9 sq mi (28.0 km2)
Land	10.8 sq mi (27.9 km2)
Water	0.1 sq mi (0.1 km2)
Population	86,395 (2012)
Density	7,900/sq mi (3,100/km2)
Time zone	Eastern (EST) (UTC-5)
Summer (DST)	EDT (UTC-4)
Zip code	20874, 20875, 20876
Area code	301, 240

Satellite map of Churchill village showing "green belt" of regional parks and lakes as its northwest boundary. Lake Churchill was created by Churchill Investment Company.

(U.S. Geological Survey Google Maps data, 2013.) This image is licensed under a Creative Commons Attribution 2.0 Generic License.

An excerpt from article titled "Germantown, Maryland" in Wikipedia describes what was once the undeveloped land that I amassed and sold from 1962 to 1987. Graphic source: http://en.wikipedia.org/wiki/Germantown,_Maryland. This image is licensed under a Creative Commons Attribution 2.0 Generic License.

Germantown, Maryland

Germantown is an urbanized census-designated place in Montgomery County, Maryland. With a population of 86,395 as of the 2010 United States Census, Germantown is the third most populous place in Maryland, after the city of Baltimore, and the census-designated place of Columbia, Maryland. If Germantown were to incorporate as a city, it would become the second largest incorporated city in Maryland, after Baltimore. Germantown is located approximately 25 miles (40 km) outside of the U.S. capital of Washington, DC, and is an important part of the Washington, DC metropolitan area.

The original plan for Germantown divided the area into a downtown and six town villages: Gunners Lake Village, Kingsview Village, Churchill Village, Middlebrook Village, Clopper's Mill Village, and Neelsville Village. The Churchill Town Sector at the corner of Maryland Route 118 and

Middlebrook Road most closely resembles the downtown, or center, of Germantown, due to the location of the Upcounty Regional Services Center, the Germantown Public Library, the Black Rock Arts Center, the Regal Germantown Stadium 14 and a pedestrian shopping area that features an array of restaurants. Three exits to Interstate 270 are less than one mile away, the Maryland Area Regional Commuter train is within walking distance, and the Germantown Transit Center provides Ride On shuttle service to the Shady Grove station of the Washington Metro's Red Line.

Germantown has the assigned ZIP codes of 20874 and 20876 for delivery and 20875 for post office boxes. It is the most populous Germantown in Maryland and is the only "Germantown, Maryland" recognized by the United States Postal Service, even though there is one in Anne Arundel County, one in Baltimore County and one in Worcester County.

much in favor of the benefits that would accrue to the state as a result of New Town development, and he agreed to sign the bill. I recall that I felt quite gratified that I had played an important, behind-the-scenes role in the preparation and passage of this vital piece of legislation.

From the time I purchased the first parcel to the time I sold the last, 25 years had elapsed.[28] During that long period, I had invested a tremendous amount of thought, time and effort in pursuing this project to completion. So, when the last parcel containing 107 acres was sold to the Marriott Corporation for nearly $18 million, I had a great feeling of elation and pride. Not only had my Germantown venture been a huge financial success, but my role had resulted in the birth of a thriving and vibrant new community.[29]

ANOTHER FASCINATING REAL ESTATE OPPORTUNITY COMES ALONG

Two Major Maryland Banks "Come a Courtin'"

Being in "the right place at the right time" is often a primary factor in the creation of an opportunity for success. In the situation I am about to describe, it was not my being in the right place but my office being there – at 215 North Calvert Street.

One day, sometime in 1967, I got a telephone call from the CFO of Maryland National Bank asking if he could come over to see me. While I cannot recall his name, he was a person whom I knew in the business world, so I said "sure," having no idea whatsoever what he wanted to discuss with me. He said he would "come right over."

My curiosity was obviously piqued, for I was not sure whether he was bringing good news or bad news. As it turned out, the news was great news and very hard to believe.

This gentleman arrived about half an hour later with two other executives of the bank. At once he proceeded to tell me how important it was for Maryland National, which was the largest and most rapidly growing bank in Maryland, to be able to process daily the checks that came through its banking system and to get those checks into the Federal Reserve Bank before 4:30 PM so that each day's checking transactions would reflect the maximum balances available for overnight lending to other banks.

My visitor then pointed out to me something of which I was aware but which had no significance to me. This was that the main branch of the Federal Reserve Bank for Maryland was almost directly across the street from my office. He said that if I could acquire the rest of the properties in the 200 block of North Calvert Street, the bank would like to build a back-office building of about 200,000 square feet where checks would be processed and where they could then be "walked" across the street at the last moment and deposited in the Federal Reserve Branch. Wow!

Obviously, I was interested. They indicated that the bank was thinking of a deal where once I had accumulated the properties from 213 North Calvert Street up to the corner of Calvert and Saratoga Streets (a footprint of 20,000 square feet), the bank would revalue the accumulated footage and purchase it. Or if I preferred, the bank would pay us a ground rent for a 15-year period with the right to buy the ground rent thereafter at its appraised value. I promptly told the bank's representatives that I would not have any interest in such a proposal but that I would get back to them with one that I thought would be more suitable.

Several weeks later I again met with the Maryland National officials in my office. My proposal was to have Calvert Parking Corporation, a jointly owned Englar/Hoffberger company, that owned a public "Off-Street" parking garage in the 200 block of Calvert Street: (I) acquire all of the other properties in the block from 213 north to the corner (creating a footprint containing 20,000 square feet); (II) build a 14-story office building containing one underground level for tenant parking and a three-level aboveground public parking garage (all of which construction was to be financed 100% by Maryland National Bank) and; (III) ten floors would be leased to the bank for its back offices. One floor would be the headquarters of the National Brewing Company (since Jerry had expressed a desire to move the executive offices of the brewery away from the production facilities in Highlandtown), and three floors would be for public parking. An additional two floors would be built below ground for tenant parking.

Within that brief two-to-three-week period, I had been able to get Will Hackerman, president of Whiting-Turner (WT), to give me an estimate of the construction costs of this facility, based on a plan developed by a very cost-conscious architect, Donald Coupard from Gaithersburg. Coupard had already designed several buildings for WT. The only undetermined major cost was for the subterranean work which could not be estimated since the site was then occupied by existing older buildings that prevented soil testing. (This subterranean work was to produce a surprise challenge and be met with a unique solution.)

The financial terms of my proposal were acceptable to the bank, and it was agreed that Calvert Parking would lease ten office floors and a certain number of subterranean parking spaces to Maryland National for 15 years. At the end of the 15-year term and at intervals thereafter, if Maryland National chose to renew the lease, it was to have options to purchase the building at stated amounts.

The ease with which the negotiations took place clearly indicated to me the bank's strong desire to be physically close to the Federal Reserve Branch. Today, in an era of electronic banking, such a need would be totally irrelevant. Nevertheless, although physical proximity to the Federal Reserve is now meaningless, the use of the facility as a back office at a modest rent continues to have significance. Maryland National exercised its first option to renew its lease at the end of 15 years and continued to occupy the building, as did its successors, for decades. I understand that the building, currently owned by the Bank of America, is at this writing no longer occupied and is being offered for sale at the same price it cost to build it in the late 1960s, a sign that it was no longer "in the right place at the right time" for the banking industry.

Soon after the signing of the lease, I was surprised to learn that Maryland National was not the only bank in town that desired to be near the Federal Reserve Branch. I received a phone call from my friend Bob Weinberg of Weinberg and Green who evidently was legal counsel for Union Trust Company, a local, well-established bank. He said he would like to come to my office with the president of the bank to discuss the acquisition of an unimproved parking lot at Davis and Guilford Streets which the Englar and Hoffberger Families owned. He explained that Union Trust wanted to build a back office at this location for the very same reason that Maryland National had desired a back office in the 200 block of Calvert. This was a real case of "déjà vu."

As a matter of fact, the lot targeted by Union Trust was not more than 100–150 feet east of the Calvert Street site to be occupied by Maryland National. While I attempted to negotiate the same kind of deal that I had with Maryland National, Union Trust held fast to wanting to retain ownership of the facility. Therefore, I put a substantial premium price on the land that Union Trust desired and agreed to lease the land to the company for 15 years at a substantial, annually increasing ground rent. At the end of the 15 years, Union Trust was to be given an option to acquire the ground rent at its appraised value.

This transaction gave the shareholders of Davis Street Garage (which merged into Calvert Parking Corporation in 1968 and became "CPC Inc.") a fabulous return on their original investment. Yet, a number of years later, when I met the president of Union Trust (who was then retired) at the Merchants Club, he said to me: "Roy, one the best things

The ease with which the negotiations took place clearly indicated to me the bank's strong desire to be physically close to the Federal Reserve Branch.

Phase one, the topping out of Maryland National Bank Operations Center, 225 North Calvert Street, *The Evening Sun*, Baltimore, 1968

TOPPED OUT—Willard Hackerman (right), head of firm that is erecting eleven-story building behind him, took time out yesterday to show the work to (from left) Thomas Mapes, of National Brewing Co.; Robert D. H. Harvey, of Maryland National Bank, and Leroy Hoffberger, of National Brewing.

I ever did for the bank was to acquire the Davis Street site. It was one of the deals that I was proudest of." I commented that I assumed that he felt that the financial terms of the deal were quite favorable to the bank. He then commented: "We were prepared to pay more."

I think that my initial reaction to his statement was to feel that I had obviously underestimated just how important that site was to his bank (just as Calvert Street was to Maryland National) and had not appropriately valued it. While I don't recall using a professional appraiser to help me determine the land value, I do know that I had looked at all of the comparable sales in the area and had used the enhanced land value that I had put on the Calvert Street site as a guideline.

The fact that they were accepted without extensive negotiations made me think that I could have probably gotten more.

For a long time, I wondered whether I should fault myself for not having gotten an appraisal. I knew in both instances that these sites had extraordinary significance to the buyers, and I had factored that into the proposals I made. The fact that they were accepted without extensive negotiations made me think that I could have probably gotten more. However, I prefer to judge my performance by what I also knew and that is that the returns on the Family's investments were fantastic. If I "left something on the table" and that made the other party happy with the deal, then maybe it would one day inure to my benefit. I believe that, at least in the case of Maryland National, it did. In the case of Union Trust, I could still "laugh all the way to the bank." And as my friend Irv Blum would say: "Sell and regret, but sell."

Let me return to the story of the actual construction of the Maryland National Bank Building for it is as fascinating as were the circumstances that gave rise to its need. First, as I recall, there were five or six improved properties that needed to be assembled to make up the 20,000 square foot "footprint." There was a three-story walk-up building, 213 (similar in appearance to 215), owned by the Rome brothers who used it as offices for their law firm; 215 that was owned by the Real Estate Holding Company, a Hoffberger entity; 217 that was a three-story walk-up much like 213 and 215, which was owned by a family that used the offices for its family law firm; 227 that was a consolidation of several properties that had been razed and redeveloped with an off-street parking garage that was owned jointly by the Englar/Hoffberger Families (Calvert Street Parking Inc.); and 229 that was a storefront building that was empty and for sale. The minute book of Calvert Parking Corporation (CPC Inc.), which I checked, revealed the prices that the company paid for each of these improved properties that I had acquired. The square-foot price did not vary to a great extent, indicating that I had been able to successfully acquire the properties covertly. Had it not been the case, the prices of these properties would have soared.

Once Don Coupard, the architect for the building, had completed the working drawings, Whiting-Turner was ready to begin construction. The first step was the razing of all the buildings on the site. Knowing that 215 was a piece of the Family's history, I had hired a well-known local artist, Nathan Glushakow, to make some pen and ink sketches of both the inside and outside of 215 as well as of Morty Hollander, Beulah Saltz, Irv Blum and me engaged in our respective activities as lawyers, secretary and client. These sketches are now in the new offices of Keystone.[30]

After demolition was completed, excavation commenced. As the hole got deeper and deeper, water began flowing in between the sheeting. The mystery of the source of this flooding was soon discovered by WT when it examined an old map of the harbor and found that a branch of the Jones Falls had formerly wended its way near Calvert Street on its path to the harbor which, in olden times, was actually as far north as the 200 block of Calvert Street. Having evidently been confronted with similar problems before (i.e., how to keep water from flowing back into the excavation), WT installed a series of "well points." These are pumps that created pressure around the perimeter of the site which prevented the water from the Jones Falls from being able to resume its natural course and flood the excavation.

I was told that these pumps had to be kept in place not only until the concrete was poured around the perimeter of the site, but until the entire building was completed. I was further told that if this were not done, the force of the water seeking to return to its natural course would not only cause the concrete subterranean walls to collapse, but would lift the entire structure off of its foundation, right out of the ground.

I assumed that at a certain height the weight of the building would be sufficient to keep the entire structure securely in place and the water out of the excavated garage basement. I remember anxiously waiting to see what, if anything, would happen when it was decided that it was time to remove the well points. Nothing did happen as far as I know, nor was any other problem encountered during the completion of that phase of the project.

Drawing by Nathan Glushakow showing me at Uncle Sam's desk following his retirement, 1960

As the last sentence of the previous paragraph indicates, what I have been describing was not the entire story of the evolution of the Maryland National Operations Building. As the Maryland National Bank grew, so did its need for additional back-office space. Back-office space is space that is needed for clerical and administrative purposes and consists largely of open areas separated by cubicles. This space need not be located where the expensive executive offices and/or retail banking facilities of the bank are, but can be remote from the high-rental areas required for executive offices and retail banking. The 200 block of Calvert was ideal for this type of operation since it was within easy walking distance of the central financial district of Baltimore, where the main offices of the bank were located.

Early in 1973, my friend at Maryland National (with whom I had negotiated the initial deal for the development of the back-office building) asked to meet with me. He was interested in the possibility of CPC acquiring the surface lot used for public parking just to the south of the Maryland National Operations Building so that the office building could be laterally expanded. This lot was owned by the Equitable Bank of which I was a director. I had always hoped that Maryland National would need more space and that acquiring this lot would be the way to accommodate such need.

The chairman of the Equitable Bank was Bob Merrick, a very savvy banker and real estate mogul. Having heard about me through my uncle and also through George Englar, Mr. Merrick (as I always referred to him) had invited me to serve on the board, making me the first and only Jew in this position. Over the years, he took a liking to me, hopefully because he had observed that I generally knew what I was talking about, particularly in regard to real estate and real estate financing. [31]

Knowing that the decision concerning the bank's willingness to sell this lot would ultimately be made by Mr. Merrick, I arranged to meet with him to discuss the possibility of CPC acquiring it. I recall that I was forthright about why I was interested in buying the lot as Mr. Merrick was too astute not to have already figured this out. The sole issues he had to resolve were whether Equitable had a need for the lot and, if not, what was it worth under the circumstances.

Fortunately, he and, I assume, John Leutkemeyer, the president of the bank, decided that the lot was not likely to be of use as a branch location and could be disposed of. Unfortunately, knowing how important the use of this lot was to Maryland National, "disposed of" did not mean "sold." However, we were able to agree on a thirty-year ground lease at a significant annual rent, but with CPC having the right to redeem the rent in the 12th and 24th years. Thus, this transaction produced a footprint for an additional 7,000 square feet as the site for the additional space needed by Maryland National.

With a $3.3 million mortgage from Maryland National, 70,000 additional square feet of office space were added to the original building as well as 21,000 square feet of additional public parking. The façade of this addition was exactly in keeping with the original façade to give the appearance of one building. I do not recall the economic terms of the new lease with Maryland National, but I do remember that the duration of both leases was extended and that the option prices were obviously increased to account for the additional space. I also recall that I was quite proud of what I had accomplished and felt that I had finally "put to bed" a very interesting and successful real estate project. Not so!

Sometime in 1976, my friend at Maryland National called me once again, asking to see me. On both of the previous occasions when we met, I had been pleasantly surprised by the message he carried, but this time I was not so pleasantly surprised. He had come to tell me that, despite the addition of 70,000 square feet of office space, the bank's growth had created a need for much more back-office space than our expanded building contained and, as a result, the bank needed to move. Therefore, I concluded that being near the Federal Reserve Branch was no longer important.

When I asked him how much more space the bank needed, he said about 150,000 square feet. My first thought was that perhaps CPC could acquire the Court Square Building, which was the only remaining property in the block. It was a high-rise office building, somewhat taller than the adjacent ten-story back-office facility that Maryland National occupied and probably contained 100,000 square feet of space. I think I suggested that as a possibility, but it did not appeal to my friend. I was saddened by the news, to say the least.

While the meeting ended on an unhappy note, I hoped that somehow there might be a way to get the inside track on building Maryland National a new facility. Then, a unique thought came to me. I called Willard Hackerman and asked him how much structural strength the existing buildings had. He got back to me with two answers. The first was that the maximum structural strength per square foot that the buildings were designed to carry was 120 pounds per square foot; the second was that the load the buildings were presently carrying was 80 pounds per square foot.

> Therefore, I concluded that being near the Federal Reserve Branch was no longer important.

I then asked Willard whether we could build a vertical addition on top of the existing buildings and if so, how many more floors we could add. After having his engineers do the necessary calculations, he told me that, with the addition of a "transfer floor" to shift some of the load, the existing structures could carry six additional floors. At 30,000 square feet per floor, the potential for the vertical addition was therefore 180,000 square feet, of which 150,000 would be rentable space. I couldn't wait to call up my friend to tell him the good news, feeling that Maryland National preferred to remain where it was and that this discovery would be welcome!

I was right. When I told my friend at Maryland National the news, he heaved a sigh of relief, believing that the bank's search for a new site was over and that the back-office operation could remain on Calvert Street. A new lease agreement was negotiated along the lines of the previous two leases except, of course, the rent was substantially increased and the term again extended. The two options given to Maryland National were likewise extended to 1989 and 1993, in which year the Bank bought the building for $13 – $14 million.[32]

Thus, a long voyage (a nautical term that I feel is appropriate for a facility that, as I indicated, is floating on a stream) had ended. While its beginning was pure coincidence (i.e., 215 North Calvert Street being "in the right place at the right time"), I steered this endeavor on a fascinating and highly profitable course. So unique was the voyage that it was written up in one of the leading engineering and construction publications.

225 North Calvert Street as it appears now, *Baltimore Business Journal*, 2012

A CHANCE TO BE A BROADWAY MOGUL

Sometime in the 1960s (when Irv Blum was spending time in the New York City area with the founders of Supermarkets General, the company Irv helped to found and in which the Family had made a significant investment), Irv met two Broadway producers. He liked them and brought them to Baltimore one weekend to meet a group of his friends and to present them with an opportunity to invest in the producers' next Broadway (or perhaps, Off-Broadway) play. I was included in the group.

We met at Philip Macht's home one Sunday morning to hear their presentation. The most I can recall about the play they intended to produce was that it was a mystery story that took place in Africa. While Phil always had a non-professional flair for the theater, as did one of his sons, the rest of us were total novices. The play did have an interesting plot and the two gentlemen from New York did a terrific job portraying it.

After the presentation, we discussed the pros and cons of the play and its likelihood to be a commercial success. The general consensus was that it had a good chance to succeed, at least from an investor's perspective. As I remember, the cost of producing the play was not that great, so even if the play did not have a long run, it was likely to be profitable. Therefore, we decided to invest as a group. I am sure I did not have to put up more than $10,000, so it was no big deal.

Sure enough, the play was successful, and we received a nice return on our investment. That gave us a desire to back these two fellows in their next Broadway production. Since they liked our group, the two producers returned to Baltimore to once again give us a preview of their next show. As before, we met on a Sunday morning at Phil's to hear a presentation; and once more we decided that we wanted to be investors. Feeling more knowledgeable, we were willing to put up a larger sum.

More knowledgeable or not, we lost just about all of our money. The show was a terrific flop! The two producers were sincerely upset and said that once they really thought they had a winner, they would return to give us an opportunity to more than make up for what we had lost. Some time went by before we heard from them again. Then, out of the blue, they called Irv to tell him that they were very excited about a musical that they thought we would "love" and that they would be coming down to not only tell us about the musical but to have one of the intended performers sing some of the songs.

Again, on a Sunday, the group met at Phil Macht's home to listen to the presentation of our two Broadway producer friends. The first thing

> After the presentation, we discussed the pros and cons of the play and its likelihood to be a commercial success.

they did was to apologize for the previous fiasco and to tell us how much they were hoping we would be a part of this new opportunity to invest in what they thought was going to be a major "winner." Then they began to tell us the theme of the musical.

The story was about a dancehall girl named "Charity" who, because she had a "big heart," ended up having affairs with the wrong men, who strung her along. Each time she had an affair, she swore she would never again be so naïve, but of course she was. She, by chance, found herself involved with an Italian movie star who, like her other pursuers, finally jilted her. As fate would have it, however, immediately after being abandoned, she became trapped in an elevator with a claustrophobic, nerdy accountant who swept her off her feet. Obviously, he was different from the other men she had been involved with, but she was, nevertheless, fearful that he would also "dump" her when he found out she was a dancehall girl.

By now you may know that the name of the musical by Neil Simon is "Sweet Charity," which evidently opened on Broadway at the Palace Theatre in 1966. Gwen Verdon played "Charity" on the stage, and the production was the nominee for twelve Tony awards. The role of "Charity" in the movie was played by Shirley MacLaine.

I wish I were telling you all of this because I had been an investor in this phenomenal play and movie that earned millions for those who did invest. However, after the two producers told us the plot and after we heard two or three of the songs sung by whomever it was that they brought with them, we got in a huddle, as usual.

I remember our conversation and that we even laughed because we concluded that if this was the way our two Broadway friends were going to get us our money back, how good friends were they? I don't know why we were so hesitant and unappreciative of the opportunity we were being offered. Some of the fellows in the group were amateur musicians, as I certainly was, but none of us liked the melodies of the songs. We must have been tone deaf that day.

Needless to say, we passed up the opportunity of a lifetime to "make it big" by backing an unbelievably successful Broadway musical. I never saw the two gentlemen again after we turned them down, and I must assume that they did not have a high opinion of us as astute investors. I have watched and thoroughly enjoyed the movie a number of times although I do not recall that I ever saw the play. The music is great. What happened that Sunday bewilders me, but so much for my inept go at being a "Broadway Mogul."

Needless to say, we passed up the opportunity of a lifetime to "make it big" by backing an unbelievably successful Broadway musical.

Irv's passing in August 1973 was almost surreal.

Irv's passing in August 1973 was almost surreal. I remember his coming into my office and telling me that he had contracted a virus that had lodged in his kidneys. I asked him about the symptoms which he said were nausea and "frothy urine," indicating an excessive amount of protein. He began missing work but would come in on days when he felt somewhat better. The next thing he told me was that his kidneys were shutting down and that he was going to have to be dialyzed. I was shocked and deeply saddened, not knowing what was in store for him.

Almost overnight he was admitted to Hopkins where, in a short period of time, things went from bad to worse. I would visit him with Morton Hollander, and we could see that he was gravely ill. The last time we visited him we went to where we thought he was being dialyzed. When we entered the room, Irv was lying on his side, facing the door where we entered. The doctors had a tube inserted in a hole in his back and were suctioning out fluids of some sort. Irv had developed a fatal yeast infection. He waved us off, and we turned around and left; but I shall never forget seeing the pain in his face. Irv died a few days later.

When I learned of his death, I went to Irv's home where his wife, my cousin Lois, and their three children greeted me with hugs and tears. My cousin Jerry Hoffberger, Irv's brother-in-law, was also there, and we embraced and sobbed. Irv was buried the next day at Baltimore Hebrew Congregation cemetery. I was too stunned to remember much about the funeral or what the rabbi had to say about Irv. I do remember that the mob who attended were all in a state of shock. I am moved right now as I write this, since recalling his passing brings back memories of so many wonderful occasions we shared and of how much I have missed him.

Irv and I worked together on the acquisition, development and financing of some exciting real estate projects. He was a brilliant businessman, as well as a remarkable community leader whom I admired and cherished. I like to think that he had taken a special liking to me as well because I believe he thought that I was smart, reliable, honest, hardworking and creative. We also shared Jewish and general communal interests and, not to be slighted, a similar sense of humor.

While I cannot remember the exact time of the event that I am about to describe, I know that Irv and I were in a transaction in which we had a property that we were offering to sell at a price we felt was fair. Someone had expressed interest, and Irv and I met with this person at his request. At the meeting, the person who had expressed interest went on and on about what was wrong with the property and why it wasn't worth what we wanted.

Irv Blum, who was my cousin by marriage to Lois Hoffberger, Uncle Sam's daughter, 1950

After about an hour of listening to his bad-mouthing the property, both Irv and I were getting a bit annoyed so I *thought* I said to this person: "Look, I've heard all you've had to say, and further conversation is unnecessary." But, evidently, I had actually said, "Look, further conversation is unnecessary; *I've said everything I want to hear.*" The meeting ended and the fellow departed. After his departure, Irv started laughing, uncontrollably, and I asked him what was so funny. He then told me what I had said. The comment, though unintended, was a Freudian slip that was so funny but often so true that I had two plaques made – one for Irv and one for me. Mine sits on my desk to this day, and I sometimes have fun using it to make a point.

> The comment, though unintended, was a Freudian slip that was so funny but often so true that I had two plaques made – one for Irv and one for me.

The fact that Irv and I worked so harmoniously as a "team" got to be known in the real estate community. As a result, we were approached by David Kornblatt, a real estate broker who, because of his good connections with the executives of the First National Bank, was given the exclusive opportunity to develop a new headquarters building for the bank. Believing that both Irv and I would make good partners and needing equity, he asked us if we would be interested.

The project consisted of a 250,000-square-foot office building, about 70% of which was to be occupied by the bank. David also said that the bank's legal counsel – Piper and Marbury, a very prestigious law firm – was to take space on several floors. I suggested that Whiting-Turner be the contractor and that Willard Hackerman be a partner. David did an excellent job finding tenants for a major portion of the building before construction was completed. I acted as legal counsel for the Limited Partnership and negotiated all of the leases together with David. The project was highly successful and was eventually sold for $40 million, minus the outstanding mortgage.

In about 1959, Irv had been serving as the president of a public company called Baltimore Trotting Races Inc. (BTR) which had built and operated a half-mile trotting track about 15 miles north of Baltimore, adjacent to U.S. 40. Unfortunately, the venture had not been very successful, as the company was unable to attract enough people to attend its limited racing dates and bet on the races. BTR also acquired another half-mile flat track from the Harford County Fairgrounds and added those racing days to its calendar, but this still did not significantly increase the company's profitability – much to the shareholders' regret. Both facilities were located on large tracts of land that lay fallow, unless used for parking or fairgrounds activities.

Finally, in about 1965, BTR decided that the racing operation was not viable, and it decided to try to sell its racing dates to the thoroughbred tracks (Pimlico, Laurel and Marlborough), with the approval of the Maryland Legislature, and to then develop these two well-situated tracts of land. After a good deal of lobbying effort, the Legislature finally agreed to the sale. BTR then entered into a joint venture with Maryland Properties (called Pulaski Industrial Park Associates or PIPA) for the development of the tract outside of Baltimore for industrial and commercial purposes. It was also decided that the parcel of land in Bel Air, the Harford County seat, should be developed as a shopping mall.

Irv asked me to assist him with planning for the development of these two ventures, which I willingly did. Unfortunately, our joint venture for the development of PIPA went very slowly, causing our partner to default in about 1971. Irv and I soon concluded that we did not have the organization or the time to take over the full responsibility for developing both of these properties, so we again thought about finding a developer partner.

Having worked with Sidney Friedberg on the initial public offering of Fair Lanes stock, Irv knew that Fair Lanes had a development team that built Fair Lanes bowling centers and any adjacent facilities these sites permitted; so he approached Sidney to see if he would be interested in joining forces with us in the development of BTR's two properties. He was, and Irv and I started discussions with Fair Lanes on the terms of our turning over responsibility for the development of our properties. It was at this point that Irv became ill and was not able to work with me to conclude the negotiations.

The merged company, formed in June 1972, was called BTR Realty Company Inc. (BTR). It needed to raise capital to operate but was struggling to do so. The investment banker BTR had approached felt the company did not have a feasible operating plan that investors could relate to and also seemed to lack executive leadership and a strong board.

Finally, BTR's board decided that the company needed a new focused image which would concentrate on the acquisition and construction of strip shopping centers located primarily in the Mid-Atlantic states. To accomplish this, BTR decided to become a Real Estate Investment Company (REIT) under the name of Mid-Atlantic Realty Trust Inc. (MART). Patrick Hughes, who was originally the CFO for Fair Lanes and had been moved by Fair Lanes to BTR as such, was elevated to the position of president. I was selected to be the chairman of the board. Pat put together an excellent group of astute retail real estate developers and managers, and a new board of experienced real estate owners, appraisers and operators was assembled.

Over a ten-year period, Pat and his team spearheaded Mid-Atlantic into a successful owner and operator primarily of strip shopping centers. Along the way, Mid-Atlantic acquired by a tax-free merger the extensive shopping center holdings of a man by the name of Jack Pechter. At the end of ten years, Pat, aided by members of the board, negotiated the sale of Mid-Atlantic for $680 million to a major regional shopping center REIT called KIMCO. This was quite a financial coup and brought a glorious ending to a shaky racetrack endeavor that had morphed into a successful shopping center enterprise.

Irv would have undoubtedly played a significant role in this success story, and there is not one thing that I have done since his passing that would not have been rendered more enjoyable, and no doubt more profitable, had Irv been by my side. Much like my father's, Irv's wisdom and counsel have been an inspiration to me, and I will always remember and revere him.

Much like my father's, Irv's wisdom and counsel have been an inspiration to me, and I will always remember and revere him.

THE MERGER OF HOFFBERGER AND HOLLANDER WITH GORDON, FEINBLATT AND ROTHMAN

The construction of the Maryland National Bank Operations Building, partially on the site where my offices were located, necessitated my moving the firm. There were then about five or six lawyers working in the firm, including Morty and me and our secretarial staff. In addition, there were two persons in our accounting office. For over twenty years, "215," as the law office was referred to by members of the Family, had been my home, and while it had required walking up and down three sets of stairs, it was quite functional and well located.

About the time that the move became necessary, the law firm of Gordon, Feinblatt and Rothman purchased (and was renovating) the Garrett Building at 233 East Redwood Street, which was about three blocks south and one block east of "215." They were looking for tenants. Morton and I knew most of the partners of Gordon Feinblatt and thought highly of them. We also thought that the lawyers in my firm would get along well with their partners and associates.

In addition, the Blum Family (Irv and Alvin) had located the offices of their new finance company on the eighth floor. It so happened that the size of the ninth floor was adequate to accommodate all of the offices we needed for Hoffberger and Hollander, and there was also room on the tenth floor for the Keystone Real Estate Holding Company to move to the "Garrett Building," as the Family would henceforth refer to our new location.

This move must have occurred around 1967, and I began using some of the real estate and tax lawyers at Gordon Feinblatt on various Family matters and in some of the deals that Irv Blum had generated.

Sometime in 1971, David Gordon and Gene Feinblatt approached Morty and me to see if we would be interested in a merger of Hoffberger and Hollander with Gordon Feinblatt. They proposed that Morton and I, as well as two other experienced lawyers who had worked for me for several years, become partners of the new firm, which was to be called "Gordon, Feinblatt, Rothman, Hoffberger and Hollander." The other members of my firm were to become associates.

Having acquired considerable respect for the legal talents of the partners of Gordon Feinblatt, Morty and I decided in 1972 to accept their merger proposal. However, I decided I did not want to become a full partner which would have required me to spend time with non-Family clients. So much of my time was spent in doing my own real estate deals for the Family and in attending to other Family business matters – not to mention the time I was spending on numerous community activities – that there was little time left to practice law on behalf of others. As a result, I became "Of Counsel" to the new firm, a position that I still occupy today. During this entire forty-year period, I have not received a single penny from the firm in fees or salary, although I have brought the firm a great deal of legal business. That may seem a little lopsided, but having the freedom to fulfill my responsibilities to the Family and to pursue my many community activities was of primary importance to me.

I developed an excellent working relationship with a number of the partners for whom I had a great respect and fondness. I believe the feelings were mutual. In particular, my relationship with Gene Feinblatt, who married my cousin Lois several years after Irv died; Larry Greenwald, who tried the Grecian Formula case; Sandy Weiss and Herb Goldman, who assisted in the Motor Freight bankruptcy; and Louis Kann, with whom I worked on numerous real estate transactions, come to mind. I still see some of them at an annual Christmas party held by Linda and Zelig Robinson, a very talented merger and acquisition lawyer and a real Renaissance man. Most of the old gang are now retired or deceased, but a few are still actively practicing law, although some are at other law firms.

Today, most of the lawyers at my firm know me by name only and to my embarrassment, because I so seldom set foot in the Garrett Building, when I run into those who do know me, I am often not able to recall their names. Nevertheless, I still harbor real fondness for my old colleagues. [33]

THE OPPORTUNITY TO RETURN TO LONDON IS IRRESISTIBLE

In 1972, Sir Lacey Vincent, the director of L.E. Vincent & Partners Ltd., Grecian Formula's European distributor, died and Max Bumford, his partner, who resided in Paris, had to assume responsibility for the distribution of Formula 16. Although quite successful as an investor and entrepreneur, Max was not a hands-on executive, nor did he want to be.

When I learned of what had happened, I was concerned about the future of our U.K. business, so I called Max and asked him if I could be of any assistance. As best I can recall, he had fired the man whom Sir Lacey had relied on to actually manage the marketing of Formula 16 and had just hired a new manager. Fortunately, Max realized he was not capable of overseeing or providing direction to the new man so he asked if I would be interested in helping him. I, of course, found this prospect irresistible.

I told Hilde what I would like to do and she, being European and liking the thought of living in London for a while, readily agreed to the idea. Jack, our older son, was then five and Douglas was two. I had already asked Lady Helen Vincent, Sir Lacey's widow, if she could get Jack into a good kindergarten, which she unhesitatingly agreed to do. We were then living at 16 East Mount Vernon Place, but we did not have any concern about closing the house and turning on the alarm system. Thus, we packed up and flew off to London to reside in a lovely cottage at Rutland Gardens in Knightsbridge. The cottage belonged to Countess Beatty, the granddaughter of the famous Admiral Beatty, 1st Earl Beatty, of World War I fame.

As it turned out, the cottage was perfectly located for all of the basic needs we had in order to adapt to life in London. Most important was that it was within walking distance of the well-respected public (in England, "private" schools are known as "public") school that Lady Helen had found for Jack. Driving in London (on the wrong side of the road) was out of the question. The school was called Hill House and was run by a retired colonel who interviewed Hilde and me when we brought Jack on his first day.

As part of the process, the colonel asked us if we knew the two most important things Hill House was going to do for Jack. I said, "Teach him to read and write." He immediately responded, "No." He then mentioned something having to do with character, the exact nature of which I do not recall, but since Prince Charles had been a student at the school, I assume it had to do with some trait that the "royals" consider

> I told Hilde what I would like to do and she, being European and liking the thought of living in London for a while, readily agreed to the idea.

admirable. He then followed with the second most important thing Hill House was going to do: "Teach Jack how to swim." He asked me if I knew how many youngsters drowned in England each year. I said, "No," to which he responded, "Several thousand."

Needless to say, I was a little put off by the colonel's educational priorities, but I concluded there must be something more to Hill House than what the colonel had articulated. So, we registered Jack. Going to Hill House necessitated our getting an appropriate wardrobe for him. Hill House's colors were various shades of brown and white, so he had to wear brown short trousers in the summer and brown knickers in the colder weather, with brown socks. White shirts were also mandatory. Jack seemed to accept the idea of a uniform, and since he already knew how to swim, we felt he was going to fit in quite well with the other, mostly British, upper-class boys in his class.

With Douglas being only a toddler, we wanted to get a "proper" nanny for him. Again, we called on Lady Helen, since she knew what agencies had the kind of nanny we would like. Before too long, we ended up with a well-spoken English woman in her forties who had all of the right credentials and recommendations. Her name was "Nanny Hobbs."

Once we obtained the right pram (baby carriage) from Peter Jones Department Store near Sloane Square (the place for buying a "proper" pram), Nanny Hobbs would take Douglas to Hyde Park where she would sit with the other nannies in a certain section where children of upper-class English families were taken. There was obviously a game of "one-upmanship" that was played by the nannies based on how elaborate the pram was, what kind of linens and blanket the baby was lying on and, of course, what standing the baby's family had in English society. Babies of American families were somewhat exempt from the final test, but were rated based on the family's prominence (wealth usually) in America. I have no idea where Douglas and Nanny Hobbs ranked, but since they kept going back to this distinct area, I assume we somehow ranked high enough not to be ostracized.

My routine was to take Jack to school in the morning and on the way home stop off to do the food shopping. Our cottage was just around the corner from Harrods, the world-famous department store that had everything anyone needed or wanted in the way of food products, clothing, furniture, jewelry, writing materials, cosmetics; you name it – and they had it! Since the refrigerator in the cottage was quite small, as were most English refrigerators of that time, food shopping was a daily task. Near Harrods was a greengrocer where I bought our fresh vegetables and fruits. Also in the area were a number of restaurants

My routine was to take Jack to school in the morning and on the way home stop off to do the food shopping.

(Indian, Italian and French) as well as some good English pubs. What more could one ask for?

On the corner of Rutland Gardens and Knightsbridge Road, which bordered Hyde Park, was the Westminster Synagogue. It was located in a large, five-story, 19th-century Victorian house that had replaced an older house built by the Duke of Kent for his mistress. Thus, the name of the newer house bought by Westminster Synagogue in 1960 was "Kent House." The sanctuary was located in the former ballroom on the second floor at the top of a beautiful staircase. On the third floor were the living quarters of the rabbi and his family. Finally, on the fourth and fifth floors were large rooms filled with damaged Torahs that had been rescued from Communist Czechoslovakia by a group of British philanthropists. They had set up a charitable trust and used its income to pay a scribe to repair these several hundred Torahs and make them Kosher. The Torahs would then be donated to congregations all over the world for a contribution to the trust.

Hilde and I decided to become members of Westminster Synagogue, and on the High Holy Days we would attend services which were Reform and mostly in English. The rabbi, Albert Friedlander, was born in Berlin, Germany. He had escaped from Berlin in 1940 and sought refuge in the U.S. where he was ultimately ordained a rabbi at the Hebrew Union College. After serving as a pulpit rabbi in several U.S. synagogues, he was invited to replace the previous rabbi of Westminster Synagogue, who had died. It so happened that when I had previously lived in London, while working with Douglas Fairbanks in the sixties, I had attended services at Westminster and had met the former rabbi. Albert was a renowned scholar on the Holocaust and specialized in the development of interfaith dialogue in Germany. He was soft-spoken, but very charismatic. He authored a number of books on the Holocaust, including one with Elie Wiesel.

Albert had a lovely English wife named Evelyn who was a scholar in the history of the Jews of Europe. Evelyn was researching *genizah* found in the rubble of destroyed European synagogues. *Genizah* are discarded religious objects which by Jewish law cannot be destroyed and were therefore hidden in places where they were likely to survive. The rafters of many centuries-old European synagogues became hiding places for these objects. When these ruined buildings were being restored or torn down, countless *genizah* were discovered. Evelyn researched many of the objects and was working on an exhibition to show how they gave insight into hundreds of years of Jewish European history.

It so happened that when I had previously lived in London, while working with Douglas Fairbanks in the sixties, I had attended services at Westminster and had met the former rabbi.

Hilde had taken a liking to a traditional tea and coffee café known as Richoux which was located on Brompton Road in a posh area of residential apartments and specialty shops. There she had met, on several occasions, a woman whose name was Avril Gordon. Avril was about Hilde's age, in her late thirties, and her appearance and demeanor were as Anglo-Saxon as one could imagine. Their acquaintance, at that point, was limited to seeing one another at Richoux. Neither had attempted to create any further social relationship.

On Purim we decided to dress up Jack and Douglas in costumes appropriate for the occasion and take them to the Purim party at Westminster Synagogue. We, of course, did not expect to know anyone there, but we thought the kids would enjoy the festivities. Not long after we had arrived, Hilde said to me: "Roy, that woman over there is the woman that I mentioned to you whom I see at Richoux. I can't believe it." She then went over to say hello and to introduce me to Avril. Avril was there with her husband, Tony Gordon, and their two very pretty daughters about the same ages as Jack and Douglas.

Hilde said to Avril, "I had no idea that you were Jewish. With your blonde hair and turned up nose, I was sure you weren't." Avril went on to explain her parentage – Jewish father and non-Jewish mother. She said that she considered herself Jewish and had married Tony, an Orthodox (although then non-observant) Jew who had a somewhat dark complexion and, from his demeanor, was definitely ethnically Jewish.

From that meeting on, the Gordons became our closest friends throughout our stay in London. Tony, as it turned out, was a successful real estate developer during those booming times and had amassed a good bit of money. Avril had inherited a fortune from her mother, who lived in Paris. The economy was good, and their style of living showed that they had benefited from it more than most. During the summer, we spent a month together in a house Avril had rented in a little French town near San Tropez. While that was a long time for me to vacation, it was for the most part very enjoyable.

After we came home from London, the real estate bubble burst and Tony got wiped out. Since at one time early in his life he had been a talent agent, a profession he really loved, he decided to switch his attention to looking for rock bands that might challenge the Beatles. Lo and behold, he found one – Boy George!

From that meeting on, the Gordons became our closest friends throughout our stay in London.

While I did not see much of Tony after we left London, he did see a close expatriate friend living in Frankfurt, Germany, Irv Tarlow, on occasion. Irv told me that Tony had found this exceptionally talented young man and his group of musicians, but did not have the money to really launch them. Not having the slightest idea who Boy George was, I told Irv to talk to Dirk Warren, our friend in Frankfurt who was in the business of distributing records. Irv did so, and Dirk expressed interest. Dirk and Tony got together, with Dirk providing the money and Tony the know-how. The rest is history. Boy George's recordings and appearances were sensational, and Dirk and Tony made a lot of money, according to Dirk.

Alas, nothing is forever. Boy George was on drugs, and Tony could not get him into rehabilitation. As a result, Boy George's rating went down until he completely stopped performing. When this occurred, Tony got Boy George to agree to go into rehab. For about two years, Tony looked for a replacement for Boy George but could not find one. When Boy George came out of rehab, Tony made an effort to revive his popularity, but Boy George went back to his old habits and faded into the dust. Tony was devastated and went into a depression.

Except on one occasion, I never saw or heard from Tony thereafter. I would see Avril when I came to London in subsequent years, but Tony would not come along. She would speak disparagingly of him, saying that he was a failure and living off of her inheritance. It was hard for me to hear how she viewed him, and to this day, I don't believe he was by nature what she painted him to be. I concluded that he had sunk into a deep depression and had become dysfunctional.

Of course, as much as our relationship with Avril and Tony enhanced our London experience, I had come over so that I could assist Max Bumford by overseeing the operation of L.E. Vincent & Partners Ltd. Max had brought in a new manager to run the distributorship whose first name, I recall, was Jack. He had experience in marketing specialty products, such as Formula 16, and seemed to have established relationships with the leading retail outlets that handled over-the-counter quasi-pharmaceutical products like ours. These included Boots, the highly successful drugstore chain, and the major department stores such as Marks and Spencer.

Jack clearly had the qualities that I felt a good salesman should have. He was personable and convincing. While his English was not "Oxfordian," he was well-spoken and, I think, college-educated. I considered him to be reasonably smart and, overall, qualified for the job.

Of course, as much as our relationship with Avril and Tony enhanced our London experience, I had come over so that I could assist Max Bumford by overseeing the operation of L.E. Vincent & Partners Ltd.

First off, I asked Jack to create a sales budget that set forth his sales goals for each year that would enable Max and me to judge his performance. I also asked him to determine an advertising budget which primarily consisted of giving retailers discounts to be used to showcase Formula 16 with in-store promotions. With these two pro-forma items and the other more fixed expenses such as Jack's salary, his expense account and the administrative overhead, I was able to create an estimated revenue and expense statement for Jack and Max. These pro-forma statements for the two years I would be in London were deemed to be achievable, in Jack's opinion, and were satisfactory to Max. Had they been achieved, everyone would have been quite happy.

As it was, our major competition was none other than Ivan Combe, our U.S. and Canadian licensee, who was marketing a product called Grecian 2000. It seems that, at some previous point, Ivan had approached Sir Lacey in an effort to buy his Formula 16 distributorship. I was told by Helen that Sir Lacey, whose health was not good, wanted to sell, but that Max refused.

In light of that, Ivan purchased the formula of a small company that was selling a product similar to Grecian Formula 16 in America. He used it to produce a product marketed as Grecian 2000, which he was selling in the U.K. as well as on the continent. As I mentioned in the "Grecian Formula 16 Saga," although the formula we had licensed Ivan to use was not patentable, it was the Grecian Formula 16 trademark that was valuable. Had George and I (and the Vincents) not decided to omit the word "Grecian" from the name of our U.K. product (having done so because the British were politically at odds with Greece), I believe that we could have competed much better against Combe, who would have had to refrain from using "Grecian" in the name of his U.K. product.

There was no doubt that Ivan had a much better marketing organization than Max did. Not only was Ivan's marketing experience far superior, but his resources to promote Grecian 2000 were much more extensive. So, while by Ivan's own admission, his Grecian 2000 formula was not as effective as the one used in Grecian Formula 16 (the formula he used in the U.S. and Canada), he had created far greater customer acceptance of his inferior product than we were able to do with Formula 16. Even though our sales were increasing, we were not able to achieve the somewhat ambitious figures Jack had projected. This irritated Max, but I tried to convince him that the fault was not purely Jack's, but included the other factors that I have alluded to.

It was then 1975, and we had been living in London for about two years. Feeling that the procedures that I had set up were being followed and that, while Formula 16 was not the leading men's hair coloring product in the U.K., its sales were growing, I told Max that I had done all that I thought I could do to be of help and that I would be returning to Baltimore. He understood and thanked me for what I had done.

Since U.K. law would have required that I obtain a work permit had I drawn a salary from the U.K. company, I had not earned "tuppence." Notwithstanding, I knew that I had rendered Max considerable assistance. Subsequent circumstances, as described in the "Grecian Formula 16 Saga," resulted in the demise of L.E. Vincent, but not of the fond memories of my stay.

On the day of our departure, a Rolls that I had ordered to take our family to Heathrow Airport arrived in the cul-de-sac adjacent to our Rutland Gate cottage. There was Jack, riding around for the last time on his two-wheel bike that we had to leave behind. Douglas was in his pram, which we also had to leave behind, as well as Nanny Hobbs. Hilde and I were loading the trunk of the Rolls with our suitcases. Lady Vincent and one of her daughters (to whom we gave the pram and the bike) were there to see us off. I certainly had (and I think the rest of the family had) an enjoyable two-year stay during which time I had become a seasoned Londoner. I had made some new friendships and renewed some that I had made on my previous stay. After two stays of two years each, I felt as much at home in London as I did in Baltimore, which is why I have continued to return year after year.

THE DEMISE OF THE NATIONAL BREWING COMPANY

"Natty Boh" Returns and "The Land of Pleasant Living" Lives On

One important reason for returning to Baltimore was the fact that the National Brewing Company was in serious financial trouble. Competition from the national breweries (Schlitz, Budweiser, Carling and Coors) had resulted in a significant loss of sales in National's core markets of Baltimore and Maryland. Being on the board of National, I had made quarterly trips back to the U.S. to attend the meetings and was aware of what was happening.

The board had already told my cousin Jerry to cut expenses to the bone, but evidently he was dragging his feet, believing National could survive this adversity. Unknown to him, Dawson Farber, National's vice president, had been keeping me informed of the dire straits facing the Family if the brewery was not kept afloat until it could be sold.

At first, Morton and I met with Jerry to express our concerns on behalf of not only the Hoffberger Family but the Krieger Family (which owned a third of the shares of National). His initial response was to ask if we thought the families would sell out. We told him that in concept we thought so, but we would have to see what sort of offer he was willing to make.

Feeling that National could be put back on its feet, Jerry, with the help of Irv Blum, devised a plan to buy (together with Irv's family) all of both families' interest in both the brewery and Merchants Terminal, which was the largest single stockholder of the brewery. The plan would have been an acceptable solution; however, upon analysis, Irv determined that it was too risky and Jerry, although anxious to be rid of the growing Family pressure, accepted his advice.

Jerold Hoffberger, my cousin and head of the National Brewing Company, 1950

Jerry was a very formidable person. He had taken National Boh from an insignificant brand in the early forties (when he returned from WWII) to its place as the dominant beer in Maryland by the early sixties. As president of the popular and highly successful Orioles, controlled by the National Brewing Company, his public image was tremendous. Everyone knew him, and he knew everyone. He was perceived as the "owner" of the team by the other major league owners and by the public – a role that he portrayed with great delight. The Orioles were on a roll, and so was National – until the national breweries came to town! Although National's sales were being severely affected by this competition, and the company was in serious trouble, Jerry remained a giant of a figure to the outside world as the owner of a revered baseball team. Because, in the eyes of the public, he was such a success, it was difficult for him to accept the reality of the brewery's impending fate. The irrefutable facts were: sell or go bankrupt. I informed him that I had discussed this with Zan Krieger and that the Krieger Family was 100% in favor of trying to salvage what we could.

Jerry finally got the message. He went into action and did an excellent job of interesting the Carling Brewing Company, a rapidly growing Canadian brewery that was owned by a wealthy South African, in acquiring the brewing assets of National in order to help expand its U.S. business. The deal was consummated in October 1975, for roughly $16 million. As an operating company, National's value would have been considerably more, but Carling was primarily interested in the brewery assets to produce its own brands, not National's. Nevertheless, the sale did include National's brand trade names, formulas and good will, but did not include the other non-brewing assets – the Pompeian Olive Oil Company and the Solarine Company, as well as the controlling interest in the Baltimore Orioles. The sale of Pompeian and Solarine was not problematic, but the sale of the Orioles turned out to be a "brewhaha"!

To begin with, Jerry wanted the Family to retain its interest in the Orioles, but some members of the Family felt that there was no economic reason to do so. National's ownership had served its purpose in that it enabled the brewery to purchase the radio and TV broadcasting rights to advertise Natty Boh, National Premium and Colt 45. The advertising slogan, "The Land of Pleasant Living," had caught fire, and everyone knew it meant enjoying life with a Natty Boh in hand. But, since the Family no longer owned National, and since the Orioles did not generate any operating return for the Family, it was hard to justify continuing to have a significant investment in baseball. Jerry reluctantly accepted the will of the board and the team was put up for sale.

When a public announcement was made that the Orioles were for sale, the local fans were furious, fearing that the team would leave Baltimore. Great pressure was put on Jerry by the mayor and governor to assure that any prospective buyer would agree to keep the team here. This put real limitations on the number of prospective buyers and thus on the price. Death threats against Jerry heightened the problem.

Several attempts to buy the franchise by various Baltimoreans failed. An offer was made by Bill Veeck, one of the most dynamic major league managers in baseball whom Jerry knew well. Contemporaneously, an offer came in from a group led by a wealthy former Secretary of the Treasury, William Simon. However, neither group was willing to agree to keep the team in Baltimore so the offers were dismissed, but not without some very hard feelings. Jerry had also been approached by Edward Bennett Williams, a very prominent Washington, DC, attorney, who offered $12.5 million for the franchise and agreed to not move the team. Believing in Williams' integrity and his ability to perform, the Family finally agreed to sell him its controlling interest.

Then, despite his promise, several seasons after acquiring the Orioles, Williams threatened to leave Baltimore unless a new state-of-the-art stadium was built to replace the old 33rd Street stadium. Consequently, with state bond money of several hundred million dollars, a new stadium was constructed in downtown Baltimore. It is a magnificent home for the Birds and one which other cities have copied.

Looking back, I have asked myself whether it was a wise decision to sell the Oriole franchise, which turned out to be a very profitable investment for Williams. However, I feel confident that from the standpoint of maintaining peace in the Family, it was the right thing to do. Furthermore, I don't think that we could have threatened to take the team elsewhere, as Williams did, as leverage for getting public funding for a new stadium.

As I recall, the total amount derived from the sale of the brewery assets, the subsidiary companies (Solarine and Pompeian) and National's controlling interest in the Orioles was about $25 million. The name of The National Brewing Company was changed to the O-W Fund, Inc. (O-W Fund or O-W), and its charter and by-laws were amended to enable it to operate as an investment company. The proceeds of the sale were to be invested by O-W primarily in marketable securities.

I cannot leave this subject of the demise of the National Brewing Company without mentioning my gratitude to Dawson Farber. Despite the fact that he and Jerry were close friends, Dawson was willing to risk this friendship out of a sense of greater obligation to our Family. I could not have so effectively challenged Jerry's resistance had it not been for Dawson disclosing to me the desperate status of the operation. Armed with this information, I was able to have the strength of my convictions that the Family had no choice but to sell out. Ultimately, Jerry got suspicious about how I knew so much about what was going on and finally identified Dawson as the person who was providing me with these facts. The relationship between these two was never the same.

Although my own relationship with Jerry thereafter was awkward at first, it gradually improved as we continued to relate to one another primarily concerning his personal financial matters. I think that he came to understand that Dawson and I had not betrayed his friendship but had done what we believed we were compelled to do to serve the best interests of the Family.

A number of years after the dust had settled and the O-W Fund, of which Dawson was a shareholder, had been merged into Davis New York Venture Fund (DNYVF), Dawson would stop by at my office whenever he needed to see his dentist, whose office was in the same building as my office. On these occasions, he never failed to thank me for having merged the O-W Fund with New York Venture Fund. I, on the other hand, had never forgotten his sacrificial act and never failed to thank him for what he had done for our Family.[34]

It is now more than 35 years since the National Brewery's assets were sold to Carling Brewing Company. Thereafter, Carling sold out to G. Heileman Brewing Company, who sold out to Stroh's, who sold out

However, I feel confident that from the standpoint of maintaining peace in the Family, it was the right thing to do.

The National Brewing Company, as it appeared as an operating brewery, 1940. Black and white photographs courtesy of National Brewing Company archives

Current Natty Boh label now owned by the Pabst Brewing Company. © C. Dean Metropoulos & Co. Documentation by DOC Artist Services

The beloved trademark of the one-eyed mustached man is increasingly seen on T-shirts, baseball caps, bumper stickers, ties and in other forms.

"Natty Boh" neon sign that surveys the city from the top of the former brew house of the National Brewing Company, 2012. This building and the surrounding area is being redeveloped by Wells Obrecht of Obrecht Commercial Real Estate. Photographs courtesy of the Obrecht Commercial Real Estate archives.

(in bankruptcy) to Miller and Pabst. The abandoned brewery buildings, which remained empty for many years, are now part of a redeveloped commercial, retail and evolving apartment real estate complex known as "Brewers Hill," that also includes the Gunther Brewing Company (in which the Family had a one-third interest).

During this tortuous history of the brewing industry in the U.S., the Natty Boh brand somehow survived, and the beer is actually being brewed today by Pabst for a growing Baltimore market where many bars, liquor stores and restaurants carry it in bottles and cans and even on tap. The beloved trademark of the one-eyed mustached man is increasingly seen on T-shirts, baseball caps, bumper stickers, ties and in other forms. In fact, I even heard one of my friends sing the Natty Boh theme song at a dinner party:

"National Boh, National Boh, I'm here to say, it's brewed on the shores of the Chesapeake Bay."

The advertising slogan, *"The Land of Pleasant Living,"* which conveyed the impression that Maryland's pleasant lifestyle included drinking "Natty Boh," is still among the phrases used to depict Maryland as a great place to live.[35] Although the demise of the National Brewery was an agonizing occurrence and a personally very unpleasant experience, the fact that the brand still lives on, and that the Mr. Boh logo and slogans are still etched in the memory of Baltimoreans, is worthy of note.

THE SHORT AND HIGHLY SUCCESSFUL EXISTENCE OF THE O-W FUND INC.

The O-W Fund Inc., referred to in the previous section, began functioning as a closely held investment company in 1975. The board consisted mainly of members of the Family: Charles H. Hoffberger, Jerold C. Hoffberger, Stanley A. Hoffberger and me, along with Zan Krieger and Morton Hollander. I served as its president. The board appointed Warburg Pincus Counselors and The Rothschild Company to serve as investment advisors, with each having a portion of the portfolio to manage. John Furth and Scott Marsh spearheaded the Warburg Pincus team, and Stan Rothschild was in charge of the Rothschild group.

As I recall, the vast majority of the investments made by the O-W Fund were in large cap domestic stocks. During the 13-year period between 1975 and 1988, at which time O-W merged with the New York Venture Fund (NYVF), the S&P 500 grew at the rate of 8.35% compounded

As our security
portfolio grew
in value, so
did the amount
of dividends,
interest and
capital gains O-W
was realizing.

annually. The times were good and the Fund grew as the S&P continued to rise. Actually, both of our investment advisors were outpacing the S&P as investment advisors are supposed to do, but often don't. By the time we merged O-W with NYVF, the assets of O-W had increased to $77 million for an annual compounded return of 9.04%.

As our security portfolio grew in value, so did the amount of dividends, interest and capital gains O-W was realizing. O-W was a C corporation and was therefore required to pay taxes at the corporate level at the rate of 35%. Thus, hundreds of thousands of dollars were going to the government (state and federal) that could have been going into the pockets of O-W's shareholders if O-W had been a pass-through entity like a partnership or an LLC. Likewise, had it qualified as an S corporation, it would have avoided paying corporate taxes. However, at the time, neither changing O-W to a pass-through entity, nor converting it to an S corporation, was possible, tax-free, under the Internal Revenue Code.

As previously mentioned, in 1986, Congress was considering a major tax reform act that, among other things, was intended to prevent all types of mergers that were tax-free. Passage would have, therefore, closed the only possible way for O-W to resolve its tax problem. Knowing this, I turned to our Washington lawyer, Covington & Burling, to focus on a provision in the code that seemed to permit an A-type tax-free merger. Covington's interpretation of this provision was that, probably by an oversight, it did not prevent the merger of a C corporation with a public mutual fund. As soon as Covington made us aware of this, Marc Blum, a friend and representative of the Blum Family, and I started on an intensive search for a mutual fund that might be interested in merging with O-W and two other smaller securities companies owned by the Hoffberger and the Blum Families. The story of how that episode played out will come next in these memoirs.

The Race to Complete Mergers Before IRS Tax Reform in 1986
Prevents Tax-Free Transactions

As a result of the Merchants Mortgage bankruptcy, Irv Blum and I saw an opportunity for him, with the help of his brother Alvin, to assist Merchants in working its way out of all of the loans that had been foreclosed on by the banks. We agreed that Blum's Inc. would buy a one-half interest in Merchants, based on the deep discounting of the value of the foreclosed properties, and that Irv and Alvin would then help liquidate the foreclosed real estate. More importantly, we also agreed that Blum's would acquire a one-half interest in the Real Estate Holding Company (REH), giving it the benefit of Irv's investment acumen.

This was in the early seventies, and during the next 15 years both Blum's and REH Co. had, after liquidating the Merchants' properties, become private investment companies owning public marketable securities. Both companies had been quite successful in the equity market and were therefore paying significant corporate taxes from dividend income and capital gains. This caused the boards of both companies to begin to think of ways that the corporate-level tax could be eliminated.

As previously mentioned, in 1986 Congress was considering a major reform of the Internal Revenue Code (IRC). Not previously discussed was a provision being contemplated that would permit C Corporations (which is the type of corporation practically all of the Family companies were at that time) to liquidate at a tax rate of 20%, a rate substantially below the previous rate. Thus, there appeared to be an opening to avoid future onerous corporate-level taxation by liquidating the corporations and converting them to LLCs or partnerships that are not taxable.

Morton Hollander, Gene Feinblatt, Marc Blum and I, all being lawyers at GFRH&H, gave serious thought to this opportunity. The companies that we were considering liquidating and converting to LLCs or Limited Partnerships were REH Co. and the O-W Fund Inc., the successor in name to the National Brewing Company which, as previously mentioned, had sold its assets in 1975 and had become an investment company headed by me. Marc Blum likewise desired to convert his family's company, Blum's Inc., into a pass-through entity that would avoid future corporate taxes. While the lower rate was an incentive to liquidate the above-named companies and thereafter continue as pass-through entities, we nevertheless concluded that the overall tax that would still be required would be too great. The stock of these companies

> This was in the early seventies, and during the next 15 years both Blum's and REH Co. had, after liquidating the Merchants' properties, become private investment companies owning public marketable securities.

had no significant cost basis, or in the case of the O-W Fund, had increased in value to such an extent that the tax on the gain would have been enormous.

Thus, I continued my search for some other solution and decided to consult my friends at Covington & Burling. They opined that since the IRC was silent about the ability of a C corporation to merge with a public mutual fund, an A-type reorganization of these companies could be done on a tax-exempt basis. This was great news so I immediately informed Marc Blum, and we promptly began our search for potential mutual fund candidates. Time was of the essence since the above-referred-to IRC provision was slated to be changed under the legislation effective January 1, 1986, known as the Tax Reform Act of 1986.

There were about 1,200 mutual funds in existence at that time so we had to set up criteria that we deemed important to the Blum and Hoffberger Families if we were to merge our companies into a public mutual fund. First, we wanted a fund with a sound long-term performance record. Second, we wanted a fund with an acceptable distribution record. And third, we wanted a fund that would permit us to have some representation on its board. In order to narrow the field in regard to the first two criteria, we decided that the fund had to have been in existence for at least 15 years so we could see how it had performed over that period.

In order to comb through 1,200 mutual funds for this information, we had to have someone develop a computer program that would electronically give us all of the mutual funds that met our criteria. Marc had a friend by the name of Ted Rosenberg who was a computer geek and a very bright person. In short order, he developed a program that gave us a list of funds that met these two criteria.

For comparative purposes, we refined the criteria by establishing a minimum average annual total return as well as a minimum average distribution that the funds on the list had to have met over the 15-year period. This, obviously, narrowed the list to enable us to focus our attention on the top ten funds.

During this process, Marc happened to meet a friend at Alex. Brown and Sons, whose name was Benjamin Schapiro. Marc confided in him what we were attempting to do, and Ben asked him whether a fund called "New York Venture Fund (NYVF)" was among those we were considering. Marc must have told him "no" but that he would check the larger list to see where it ranked. When he did, it turned out that NYVF was 11th.

As we investigated further, we discovered that NYVF also met the two criteria we had established. Marc then contacted Ben, who knew the principals at NYVF quite well, to find out if they would have any interest in doing an A-type reorganization with our companies. Their response was "yes." In addition to receiving an expression of interest from NYVF, we also heard from one of the Guardian mutual funds that we had contacted, and it likewise expressed interest in such a merger transaction.

While we now had two mutual funds interested in a tax-free deal, both Marc and I were leaning toward NYVF. Marc, through Ben's introduction, had had a number of telephone conversations with Jeremy Biggs, the vice-chairman of Fiduciary Trust International and a member of NYVF's board, concerning the merger. Marc was impressed with Biggs' investment philosophy and with the fact that NYVF was being managed by Shelby Davis, the son of Shelby Cullum Davis, a man who had made a great fortune in owning insurance company stocks. I was impressed that he and his father were both Princeton alumni.

Being anxious to proceed, Marc and I made two separate appointments to meet with representatives of NYVF and Guardian in New York. First, we met with three executives from NYVF – Martin Proyect, the president; Shelby Davis; and Jeremy Biggs. They all were very serious about doing the deal, particularly since the Fund, at that time, had total assets of only $400 million and we were offering to add assets of up to $123 million through the mergers. As evidence of their eagerness to increase their assets by over 30% and knowing of our desire to have representation on the NYVF board, they offered us three seats on the board. We had a nice lunch and then left for our second appointment with Guardian Mutual Fund. Feeling quite elated, we were looking forward to a similar warm reception.

Guardian was a considerably larger fund than NYVF so the enticement of an additional $123 million did not appear to have the same importance to the one executive with whom we met. While he clearly expressed interest in entertaining an A-type reorganization with our companies, he made it clear that Guardian would not be interested in our having any representation on its board.

I can hear him saying: "We'll invest your money carefully and intelligently. If you want to call us from time to time and ask any questions, we'll be glad to answer them. But we don't need any additional advice on how to invest our funds."

That having been said, Marc and I thanked him for his time and left, knowing that we could not (nor did we wish to try to) sell the Family on turning over $123 million of securities to an organization that would treat us as total strangers, even if it did have a good track record.

From then on, NYVF became our sole focus of attention. Wishing to promptly proceed with the legal steps necessary to effect a tax-free A-type reorganization, both the REH Co. board and the board of Blum's Inc. promptly adopted resolutions that stated their intentions to engage in such a transaction with NYVF. The terms of the merger were simply that Blum's Inc. and REH would turn over their marketable assets, amounting to $46 million, to NYVF in exchange for shares of NYVF, most of which were required to be put in a ten-year Voting Trust, giving NYVF trustees the right to vote these shares. The reason for restricting our right to vote was to prevent us, as owners of so many shares, from having so much potential influence on the selection of the Fund's manager. Marc and Gene Feinblatt would become directors of NYVF, and if and when O-W agreed to merge, I would too.

The Plans of Reorganization were circulated to the shareholders of the respective companies and were approved overwhelmingly at respective stockholders' meetings. The two closings took place, and the mergers were consummated prior to December 31, 1985.

However, the O-W Fund board members, particularly Morton Hollander, "Reds" Charlie Hoffberger and Gene Feinblatt, were hesitant to place control of any more of the Family's assets in NYVF hands. O-W Fund's net worth was about $77 million by this time, having grown from $25 million. Its investment advisors, Warburg Pincus and Rothschild Management, had done a good job and the market had been most kind. The addition of O-W's marketable assets to what we and the Blums had already turned over to NYVF would have meant that all of both families' marketable securities (amounting to over 30% of NYVF's total assets) would have been in one basket. Therefore, the majority of the board was reluctant to take any definitive steps that would enable O-W to merge with NYVF, despite the fact that if the 1986 Tax Reform Act passed Congress, it would prevent any future tax-free mergers with mutual funds beginning January 1, 1986.

Both Marc and I felt that the majority directors were wrong not to at least pass a resolution, before January 1, 1986, stating that we intended to enter into a tax-free A-type reorganization with NYVF. Even if we did not proceed any further, no harm could be done. By going on record that O-W intended to enter into a merger transaction, we felt O-W would have an opportunity to be "grandfathered" out of the 1986 Tax Reform Act.

Marc Blum Esq., my friend and advisor

We tried to convince those who were opposed to a merger that such action by the company was the wise thing to do.

We tried to convince those who were opposed to a merger that such action by the company was the wise thing to do. We knew that Morton and Gene were really "dug in," so it was "Reds" Charlie who we hoped would change his mind. At the next board meeting of O-W, this matter was again discussed and a resolution to proceed with the merger was introduced. Charlie (with some urging from Marc and me, whom he greatly trusted and respected) changed his vote, and the motion to state our intentions to merge with NYVF carried 4 to 3.

Unfortunately, by the time the O-W board acted, it was already too late to complete all of the required legal steps in 1985 to effect the merger. We had circulated the Plan of Reorganization to O-W's shareholders and received an affirmative vote from the majority. Likewise, NYVF had completed all of the legal steps it needed to take on its side to enable the merger to take place.

However, before the O-W Shareholders Meeting could be held to affirm the majority vote of the shareholders, the IRS (knowing of the first mergers that had taken place in 1985 and possibly having heard of another private company that intended to effectuate a merger with another mutual fund) issued a very damaging memorandum. In effect, it said that the regulation in the existing tax code (that Covington said permitted O-W to merge with a mutual fund) was intended, although silent on the subject, to prevent such an A-type reorganization. Although O-W had but this one final step to take to complete the deal, we were effectively stopped in our tracks by this memo.

Since Rod DeArment of Covington & Burling had been keeping me apprised of what Congress' intentions were concerning mergers between C corporations and public mutual funds, I met with him and several other Covington partners to tell them of our dilemma and why we felt strongly that the IRS had stretched the meaning of the existing provision in an effort to prohibit any more tax-free mergers before the passage of the 1986 Tax Reform Act. They agreed and recommended that we lobby key members of the Maryland congressional delegation to support our position by advocating that Congress pass a special piece of legislation couched in terms that would "grandfather" only the O-W merger with NYVF from the 1986 Tax Reform Act.

Such legislative bills are not unusual, but they require a sound legal and moral justification in order for delegates to support them. Rod and I hit the road and called on our two Maryland senators, as well as most of the Maryland House members, to explain the appropriateness for making a special exception of the O-W pending merger. Rod, who was well-known on the Hill, having been Senator Dole's chief of staff, called on some of the key Republican Senate and House members to obtain bipartisan support.

I can recall that the last holdout in the Maryland delegation was Senator Paul Sarbanes, who after very carefully analyzing the legal basis for our request finally concluded that he could justify his support. His concern was the possible allegation of favoritism since he and I were friends. The special bill passed both houses, but it was not until 1988 that the O-W merger with NYVF actually became a reality. I then became a director of NYVF although I had been serving as a consultant to the advisor since 1986, at the same salary I had received from the O-W Fund. Thus we had concluded the last tax-free merger of a private C corporation and a public mutual fund.

Over the many years in which the Family has owned Davis New York Venture Fund (DNYVF) shares, it has greatly prospered from its investment which has delivered an average annual compounded total return of about 12.5%. Despite this, the fact that the Family had so much of its wealth concentrated in a single holding, which tended to be volatile, caused me to believe it was time to diversify. Moreover, when the Davis family took over control of the Fund (resulting in a change of the Fund's name to the Davis New York Venture Fund – DNYVF), they also changed the distribution policy by not realizing capital gains and paying them out to the shareholders. This decision may have been good tax policy, but it substantially reduced the Family's main source of passive income. Since the large distributions of DNYVF had been one of our important reasons for having chosen to merge with Davis, this change was an additional reason to diversify.

My son Douglas and my cousin Harry Halpert commenced a two-year, exhaustive process of selecting a major advisory firm to assist in such diversification and reinvestment of the net proceeds to be derived from the sale of DNYVF shares by the Family. A well-designed investment program was established for the Family trusts that varies the allocation of securities based on the longevity of each trust and the age of its life beneficiary. KRC (the family's investment administrator created as a subsidiary of Keystone) was engaged to manage this program and Northern Trust Company was selected to be the investment advisor. An investment committee, consisting of qualified Family members, was created to assist Douglas as president of Keystone in his decision making.

The process of diversifying out of most of the Family's holdings in Davis is now taking place and my feeling is that we are doing the right thing to preserve and hopefully grow the Family's wealth in a more prudent manner. Our decision to merge with the Davis New York Venture Fund

> The process of diversifying out of most of the Family's holdings in Davis is now taking place and my feeling is that we are doing the right thing to preserve and hopefully grow the Family's wealth in a more prudent manner.

was no doubt a very wise one. It created a holding of several hundred million dollars for the Family at one point, and, although two market crashes have diminished this, DNYVF still represents the Family's single largest source of wealth. While our journey with Davis has been a long and successful one in which I am proud to have played a major role, it was prudent to diversify.

SERVICE ON THE BOARD OF (DAVIS) NEW YORK VENTURE FUND

Following the completion of the merger, and after serving as a consultant to the advisor of NYVF for three years, I went on the board of NYVF where I served as a director until 2000 when, having reached 75, my retirement was mandated. Thereafter, I served as an emeritus director for three more years as permitted by the bylaws.

The board consisted of ten to twelve interesting, experienced and astute persons – at first all men, but later including women. I learned from all of them and formed a friendly relationship with several – i.e., Martin Proyect, who was for most of my tenure the president of NYVF; Chris and Andrew Davis, the sons of Shelby Davis, whose family purchased control of the advisor company from Martin; and Chris Sonne, whose family merged its privately owned security holding company with NYVF not too long after O-W did.

During the time that I served as a director, there were several events that stand out in my mind. One was Martin's decision to sell his controlling interest in the advisory firm to the Davis family. There was evidently a difference of opinion between Martin and Shelby Davis, who was critical of how Martin was marketing the Fund's shares. Shelby had evidently made Martin an offer for his controlling interest in the Advisor (i.e., the firm making investment decisions for the Fund) that was too good to turn down, but Martin retained a minor interest.

Although the Davis family now controlled the Advisor, for some reason Martin felt that he should still be president of the Fund. However, when the board voted on the election of officers, Martin lost. This was a devastating blow to him because some of his oldest friends on the board had voted against him. They felt, as I did, that because the Davis Family had not only made a substantial investment in the Advisor, but had also invested a huge amount of the family's money in the Fund, they were also entitled to control the Fund.

> During the time that I served as a director, there were serveral events that stand out in my mind.

The most
surreal and
unquestionably
memorable
experience that I
had while serving
on the board
occurred
on September 11,
2001.

As I recall, Martin thereafter sold the rest of his interest in the Advisor to the Davis Family and resigned from the board. Right or wrong, Martin's decision to leave the Fund saddened me for, in truth, it was his warm, welcoming personality that had been a factor in our selection of NYVF when Marc and I were originally seeking a home for our family investments.

The most surreal and unquestionably memorable experience that I had while serving on the board occurred on September 11, 2001. The board at that time usually met in New York in the board room of Fiduciary Trust International, located on the 94th floor of the South Tower of the World Trade Center. Notices of the meeting, which was scheduled for 9 AM, had been sent to all directors several weeks before the meeting, and I had indicated that I would attend. However, for an unstated reason which turned out to be purely logistical (i.e., to make it easier for the large number of directors and staff coming from Tucson, Arizona, where the administrative offices of DNYVF were located), the location of the meeting was changed to Chicago. Since I was then an emeritus director, without a vote, I decided that I would not travel that distance to attend.

While I seldom watch TV in the morning, I had my set on when the second terrorist-piloted plane struck the South Tower at the 94th floor at about 8:45 AM. I couldn't believe it. I continued to watch and listen as the commentator was relaying the apparent indecision of the fire and police departments about whether to tell the people inside the two towers to abandon the buildings. Obviously, people, on their own, decided to leave the buildings and I could see many of them running away from the site of the Towers.

Finally, the fire and police departments must have concluded that both towers were in jeopardy of collapsing. Desperately, they and others sought to assist as many people out of the buildings as possible. But time ran out, and first the North Tower and then the South Tower collapsed like accordions. I could see people escaping from the site as fast as possible. Smoke and thick dust filled the air. There was utter chaos. As I sit here typing my recollection of this horrendous event, I am feeling a sense of anxiety and sadness for the thousands who were trapped in the burning and collapsing Towers.

Although I would have been entering the South Tower via the PATH train coming from Newark and arriving at the South Tower at about 8:45 AM (had the DNYVF meeting not been changed to Chicago), I do not feel overwhelmed by the thought that had the board meeting not been changed, I probably would have perished. When I tell this story to others, they gasp. But, I have come to believe that G-d works in strange ways and that it was just not my destiny to be where the 9/11 tragedy struck, with its global (but, thank G-d, for me not personal) consequences.

KEYSTONE REALTY COMPANY INC. AND CPC INC.

Their Origin, Purpose and Growth

Earlier in these memoirs, I mentioned the role of both Keystone and CPC Inc. in the real estate and mortgage operations conducted originally by my Uncle Sam and then by me. Uncle Sam's modus operandi, following World War II, had been to sell small parcels of large tracts of land owned by Keystone to two or three trusted small home builders to enable them to construct houses in the northwest part of Baltimore City. Using the financial resources of Merchants Mortgage to finance the acquisition of small, subdivided residential parcels of the acreage owned by Keystone and the construction of the houses thereon, they then used the resources of Union Federal Savings and Loan to finance the purchase of the finished homes by the ultimate buyers.

In the booming housing market that existed in the 1950s, this was a safe way to dispose of Keystone's land holdings at a profit that consisted of cash and/or the receipt of ground rents from the sale of the leasehold interest to the buyers. Thus, when I came on the scene, I initially continued the same procedure set up by my uncle for the disposition of Keystone's undeveloped land. I also decided to sell off Keystone's Class B and C office and retail properties located downtown, since I saw no real growth potential in their ownership. Downtown, in general, was in need of renewal. Suburban commercial development in the counties had begun to attract both office and retail tenants and properties were becoming vacant.

After the disposition of all of Keystone's downtown properties (leaving only one industrial building that my son Douglas ultimately sold at a considerable profit) and the sale of its undeveloped land, I felt that future acquisition should be by other newly created entities. The tracts of land that interested me were farmland located in then somewhat-remote areas of Baltimore County that were not, at the time of their purchase, served by public sewer and water. In effect, I was buying land zoned as farmland, at very reasonable prices. However, through my engineer

In effect, I was buying land zoned as farmland, at very reasonable prices.

and land planner, I was made aware of the county's Five-Year Land Use plans which, in general terms, set forth a timetable for when and where public utilities would be extended. All of this information was available to developers to enable them to plan, but few developers had the money to "land bank" for future development. What was required to take advantage of this information was the ability of the buyer to provide the annual cash needed to carry the standing mortgage on the land and the real estate taxes for about a five-year period. The male members of the Family who worked in our businesses had that capacity and as a result realized substantial capital gains from the sale of their stock.

In all, I acquired three or four of these relatively large parcels for the male members of my generation. As a result of the success of these ventures and the vast experience and confidence that I had gained, I was fully prepared and was looking for the opportunity to follow this procedure on an even larger scale, but in the booming Washington suburban area. When Jerry brought Fairchild Industries to me, as previously described in the story of the New Town of Germantown, I was confident this was the opportunity of a lifetime to use my skills in a highly creative and rewarding way.

While this activity was taking place, the venture described in the section titled "Another Fascinating Real Estate Opportunity Comes Along" presented itself. As recalled therein, this enterprise required the acquisition of all of the properties on the east side of the 200 block of North Calvert Street. Among these properties were the building where my office was located (owned by the Real Estate Holding Company) and the Calvert Parking Garage (owned by Calvert Parking Garage Inc.). I decided that Calvert Parking Garage Inc. should be the vehicle through which the accumulation of the required properties should occur. This was done and the rest of the story has been told previously.

However, continuing to use the existing name of the Calvert Parking Garage Inc. as the owner of the Maryland National Bank Operations Building did not seem appropriate. So, in 1968, I decided to amend its charter by broadening the powers of the company and changing its name, using the first letters of its existing corporate name as the new name of the company. Thus, CPC Inc. was born.

Soon thereafter the Union Trust Company entered into a 15-year lease of the lots owned by Davis Street Parking Inc., which were located across the street and to the east of the Maryland National Bank property. Since the Englar Family was 50% owner, as well as partial owner of CPC Inc., I decided to merge the two companies to simplify our accounting and operations.

CPC's annual operating net profits were considerable, enabling it to not only pay significant dividends but to accumulate cash for other investments. Then, when Maryland National decided to exercise its option to purchase the building it occupied and Union Trust Company acquired the land lease on which it had built its operations center, CPC faced horrendous capital gains taxes. Rather than accept cash at the settlement with Maryland National, I decided to do a Section 1030 like-kind exchange to delay the tax.

This proved to be not such a wise decision since the property involved in the exchange, which was a newly built apartment project in Richmond, Virginia, turned out not to be a good investment. Thus, after about six years of mediocre returns, I again did a Section 1030 exchange, this time with the largest apartment REIT in existence, Equity Residential, for which CPC received certificates convertible into shares. Until it actually converted its certificates (which my son Douglas did in 2011), the tax on the exchange was deferred. While CPC Inc. probably did not net out of its conversion and sale of Equity Residential shares what it would have netted had it accepted cash from Maryland National in the first instance, its partial recovery from a bad investment in Richmond was most satisfying.

With accumulated cash, CPC acquired a limited partnership interest in a number of residential and commercial real estate projects. It made several investments in suburban office buildings with Jon Kolker, most of which turned out to be excellent. It also made several investments in apartment projects with my friend and real estate dealmaker Jonas Brodie, which likewise proved to be quite profitable. When my son Douglas took over the operation of CPC in 1989, he expanded the number of real estate partnership investments and built a diversified portfolio of marketable securities.

CPC is today a diversified investment company with a policy that permits it to invest in real estate, marketable securities and private equity. Douglas continues to seek out and find a variety of passive investments which have considerable potential for profit with a reasonable risk profile.

When Douglas became the operating head of Keystone, it had a large investment in Davis shares. He has since diversified out of Davis and into a portfolio of national and international securities.

THE FAMILY OFFICE (KRC LLC)

By being on the board of Davis, I learned about how most mutual funds distribute their shares and service the accounts of their shareholders. By virtue of an SEC regulation (that did not exist a few years earlier when O-W Fund merged with NYVF) known as Section 12(b)(1), mutual funds are permitted to pay a fee, not to exceed 0.25% of the net asset value of a share, to brokers, trust companies, banks and servicing agencies for their services in distributing, promoting and selling their shares as well as for administrating the accounts of shareholder customers.

As I learned more about what type of services trust companies and servicing agencies were rendering to Davis shareholders, I began to realize that Keystone, which my son Douglas was running, was performing the exact same services for the Family trusts that publicly owned organizations were rendering to other Davis shareholders and for which they were receiving a 12(b)(1) fee. After carefully studying the material that set forth which organizations were entitled to receive a 12(b)(1) fee, I met with Martin Proyect to discuss the possibility of Keystone qualifying to receive such a fee on the large number of shares that the Family owned.

I asked Martin whether our Family holding and servicing company, Keystone Realty, would have been able to qualify to receive the 12(b)(1) fee had the fee existed at the time of the merger. After thinking about it, he agreed that it probably would have. Martin then checked with NYVF's legal counsel who likewise agreed that Keystone, if it or a subsidiary qualified as an SEC-approved investment advisor, could receive the fee on shares owned by Family trusts and individuals with whom it had a servicing agreement. The matter was then brought before the NYVF board which approved the payment, provided a qualified entity was formed.

I informed Douglas of this and he immediately went about engaging legal counsel to assist him in the formation of an SEC-approved investment advisor as a subsidiary of Keystone. The investment advisory firm was called "KRC LLC" and was headed by Douglas, who had qualified as an investment advisor under the SEC regulations. Once this was done, he sent out servicing agreements to the trustees of the Family trusts and to certain individuals in the Family who owned a significant number of Davis shares. Whereas previously Keystone had charged a fee to the trusts for accounting and administrative services, it no longer had to do so. The 0.25% fee now being received was generating far more revenue for the services KRC was rendering than Keystone was formerly receiving. What a win-win situation for the Family and for Keystone!

> By being on the board of Davis, I learned about how most mutual funds distribute their shares and service the accounts of their shareholders.

As previously
mentioned,
sometime in
2005, I began
advocating the
importance of
diversification
of the Family's
holdings in
DNYVF with
Harry
and Douglas.

As previously mentioned, sometime in 2005, I began advocating the importance of diversification of the Family's holdings in DNYVF with Harry and Douglas. That meant the sale of all or a large portion of DNYVF shares. Having gone through the stock market disaster of 2001–2002, which significantly impacted Davis shares, they were receptive to the idea. Thus began a long process of determining which major investment advisory firm could best assist in creating the appropriate investment portfolio for each of the Hoffberger individuals and trusts over the long term. Eventually, an investment advisor was selected (Northern Trust Company) and an investment policy was crafted to guide KRC in the disposition of Davis shares owned by the Family trusts and the reinvestment of the net proceeds.

The process took a long time, and in 2008, the Family's holdings in Davis were again subjected to a devastating decline of over 30% in value. In 2009, DNYVF shares recovered about 50% of their lost value. Douglas informed me that the Family's investment advisor (Northern Trust Company) had begun selling shares of Davis in an orderly fashion. Fortunately, the extension of the Bush tax cuts lengthened the time frame (until 2013) during which the 15% capital gains rate would still be effective.

I am satisfied that selling most of the Family's holdings of DNYVF shares was a sound decision. While we had done quite well with Davis, having realized an average annual total return of about 12.5%

compounded over the 23 years we had been invested in the Fund, the risk of having all our eggs in one basket proved to be far too great.

I have now intentionally relinquished active participation in the decision-making process that has brought our Family to this point. Douglas, as CEO of KRC, has put together an Investment Committee, consisting of himself, Harry and their cousins Peter Lebovitz and Keith Rosenbloom, all of whom are well qualified to act in an advisory capacity to Douglas. I am optimistic that they will do an excellent job of overseeing the Family's wealth well into the future.

MERCHANTS TERMINAL / HOFFBERGER HOLDINGS INC. (HHI)

The "Cousins Council" Is Formed in an Effort to Maintain Unity

Throughout my entire legal and business career, I have been involved in one capacity or another with Merchants Terminal Corporation (Merchants), now known as Hoffberger Holdings Inc. (HHI).

In the early 1950s, Merchants acquired Terminal Refrigerating and Warehousing Company (TR&W) that operated two refrigerated warehouses in southwest Washington, DC, both of which were subsequently condemned by the District in connection with its Downtown Urban Renewal Plan. For the first time, instead of reinvesting the proceeds in an operating business, Uncle Saul Hoffberger, then president of Merchants Terminal, decided to invest the proceeds in conservative marketable stocks.

Not too long thereafter, Merchants received an offer (which I recall was $6 million) from the Gulf Oil Company to buy its fuel oil distribution business. I recall having lunch with Uncle Saul and "Reds" Charlie at the Belvedere Hotel in the final phase of their negotiations and hearing their rationale for selling. The competition was getting tougher and the customers were getting rougher. The offer was accepted and, again, the proceeds were invested in conservative marketable stocks.

Having only been out of law school for a few years, I was only marginally involved in both of these transactions, which Morton Hollander handled. I therefore had no conversation with my Uncle Saul concerning his rationale for investing in the stock market and thus did not attribute any possible undisclosed motive to his decision. But, looking back, I can now think of two possible (perhaps likely) reasons for his having chosen to invest in marketable securities: the first being his decision to diversify Merchants' holdings into other than our illiquid existing businesses, or

The competition was getting tougher and the customers were getting rougher.

a new operating venture, and the second, less obvious, that marketable securities could be easily sold to raise money.

Uncle Saul liked me, and so, on occasion, he confided in me the fact that he was very frustrated by the lack of attention that both my brother Bert and cousin Jerry paid to his advice concerning the respective businesses they were running. It had been understood that when Bert and Jerry were put in charge of their businesses, they would periodically report to Uncle Saul to keep him informed (since Merchants had large holdings in both of their companies). Evidently, this was not being done and I even think they had both told him to "butt out."

No doubt this disturbed Uncle Saul to the point that he decided to ask to be bought out. This thought could well have been on his mind when the decisions, mentioned above, to invest in liquid assets were made. He told my father that he had lost confidence in Bert and Jerry and that he felt their businesses were headed for trouble (which prediction ultimately came true, but I doubt because they were not listening to him). He further stated that he did not have any sons who could succeed him and protect his Family's interest. My father was sympathetic to his expressed desire, particularly since Uncle Saul seemed to be quite distraught by having been ignored and rejected by two members of my generation.

As I recall, Uncle Sam was dysfunctional by this time and did not participate in any of the buy-out discussions, so it was up to Morton Hollander and me to negotiate the buy-out with Uncle Saul. I have forgotten how Morton and I arrived at the prices that we felt were fair for his various closely held stocks, but whatever method we used produced values that were not far from his asking prices. I believe our biggest disagreement was over the price for his National Brewing Company stock. While we thought he wanted too much, my father asked Morton and me to "bend over backwards to be fair" and to "give him the benefit of the doubt," two of my father's often-used expressions. I recall that several hundred thousand dollars were at stake, which we conceded to give him.

"Reds" Charlie Hoffberger, 1995

At this point "Reds" Charlie became president of Merchants, which then consisted of a refrigerated public warehousing business operating two warehouses in Baltimore and one in Landover; a portfolio of marketable securities; 100% ownership of the stock of Motor Freight Express (operated by my brother Bert, who did not get along too well with "Reds"); about 17% ownership of the stock of the National Brewing Company (which was run by my cousin Jerry, with whom he did have a close relationship); 100% of the stock of TR&W of which he was president (which owned a portfolio of stocks and bonds); and 100% of the stock of the Pompeian Olive Oil Company (which was run by my father and my younger brother, Stanley).

"Reds" Charlie relied over many years on Morton Hollander for advice, but he also valued my opinion and liked me (as I did him) both as a friend and someone with good business judgment. With the departure of Uncle Saul it was decided that all of the cousins who were involved in operating one of the Family's companies, together with Morton and me, would meet periodically with my father to discuss various business matters. My father died in 1963, but this process of the "Cousins Council" continued through the sixties, a time when our businesses were growing.

Both Bert and Jerry would from time to time bring to the group proposals for the acquisition of other companies in their respective industries. Over time, the group gave Jerry the okay to acquire several relatively small marginal breweries. One was located in Detroit, one in Orlando and one in Phoenix. The idea was to continue to sell their existing brands but to gradually introduce National Boh and Colt 45 (also produced by National) in those areas, with the hope that we could make these two brands strong regional contenders.

Likewise, Bert was authorized to acquire two other trucking companies that he felt would create more synergy for his transportation system. However, his proposal to acquire yet a third company was turned down by the group, which had dire consequences for Merchants Terminal and also for my personal relationship with him.

"Reds" Charlie was much more conservative than Bert and Jerry in his desire to expand the refrigerated warehouses. However, the obsolescence of the Monument Street multi-storied warehouse and the fear that a competitor might locate in the newly created Maryland Food Market in Jessup caused him to seek and get approval to build a large warehouse at the Jessup Market.

As I have indicated, the sixties were a euphoric period of expansion for our Family businesses and while I feel that our decisions were rational, we did not (perhaps could not) realize how rapidly "big" business and the government's decision to deregulate (i.e., let competition set prices) would play havoc with our operating companies. I also believe that we had too much of a tendency to want to please each other in our decision making for fear that if we did otherwise, a Family fight would ensue. This inclination to placate each other by not saying "no" to each other's proposals (when "no" might have been what was warranted) did keep us together until, finally, our saying "no" to Bert resulted in a devastating personal and business tragedy.

I also believe that we had too much of a tendency to want to please each other in our decision making for fear that if we did otherwise, a Family fight would ensue.

HHI owned Motor Freight Express (MFX) which, as previously mentioned in these memoirs, was headed by my brother Bert. Also, as I previously said, he became infuriated with the cousins' decision not to permit him to acquire a third trucking entity, and especially at me because I had been a part of that decision. Motor Freight was not doing particularly well at that time and, while I do not recall how Bert proposed to finance the acquisition, it seemed too risky for the group, including me.

But this rejection of his proposal was not alone what gnawed at him. Bert felt that all of his cousin Jerry's proposals to buy other breweries were just as risky as the group felt his proposal was, yet the group approved them. To him, this was pure favoritism, which he could not tolerate. Furthermore, the fact that Jerry permitted the public to believe he was the owner of the Orioles (not the Family) did not sit well with him.

In now trying to recall the circumstances that may have justified the group not to approve Bert's request, I believe I voted with the group because Bert's request would have meant that Merchants would have to invest significantly more money in MFX to make the purchase possible, and there was not sufficient evidence that the addition of another trucking company would resolve MFX's problems. In the case of Jerry's requests, while the ventures may have been just as risky as Bert's, the National Brewing Company had the wherewithal (capital) to make the acquisitions.

I went to see Bert after he announced he was quitting. He told me that I should be aware of the fact that none of the men under him were capable of running MFX and suggested that we sell the company. I conveyed his words to the "Cousins Council" which, unfortunately, did not heed his advice. Bert left to become president of a competitor, Jones Motor Freight Company, which he ran very successfully for two or three years until he decided to retire.

When Bert left, I joined the board of MFX and, together with "Reds" Charlie and Morton Hollander who were both already on the board, we represented the Family. The rest of the board was made up of the then top-operating executives. The operating results shown at each monthly meeting revealed little or no improvement in business, and while plausible predictions of better times were made by management, none proved to be true. We went through the two executives who had assisted Bert and who he said could not run the company. Neither could. Finally, a new man, who had at one time worked for MFX, was brought back to head the company. He, too, struggled to keep the company

> When Bert left, I joined the board of MFX and, together with "Reds" Charlie and Morton Hollander who were both already on the board, we represented the Family.

going, and with deregulation of rates by the government, the final blow had been struck.

Therefore, we began a rather desperate search for a buyer. Only one prospective buyer emerged, and that was Consolidated Freight, a large national trucking company based in California and Honolulu. I, together with two partners of Gordon Feinblatt, entered into protracted negotiations that involved months of examination of MFX's operations and books by Consolidated's representatives. Ultimately, they recommended that the company's assets be acquired. It looked like we had a deal, so armed with a fully negotiated agreement, I and two lawyers from GFRH&H who had worked with me in the negotiations (Herbert Goldman and Sandy Weiss) flew to California to await the decision of the board of Consolidated that was meeting in Honolulu.

For some reason, we were all pretty sanguine about the board giving its okay, but it was not to be. Word came to us at the hotel where we were staying that the deal had been turned down. *Quel dommage!* Our last prospective purchaser was gone, so we departed L.A. feeling MFX could not continue to operate much longer. Merchants Terminal had been funding the monthly shortfalls in cash, and its board was getting anxious about how much longer it made sense to continue to put good money after bad.

Now that it appeared that bankruptcy was a real likelihood, we sought legal advice, first from GFRH&H and then from Covington & Burling. The seriousness of the situation became even more acute when it was discovered that an amendment in the ERISA Act dealing with Multi-Employer Pension Plans made Merchants Terminal (as the parent of MFX) liable for MFX's proportionate share of any shortfall in the funding of any such plan. MFX was involved in about ten or so such plans with various Teamster Locals, each of which was underfunded, thereby making its share of the underfunding amount to millions of dollars. Being aware of this, the board of Merchants Terminal was in a quandary. Should it permit MFX to go into bankruptcy and expose the parent company (Merchants) to multimillions of dollars of liability to the unions, or should it keep feeding MFX money to keep it afloat, hoping that someone could turn it around?

To help us decide we sought the advice of Bert, who had just retired from Jones Motor Freight. He advised us that MFX had no chance of succeeding unless most of its trucking fleet was replaced with new vehicles. Obviously, this would entail millions of dollars of additional investment by Merchants Terminal, with no assurance of success. I remember that, when "Reds" Charlie balked at Merchants Terminal

For some reason, we were all pretty sanguine about the board giving its okay, but it was not to be.

continuing to put up more money, a special board meeting was called at which Gene Feinblatt was asked to help lay out the pros and cons of a decision to allow MFX to go into bankruptcy or continue to operate.

After the presentation and a long discussion, the board still seemed unable to come to grips with the consequences of either option. I finally stated that I felt that bankruptcy was the lesser of two evils. I had done an analysis of the value of the assets of MFX and the extent of MFX's full liabilities. While the potential loss was staggering, I concluded that Merchants was not in jeopardy of being forced into bankruptcy, and, furthermore, there was the likelihood that Covington & Burling could negotiate for MFX to pay substantially less than the full amount of its potential pension fund liability. My conviction carried the day, and, as nervous as the board was, it was agreed that MFX should go into bankruptcy.

Now, the work of liquidating MFX's assets began. The person who was then heading MFX agreed to stay on until the operating assets had been sold. The disposition of the trucking fleet was not that difficult, but the disposition of the trucking terminals proved not as easy, and took several years to complete.

Negotiations with the unions by Covington & Burling (Arvid Roach and Harris Weinstein) took more time and skill, but in the long run significant compromises were obtained. The end result of about five years of work was that Merchants Terminal was called on to put up about $10 million to settle MFX's obligations to the various unions and to cut its dividend to the Family in half for two years.

Based on information provided by Covington & Burling, I was advising "Reds" Charlie (and the board) on what actions to take and their consequences. This was a very serious responsibility, one that challenged me for several years. While in the beginning there was considerable trepidation on the part of the Family that MFX's bankruptcy would have dire long-term consequences for Merchants and, thus, its dividend policy, and as it became clearer that Merchants would not only survive but be back on its feet in a relatively short period, the nervousness of the Family began to abate. I believe I played a significant role in "manning the tiller" and "calming the waters," of which I am proud.

After the liquidation of MFX, Merchants Terminal's assets consisted substantially of three refrigerated warehouses and a significant holding – through its ownership of Terminal Refrigerating and Warehousing Company (TR&W) – of marketable securities, including a large block of stock in NYVF totaling 1.8 million shares.

The company still owned a large holding in National Brewing Company, which had acquired Pompeian Olive Oil Company from Merchants Terminal as it continued to expand. "Reds" Charlie was president of the company and I was vice president. Harry Halpert, who was the grandson of "Reds," was comptroller. As a result of being made an officer of Merchants, I began to be compensated by Merchants for the first time.

Both the operating division and TR&W were doing well and, as a result, Merchants Terminal was paying a large amount of federal and state taxes as a C Corporation. This was "déjà vu"– the same situation that O-W Fund had faced. Luckily for O-W, we were able to do a last-minute tax-free merger with a mutual fund that eliminated the corporate-level tax, but since this avenue was no longer available, we had to find some other solution.

In reviewing the audited financial statements one day, I noticed that TR&W was paying a considerable amount of income taxes to Maryland on its earnings from its portfolio of securities. This meant that the auditors were treating this income as having been earned in Maryland, even though TR&W was a Delaware corporation whose laws exempted such income from tax at the corporate level. My additional investigation of Maryland regulations and cases revealed the instances when a foreign corporation (i.e., a company not founded in Maryland) was subject to Maryland state tax. In essence, to be exempt from Maryland tax, a corporation could not have earned income from assets located in Maryland and could not have any paid employees in the state.

Further checking indicated that custody of some of TR&W's securities was at brokerage firms in Baltimore and that "Reds" Charlie was a paid officer of the company. Were that not the case, TR&W would not have to pay Maryland any state taxes. Why hadn't the auditors advised "Reds" that by moving custody of TR&W's securities to Delaware, and not having any TR&W employees residing in Maryland compensated by TR&W, Merchants could save hundreds of thousands of dollars of state tax each year? I did, and a relatively simple solution was devised.

First, custody of all of TR&W's securities was transferred to Delaware Trust, which leased a room to TR&W to be its headquarters. Then, an officer of Delaware Trust was made a paid officer of TR&W and "Reds" ceased to be compensated as an officer. Merchants, as TR&W's sole stockholder, elected "Reds," Morton, Harry and me to be directors of TR&W and three or four times a year we would travel by train to Wilmington, Delaware, to hold board meetings. Once this modus operandi was effected, TR&W ceased paying Maryland taxes.

In reviewing the audited financial statements one day, I noticed that TR&W was paying a considerable amount of income taxes to Maryland on its earnings from its portfolio of securities.

Not a bad start in our effort to save taxes, but it did not resolve the main problem of relieving Merchants of the federal taxes on its taxable earnings from all sources and state taxes on Maryland earnings. To do that, a tax-free way to convert the company to a pass-through entity of some sort had to be found. There was no tax-free way for the company to become a limited partnership and the IRC provisions concerning S corporations, which are also pass-through entities, limited elections to small business corporations with one class of stock and not more than 35 shareholders. Merchants Terminal, which was a small business corporation under the code, had two classes of stock and more than 35 shareholders, as shareholders were then defined by the IRC. What to do?

As luck would have it, one day in 1995 or early 1996, I read in the *Wall Street Journal* that Congress was considering amending the S corporation provisions to increase the number of qualified shareholders to 75. I immediately called Rod DeArment of Covington & Burling (with whom, as I have previously revealed, I had worked on the NYVF matter). Rod had been Senator Dole's Chief of Staff and, as such, he knew all of the "players." Rod confirmed that such an amendment was under consideration and had a good chance of passage. He sent me a copy of the bill, and Morton and I began to study its various provisions to see if there was a way that Merchants Terminal could qualify, and under what circumstances.

The first thing we concluded was that Merchants Terminal, having two classes of stock, would have to redeem its preferred shares. This did not seem to be a problem as the shares (which legally could be called and redeemed) only had a value of $1 million or so plus a $5 premium and a final dividend. The real problem that remained to be resolved was whether Merchants Terminal had fewer than 75 qualified shareholders as defined by the proposed amendment. [36]

How to determine who qualified was our next task, and it was not an easy one. Having individuals and trusts of various types as shareholders, we had to determine how many qualified, under the new law, as individuals, how many as simple trusts and how many as complex trusts to see if Merchants could take advantage of this legislation. To assist in this important task, I enlisted the support of Melvin Sykes Esq., a renowned Baltimore attorney, with expertise in trust law.

GFRH&H was also brought in to begin to draft an amendment to the company's bylaws. The amendment would assure that if Merchants Terminal qualified to be an S corporation, the bylaws would make certain that such status was not jeopardized in the future by inter vivos transfers of shares to persons who were not shareholders when the

As luck would have it, one day in 1995 or early 1996, I read in the *Wall Street Journal* that Congress was considering amending the S corporation provisions to increase the number of qualified shareholders to 75.

company converted. This would prevent the number of shareholders from exceeding 75 persons, the highest number of shareholders allowed under the new litigation. Unless this could be prevented, Merchants would be in jeopardy of being disqualified in the future and would thus lose its S corporation status.

All of this work was quite time-consuming, so we set a deadline of November 1996 to enable the company to elect S corporation status that would make the conversion effective as of January 1, 1997. Getting all of the required signatures from the shareholders was maddening, but it was accomplished in time for the filing with the IRS before December 31, 1996, thereby accomplishing our goal.

This was a very significant event for the Family, as S corporation status would mean we had on a tax-free basis eliminated all corporate-level taxes of Merchants Terminal and thereby made it possible for the company to distribute significantly larger annual dividends in a form that would change large portions of such dividends from ordinary income (taxed at the highest rate) to capital gains taxable to the shareholders at lower rates. As I recall, "Reds" Charlie lived to see this happen, although he passed away soon thereafter at age 84.

As a result of having converted Merchants Terminal (now renamed and reorganized as Hoffberger Holdings Inc., or HHI) to S corporation status, average annual distributions were well in excess of the highest annual dividend formerly paid by Merchants Terminal as a C corporation. In checking, I note the tremendous jump in annual distributions that resulted. In 1996, the year before Merchants elected S corporation status, the dividend to shareholders was one-half of what it was in 1997, the first year of Merchants' S corporation status. By 1999, the distribution to shareholders had grown to be nearly four times what it was in 1996.

With this rapid rise in shareholder distributions, I became concerned about shareholder expectations and HHI's ability to sustain the per share annual shareholder distributions in the future. Harry agreed that the issue of the sustainability of HHI's annual distributions had to be dealt with. He therefore appointed a committee (of which I was not a member) to create an investment policy intended to achieve this objective. He sought the advice of a Richmond-based investment advisor (Cary Investment Advisors).

After about a year, during which time none of the specifics of the policy were revealed, Harry presented an investment policy to the board for approval. Among other things, the investment policy set the annual distributions to shareholders by a formula based on the year-end net asset value of HHI. Once the net asset value of HHI was determined, it was to be multiplied by a factor of 2%. This formula was anticipated to reduce the annual distribution to shareholders to a sustainable level.

Shortly before the board meeting at which the adoption of the investment policy was to be considered, Harry sent a copy of the proposed policy by e-mail to each director to read. I did so and wrote Harry a long memorandum pointing out in considerable detail where I thought the proposed policy was problematic. One of the criticisms that I had was the proposed multiple by which the net worth of the company was to be determined. It was 11 times EBITDA (earnings before interest, taxes, depreciation and amortization) which, based on all of the information I had, was a multiple higher than other refrigerated warehouse companies had previously sold for. The fact is that current information about other selling prices for public refrigerated warehouses was apparently lacking, so Cary Investment used some other industry figures it thought to be comparable.

Harry Halpert, the grandson of "Reds," Chairman and President of HHI (formerly Merchants Terminal Corp.), 2012

Using this formula, the 2010 distribution was reduced substantially from the previous year. To me, it was apparent that basing our distributions on the Cary-recommended concept rather than on sustainable cash flow would likely diminish the net worth of the company. While I pointed this out to the board, it adopted the investment policy as presented by the committee.

When it came time in 2011 to determine the 2011 distribution, the board, over my objection, approved a distribution 20% higher than the 2010 annual distribution, an amount even higher than the amount the formula set forth in the company's investment policy recommended be paid. The rationale for this was that (contrary to the situation in 2010) the nature of the 2011 cash flow to be distributed involved the payment of considerably more federal and state taxes by the shareholders.

The board has fixed the 2012 annual distribution a little below 2010's distribution, a step in the right direction. Furthermore, it is anticipated that, due to the closing and sale of the obsolete Landover warehouse and to an improvement in the ratio of expenses to revenue at the Quail Street warehouse, cash flow from Merchants Terminal Corporation Logistics (MTCL), the subsidiary of HHI that owns and operates the warehouses, will experience an increase. However, it is clear that only steady increases in profitable gross revenues will result in MTCL producing more operating cash flow with which to make sustainable distributions and accumulate reserves.

Harry's attention is rightly focused on increasing the profit margin on existing business and obtaining new customers, and he believes that the results of the company's efforts to do so will be evident in 2012. But, the tension created by my constant questioning of HHI's distribution policy was obviously disconcerting to him and the rest of the board, so I began thinking that in order to maintain Family unity it might be time for me to go – i.e., to retire.

In the later part of May 2012, Peter Hoffberger, who was chairman of the compensation committee of HHI, called me on the phone to tell me that I would not be a proxy entitled to vote the shares of absentee shareholders at the annual meeting of HHI to be held on June 25, 2012. That statement, while disturbing, did not rattle or surprise me since I had previously indicated to Harry at a private meeting that I would retire as chairman in view of Harry's expressed feelings that my contrary position on various issues was interfering with his ability to operate the company.

I was emotional when I made my offer to retire, but, as previously indicated, I really meant it. After sixty years of service, it was too much to hear that my efforts were considered to be interfering with management's ability to operate, but I recognized there was truth in what he had said, i.e., that open disagreement between the Chairman and the President was detrimental to a company, even if the opposition has merit.

Several days after that stressful meeting, Peter Hoffberger arranged for a special board meeting to discuss my retirement. The board members wanted to know why I wanted to retire. While I alluded to what had happened at my meeting with Harry as the impetus for my decision, I stated that my impaired hearing and sight, which made it difficult for me to function at the level with which I am comfortable, were the primary reasons for my decision. That was a true statement of fact, but in my heart I knew that I and the present generation of the Family board members were no longer on the same page, and that, for the sake of Family unity, it was time for me to hand the baton of leadership to those who have the desire and capability to assume that role.

My retirement from HHI (and Keystone/CPC), effective as of June 2012, formally occurred in November, at which time I received a lump sum payment of retirement compensation. I appreciate Harry's and Douglas' efforts to be generous in determining the fairness of their offer and the board's expression of appreciation for my sixty years of devoted service.

> I was emotional when I made my offer to retire, but, as previously indicated, I really meant it.

SUMMARY OF MY PROFESSIONAL AND BUSINESS CAREERS

In this section, I have covered what I consider to be the significant accomplishments and setbacks of my professional and business career. Unquestionably, it has been a challenging and, for the most part, fulfilling one. Some incidents were scary and could have had fatal consequences. Some were emotionally draining, as they affected, and still do affect, my relationship with members of the Family. And some, though successful endeavors, were not followed up by me to the fullest extent and were, therefore, from my perspective, "lost opportunities."

Of equal significance to me is the fact that I believe that as I pursued my professional and business life, I gained the respect and, in many instances, the admiration of my peers. The more experience I gained, the more confidence I had that I could (with hard work) "hold my own" with the best of them. I also have been able to use my creative abilities – as my father would say, "to think around corners." In the process, I gained a good degree of "wisdom" and it is that attribute that I am most proud of. Having developed the ability to think creatively and wisely, I believe that I have served (and am still capable of serving) the Family in innumerable ways that have and will continue to contribute to its well-being.

Despite my decision to withdraw from the "firing line," I still abhor the thought of complete retirement. It is hard to let go, and I believe unhealthy. In the reunion book put together for the Princeton Class of 1947's 45th reunion (in 1992), I commented: "Retirement is the curse of the working class."[37] I believed that then and I believe it, perhaps, more now than when I wrote it. Fortunately, my communal activities (to be dealt with next) still present challenging opportunities for me to serve.

Visiting with Jamie Johnson-
Dutterer at the exhibition
*Humanoid Boogy: The Work
of William S. Dutterer*, 2014.
Dutterer (1943–2007) was
an alumnus of MICA's
Hoffberger Graduate School
of Painting's inaugural
class of 1967. Photograph by
Paula Gately Tillman

COMMUNAL AND
PHILANTHROPIC LIFE

FIRST INVOLVEMENT WITH VOLUNTEERISM: UNCLE SAM TELLS ME THAT I AM GOING ON THE LEVINDALE BOARD

> "Roy, you know that, as a Hoffberger, you are expected to be involved in the Jewish Community."

Not long after I graduated from law school and came to work for my Uncle Sam full-time in 1950, he said to me, "Roy, you know that, as a Hoffberger, you are expected to be involved in the Jewish Community." He then said that he would like me to go on the board of the Levindale Hebrew Home and Infirmary.

Now, as I have mentioned in the earlier part of these memoirs, my father was the most concerned and compassionate person I have ever known. However, to my knowledge, he was not himself involved in any organized communal work, probably because he had little, if any, time to do anything outside of running the ice division. His "acts of loving-kindness" were one on one.

In fact, it appears that, except for Saul Hoffberger's service on the board of Levindale and Sam's service on the board of the Hebrew Free Loan, the Family's philanthropic reputation derived primarily from its giving willingly of its wealth. My father and his brothers deferred to their brother Sam to decide how much money the Family should give away and to whom. All were keenly aware of Grandmother Hoffberger's dictum to "…give back to the community since it has been so loyal to us." Thus, the idea of helping others was practically in my blood, and community service was felt by me to be a Hoffberger responsibility.

As far as I know, no member of the Family in my father's generation had played a major leadership role in the "shaping" of the organizations that served the needs of the Jewish or general community. Uncle Sam was trying to change that in my generation. When he told me that he wanted me to go on the board of the Levindale Hebrew Home and Infirmary, I willingly consented and was elected to the board in 1950.

I knew nothing about Levindale or The Associated Jewish Charities nor did I then have any particular interest in care for the elderly. However, many of the directors of Levindale were old friends of my father and my Uncle Saul, so my membership on the board was welcomed by them. These men had expectations that I would be active on the various committees of the board which did the real work of actually helping to run Levindale.

As a result, I was placed on a number of committees, one of which was the Residents' Admissions Committee. That may sound a bit strange today, since admissions decisions are now made by professionals, but not so in 1950, pre-Medicare and -Medicaid.

Levindale had one social worker who served as the executive director (Joe Folkoff) and another social worker (Lou Balk) who was a case worker. Of course, there were nurses and nurse's aides, as well as housekeeping personnel on staff. Being considered a long-term "home and infirmary," Levindale did not admit elderly persons who were seriously ill, physically or mentally, at the time they applied. Levindale was not capable of caring for them. We did, however, have a wonderful older doctor on the board who gave a considerable amount of his time to Levindale pro bono, actually taking care of residents who became ill after they had been admitted.

Since Levindale is across the street from Sinai Hospital, we had an informal (later formalized) relationship with the hospital (which, like Levindale, was a constituent agency of The Associated Jewish Charities) whereby very ill persons were admitted to the hospital, when necessary, and returned to Levindale when they were well enough for Levindale's staff to handle them. As I recall, residents who became too mentally ill to be safely housed at Levindale or too disturbing to other residents were sent to a state facility for the mentally ill.

I mention all of this because, to a large extent, Levindale depended on the volunteer services of its lay board and other volunteers (women) to function. Every Sunday morning, three or four lay directors on the admissions committee were handed a four- or five-page workup, prepared by Lou Balk, on three or four persons whom we were to visit. Our job was to digest these reports before making our house calls during which we would determine whether we agreed with the social worker and the executive director that these elderly persons, whom we were seeing for the first and only time, should be admitted.

All of the men on the committee, except me, had been making these decisions for a number of years. Being either retired or active businessmen, who had run or were successfully running their own businesses (mostly clothing), they (and eventually I) felt comfortable making admissions judgments. We would ask questions like "How do you feel?" and "When was the last time you saw your doctor?" We would look in the medicine cabinet to see what and how many different vials of pills were there. We would observe how tidy the house was and how clean the applicant was. This was, perhaps, not a very professional assessment of the applicant's needs or of Levindale's ability to provide the appropriate care, but it worked.

This was, perhaps, not a very professional assessment of the applicant's needs or of Levindale's ability to provide the appropriate care, but it worked.

Another important aspect of the admissions committee's work, prior to the beginning of Medicare and Medicaid in 1965, was to determine how much money the applicant and his/her family were capable of paying for care. Not having access to government funding, Levindale (using funds allocated to it by The Associated Jewish Charities) considered itself the funder of last resort.

Thus, the committee would review the social worker's report to see what the person had in the way of a bank account, securities, a home, Social Security, pension, etc. Usually, not much! Then, it was the committee's job to interview the family members (sons and daughters) and examine their recent tax returns to see how much they were able and willing to pitch in for their parents' care. In too many instances, the children were either unable or unwilling to contribute a significant amount. The feeling of the committee is best expressed in accordance with an old Jewish adage: "One parent can take care of ten children, but ten children cannot take care of one parent."

A great deal of each board meeting was spent listening to the admissions committee report, and often long discussions took place as to whether a certain person should be taken in. In time, I began to feel that having lay people have the final say on these matters was not right. Therefore, during my term as president of Levindale, which was before Medicare and Medicaid came into effect, I recommended that we professionalize the intake process. The board decided to accept my recommendation, but there were still some hold-outs who strongly believed that turning the admissions process over to social workers, all of whom they insisted lacked the compassion needed for this type of work, was wrong.

After about ten years as a director and officer, I was next in line for the presidency. Stanley Sagner, the CEO of a large national men's clothing business, was then president. During his term it had been decided by the board that Levindale should construct on its campus a two-hundred-bed facility to house older people who were still capable of living independently (therefore, not ready to apply to Levindale), but, being isolated where they lived, would benefit from congregant living and from having a nutritious meal at least once a day (kosher, of course).

The federal government had two programs that could have been used to fund such a project. Stanley felt strongly that one of them was preferable and I the other. So, we were at loggerheads until, tragically, Stanley suddenly died. Thereafter, I became the new president, and the government program that I preferred was approved by the board.

> After about ten years as a director and officer, I was next in line for the presidency.

As president, I was given the authority to proceed. I had a great real estate lawyer on the board whose name was Robert Weinberg. Bob, who was a member of a very prestigious law firm founded by his father, was quite knowledgeable about federal government housing programs. Together, he and I handled every aspect of constructing and federally financing the facility, then called Concord Apartments.[38]

Not too long thereafter, The Associated realized that providing congregant living accommodations for the relatively well elderly to live independently was not the only problem facing the Jewish elderly in the Park Heights area. In many cases, their housing was quite old and needed repairs and renovations in order for the people to remain in their homes. Sadly, most of them did not have the resources to do the necessary work. This need for assistance gave rise to a new housing agency of The Associated called Comprehensive Housing Assistance Inc. (CHAI).[39] Because I had been the first one to direct the construction of public housing for the Jewish elderly, I was given the honor of being named its first president.

Me and other officers of Levindale Hebrew Home and Infirmary. I was elected to succeed Stanley Sagner as president at the 74th annual meeting in 1963.

A MOVE UP THE LEADERSHIP LADDER
TO THE BOARD OF THE ASSOCIATED

Having been largely responsible for Levindale switching from a lay-dominated to a professionally run organization and having laid the groundwork for the creation of CHAI, the powers that be at The Associated thought that I should be nominated to its board where I could apply my experience and talents to the resolution of other community-wide problems. I became a board member in the early 1960s when Harry Greenstein was the professional executive director. Thus began my fifty-year Associated "career."

Fundraising became one of my first major responsibilities. As the plaque on my office wall indicates, I was general chairman of The Associated Jewish Charities and Welfare Fund Annual Campaign in both 1968 and 1969. This was truly a challenging and demanding job, for I needed to instill in both my fellow workers and the general community a sense of responsibility for providing the resources to fund the agencies serving Jews in need here and in Israel.

The campaigns involved hundreds of workers who solicited thousands of persons. It was a job that, after one year, truly had burned me out, but for some reason I was asked to take the chairmanship for a second year. Buoyed by the birth of my son Jack on May 27, 1969, which I announced at the final workers' meeting at the successful conclusion of the 1968 campaign, I agreed to a second year. However, I knew that I could not be as hands-on in the second year as I was in the first, so I relied on the person under me, who would be the next campaign chairman, to solicit more of the major contributors.

Following the death of Harry Greenstein, a man by the name of Bob Hiller became the new executive director. He and Irv Blum, who was the incoming president, created a new order of governance and responsibility, a ladder of chairs leading to the presidency. I was asked to serve as the vice president of planning and budgeting, a job which I nervously accepted since it required a yet-undeveloped set of skills. Anxious or not, I convinced myself that "having been in the back and discovered" (as my father would have said), I could handle the responsibilities of the job.

From there, I moved up to first vice president/president-elect (or something like that), which meant that I was next in line for the presidency. Frankly, I don't remember what the responsibilities of this office were, but by that time I was quite confident that I could handle them and that I was ready to ultimately step into the presidency.

HOFFBERGER TO HEAD ASSOCIATED

LeRoy E. Hoffberger, well-known Baltimore attorney, was elected to succeed Bernard Manekin to the presidency of the Associated Jewish Charities and Welfare Fund at the Associated's 58th annual meeting which took place at the Baltimore Hebrew Congregation.

Mr. Manekin retired after serving two years in office.

The slate of officers, which was submitted by Calman J. Zamoiski, Jr., chairman of the nominating committee, also included: David Hirschhorn, first vice-president; Richard Davison and Willard Hackerman, vice-presidents in charge of administration and of social planning and budgeting, respectively; Howard B. Miller and Suzanne F. Cohen, treasurer and assistant treasurer, respectively; and Sanford G. Jacobson, secretary; and Judith Sykes, assistant secretary.

Twelve new directors were elected to two-year terms: Rabbi Donald Berlin, Manuel Dupkin, II, Herbert D. Fried, Bunny Howard, Michael M. Kalis, Alvin D. Katz, Laurence M. Katz, Dr. Joseph M. Miller, Ann Pearlstone, Eleanor K. Rosenberg, Stanford Z. Rothschild, Jr., and Stephen M. Thaler.

Elected to serve second two-year terms were: Grace Abramowitz, Herbert J. Belgrad, Dr. Morton K. Blaustein, Irving F. Cohn, Samuel I. Frank, Martin S. Himeles, Theodore W. Hirsch, Leonard Jed, Dr. Bernard Kaplioff, David W. Kornblatt, Sharan Kushner and Herschel Levin.

In his brief acceptance speech, Mr. Hoffberger pointed out that the Associated was embarking on a new era with a new president, a new executive vice president (Stephen D. Solender, and the prospect of moving into a new building within a year.

"We're also facing an era of change, growth and broader responsibilities," he said. "Our aged population is growing rapidly; Soviet Jewish refugees are arriving in our community in increasing numbers; the level of Jewish education must be up-graded, and every Jewish child must be given the opportunity to receive a Jewish education if our Jewish community is to remain strong and viable; and Israel is facing serious social problems as she prepares for peace.

"We must find new ways and new means to meet these challenges," he continued, "and also new ways to provide the funds that will enable us to meet our obligations."

Mr. Hoffberger pledged his own efforts to carrying out his responsibilities saying, "I fervently hope that my administration, like that of my distinguished predecessors, will make a lasting impact on our community and so help safeguard it for our children and our children's children."

Long active in community affairs, Mr. Hoffberger is a former president of the Levindale Hebrew Geriatric Center and Hospital, a major beneficiary of the Associated's annual campaign, and former chairman of Comprehensive Housing for the Aged (CHAI), the Associated agency responsible for housing for the Jewish elderly.

He is also immediate past chairman of the Associated's Health and Institutional Services Committee, one of its seven standing committees, and has just completed a term as the first chairman and prime organizer of the Associated's Ir Ganim Planning Committee, the committee responsible for the rehabilitation of the poverty-ridden suburb of Jerusalem.

LeRoy Hoffberger

Photo courtesy of the *Baltimore Jewish Times*, 1979

However, by choice, that was not to be – at least not at the time expected. As related earlier in these memoirs, it was then that Hilde and I took our family to London for a two-year stay.

Upon my return to Baltimore in 1977, I wanted to get back in line for the presidency of The Associated. Bob Hiller was quite happy to have me step back in as vice president/president-elect, which I did for two years. During much of this time, the Jewish community was confronted with a very contentious issue that arose when the Jewish Community Center (JCC) decided that it wanted to remain open on the Sabbath. This was contrary to the bylaws of The Associated, and I felt it was also an affront to the Orthodox community. Therefore, I took the lead stand that The Associated, whose approval was required, should deny the JCC the right to open. I was quite outspoken about how hypocritical and hurtful I thought approving the JCC's request would be.

Bernie Manekin, the then-chairman of The Associated, appointed a three-person committee, of which I was one, to seek a compromise satisfactory to the Orthodox community. With the consent of Rabbi Herman Neuberger, the head of Ner Israel Rabbinical College and the man whose stamp of approval was needed to resolve this issue, it was decided that the outdoor swimming pool and grounds at the Owings Mills JCC could be used during the summer, but none of the other facilities could be open. This solution satisfied the majority of the board of The Associated, but there was a minority that was deeply dissatisfied. I knew that while G-d would not change his mind about the sanctity of the Sabbath, one day the board might change its decision.

Retiring AJC president, Bernard Manekin, turns over the gavel to me in 1979.

A dangerously divisive issue had been resolved, and for twenty years no effort was made by the JCC to change the status quo. However, in 1997, using almost the same arguments it had used in 1979 for opening on the Sabbath, the JCC board voted to open the athletic facilities on the Owings Mills campus and brought the matter, again, to The Associated board for its approval. Although I had anticipated this, I was as incensed as previously that a decision granting approval was about to be made. I will deal later with my desperate last-minute efforts to express my feelings, now as a religious Jew, against such an action.

HAIL TO THE PRESIDENT

In June 1979, I was elected president of The Associated for a term of two years. Just when I took office, Bob Hiller resigned to take a position in New York reorganizing the Council of Jewish Federations (the coordinating agency for all of the Federations around the country, which was having fiscal as well as leadership problems). Steve Sollender, who had been Bob's subordinate, became the new executive director, and since we had already established an excellent working relationship, we became a good team.

While there were many issues that I dealt with during my term as president, one stands out. Strangely, it was not a local problem that was the focus of my attention. Rather, it was a project in Israel that Baltimore had undertaken, along with all the other Federations in the U.S. and Canada, to provide financial and logistical support for poor neighborhoods in towns and cities in Israel. Each Federation had selected a community to assist. Baltimore had chosen a poor neighborhood in Jerusalem called Ir Ganim.

Presenting a scroll to the town of Ir Ganim, following Baltimore's Walk for Israel, 1978

Ir Ganim consisted of mostly poor Sephardic Jews from North Africa who needed to have better health care, as well as housing and play areas for their large families. The neighborhood had appointed a committee with whom chosen representatives from Baltimore were to work. The commitment on Baltimore's part was for five years and we had had a special campaign to raise money for this endeavor. I recall being very instrumental in raising the funds and in taking numerous trips with Steve to Ir Ganim to provide oversight needed to assure Baltimore that its money was being used in the best way possible.

Sarah Kallins and me visiting the Hoffberger Vocational High School, Ort, in Israel while I was president of The Associated, c. 1980

I stayed involved in this project for the entire five-year period and the experiences that I had with the Ir Ganim leadership were most rewarding. I formed a true bond of friendship with a number of residents who I feel really looked forward to my visits. I was also most proud of a second mortgage project that I developed that made it possible for poor families to get inexpensive subordinate financing from a fund we had created for that purpose. Without that assistance, many of the families that needed additions to their houses, due to the growing size of their families, would not have been able to afford them.

Like my experiences on the admissions committee at Levindale, I again was able to feel and see, firsthand, the results of the work we were doing. Subsequently, the Baltimore federation undertook to assist more communities in Israel in tackling problems they would not have been able to handle on their own.

Zanvyl and Isabelle Krieger, Donald Schaefer and other officials of The Associated and the city breaking ground for the new Associated building on the corner of Mount Royal and Maryland Avenues, during my tenure as president of The Associated, 1979

I can remember giving my final report, as president, at the June 1981 annual board and members meeting held at Baltimore Hebrew Congregation and feeling, as I looked out at the audience, that I had provided meaningful leadership during my two-year term. What is clear to me is that it was not the office of the presidency of The Associated that left me with a feeling of fulfillment, but my hands-on involvement with recipients of assistance supplied by programs I had helped to develop.

MY COMMITMENT TO ENHANCE JEWISH DAY SCHOOL EDUCATION

A Good Plan Goes Unfulfilled

After leaving the presidency, I was asked by Shoshana Cardin, who succeeded me as chairwoman, to serve as chairman of a large committee of Jewish community leadership convened by The Associated to develop a strategic plan to enhance and finance Baltimore's Jewish Day School System. The study lasted for about 18 months, and the result was a well-thought-through plan that proposed that The Associated focus its expertise in the field of Jewish Education on teacher training and its fundraising acumen on raising scholarship funds. It was a daunting task to get all segments of the community (Orthodox, Conservative and Reform) to agree that these two issues were, in fact, the primary needs of the day school system. Unfortunately, after having created an acceptable plan to deal with these two problems, it was even harder to get the community to come up with the money ($10 million) needed to accomplish the goals of the study. Sadly, that task ultimately proved to be impossible.

When it came time to raise the money, I went to the Weinberg Foundation, then headed by Bernie Siegel, for a challenge grant. The foundation agreed to put up $5 million to be matched by the community based on a very complex formula that Bernie had developed. I then went to the persons whom I knew were interested in enhancing Jewish education in Baltimore, explained the formula to them and requested that they make sizable matching grants.

As it turned out, the persons who I thought would be interested were emotionally tied to supporting a particular day school of their choice and not the entire day school system. Although I truly believed that the Weinberg formula for the match, that required all funds to be put in a "pot," the income from which was to be allocated throughout the day school system by formula, would produce more funding for the particular school certain donors wished to support, I was unable to convince these potential givers of the validity of my belief.

After several years of trying, it was apparent to both me and the Weinberg Foundation that our efforts to raise $10 million had, for the most part, failed. There were one or two relatively modest grants, but the only sizable grant was made by me in the form of a $500,000 "zero coupon" bond. We therefore decided to abandon the campaign. Having worked so hard, I was not only deeply disappointed by my inability to raise the money required to fulfill the goals of the plan, but I was stunned by the general lack of interest in the community to support Jewish education.[40]

In 1997, twenty years after the JCC and The Associated had agreed to keep the Owings Mills buildings of the JCC closed on the Sabbath, the new JCC leadership, claiming it needed to respond to the demands of its membership, once again sought to open these facilities. Unknown to me, the board of the JCC had passed a resolution to that effect and the executive committee of The Associated had agreed to recommend it to its board for passage. I am not sure what was going on in my life that caused me to be ignorant of these actions, but once I was aware of the situation, I felt compelled to again become involved.

Literally, within a week or so of when the recommendation was to come before The Associated's board, I became acquainted with the arguments then being made for opening and compared them to my extensive notes made during the protracted discussions of this issue in 1979. When I did, I concluded that the arguments were essentially the same. That being the case, I felt that my position taken in 1979 against opening was just as valid in 1997 as it was then. The problem was that I had waited until the 11th hour to take a stand, and to make matters worse, I was scheduled to fly to London on the day before the matter was to be brought to The Associated board for a vote.

The only way I could let my position be known to other members of the board was to compose a letter that would be in their hands on the day preceding the board meeting. Not knowing their addresses, I called Darrell Friedman, the then-executive-director of The Associated, to ask him to have someone deliver a copy of these to me ASAP.

His response was something to the effect that I was certainly entitled to communicate my thoughts to the other board members, but that in view of the fact that passage was "a done deal," why spend all weekend working on a letter that would not change the outcome of the vote? I was not angry or upset with his comment since I, too, did not feel that my letter would be so persuasive as to counteract the recommendation of the executive committee. However, because all I wanted to do was to let my strong feelings about the importance of this decision be known (having played a major role in the outcome of the 1979 airing of this dispute and also having become religious by then), I felt compelled to once again challenge a move by the non-Orthodox community to desecrate the Sabbath.

To make a long story short, I wrote a four- or five-page letter Saturday night, after Shabbos, explaining that there were really no new reasons for opening that had not been aired in 1979 and that permitting the

The only way I could let my position be known to other members of the board was to compose a letter that would be in their hands on the day preceding the board meeting.

opening would be deeply hurtful to the Orthodox community and would render The Associated's observance of all other Jewish holidays of lesser religious significance hypocritical. The wording of the letter came to me like a stream of consciousness and in several hours I had expressed what I thought was a cogent and passionate articulation of the issues and why I felt so deeply against reversing a policy that had served the community so well since its inception. The letter was typed by my secretary on Sunday and posted in time for the entire board to receive it by Monday.

On Monday evening my second wife, Rebecca, and I left for London. On Tuesday night, after returning from dinner to our hotel, I got a telephone call from someone informing me that the board had voted by a large margin not to permit the JCC to open on the Sabbath and that my letter had persuaded a great many of the members to change their positions on the issue. I was, of course, both surprised and greatly pleased. My Orthodox friends thanked me profusely as they had given up hope. One of them, Eli Schlossberg, who had been keeping a record of this issue since 1979, wrote to me and in thanking me added that "he who saves the Sabbath is assured of a place in Olam HaBah – in the 'World to Come.'"

Unfortunately, the issue would not die. In 2009, a new set of officers and board members of the JCC raised this question once again. I am sure that there were those among them who were deeply resentful of the fact that they had not prevailed, over the last thirty years, to open the Owings Mills JCC on Shabbos.

Despite the fact that throughout the Torah (in well over one hundred places) the Sabbath is mentioned as the day on which G-d rested after having created the world and therefore a day on which man is to rest, strict observance of the Sabbath is no longer meaningful to most Jews, other than the Orthodox. Now that I consider myself to be a relatively observant Jew and, more importantly, to truly believe in G-d, I was even more upset that the organized Jewish Community (supposedly representing Jews of all denominations) for the sake of the convenience of the non-observant members of the JCC (or worse, for purely business reasons) would once again be blatantly hypocritical and disrespectful of the Orthodox community, which now represented an even larger portion of the total Jewish community of Baltimore than before.

When the issue was brought before the board of The Associated, I and a few others (mostly the Orthodox rabbis) argued against the JCC's request, as fervently as we could, but to no avail. The decision to allow the JCC to open passed decisively. I literally cried, not because I had lost a long-running battle, but because G-d had. What had started out as a fight on my part to prevent an indignity to the most traditional part of our community (the Orthodox community) ended in my own beliefs being violated.[41]

THE HOFFBERGER PHILANTHROPIES: HISTORY AND REORGANIZATION

In 1941, the Hoffberger brothers set up a charitable foundation by the name of Hoffberger Brothers Inc. that qualified as a 501(c)(3) tax-exempt charitable organization. While the Family's "acts of loving-kindness" preceded the establishment of the Foundation by many years, the Foundation thereafter served as the vehicle through which most of the Hoffberger brothers would make charitable grants. It also enabled the brothers to give non-marketable shares owned by them in Family-owned businesses to the Foundation, for which they would receive income tax deductions. These shares were initially not income-producing because the companies were growing and needed cash. However, cash contributions were often made by the various Hoffberger companies to the Foundation, which then was able to make grants.

Uncle Sam, my cousin Jerry and my father at the dedication of the Hoffberger Building for the Nurses' Residence at Sinai Hospital, 1959

There were five founding brothers (Harry and Abe having died) and two members of my generation ("Reds" Charlie and Charles Carroll, who were the sons of Harry and Abe, respectively). Sam served as president of the Foundation from its inception until 1961, when my father assumed the presidency. Jerold became a member in 1946 when he returned from the Army, and Morton Hollander (who had been instrumental, as the Family's tax attorney, in the creation of the Foundation) became a member in 1961. Although not a member of the board, I served as assistant secretary of the Foundation from 1953 until 1963.

Just before my father's demise in 1963, the charter of Hoffberger Brothers Inc. was amended to, among other things, change the name of the Foundation to the Hoffberger Foundation Inc. in recognition of its transition from my father's generation to my generation. Shortly after this event, I was elected to be a permanent member of the board and to serve as its president. "Reds" Charlie and Jerry were also made permanent members, as was Morton Hollander. Thus, the baton of philanthropic leadership had passed from one generation to the next, where it remained until most of the male members of my generation were deceased. At that time, the charter was again amended to accommodate the third generation of Hoffbergers, both male and female. Since there were many more of this generation than the total number of mandated board positions, a policy of rotating service on the board every six years was instituted as the fairest way to give all members of the third generation and those thereafter an opportunity to participate.

Prior to my coming on the board, Hoffberger Brothers Inc. annual grants were primarily to The Associated Jewish Charities and Welfare Fund (ranging from nearly 60% to 90%) and the balance to a number of Baltimore hospitals (primarily Sinai Hospital), educational institutions (primarily Goucher College and a school for the deaf in Israel) and various cultural organizations. Since, in the early days of the founding, the annual funds of the Foundation were limited (amounting to less than $90,000 a year until 1958), the National Brewing Company often gave substantial sums directly to various capital campaigns to supplement the Foundation's gifts.

Thus, the baton of philanthropic leadership had passed from one generation to the next, where it remained until most of the male members of my generation were deceased.

In 1969, Congress passed a major tax reform bill which gave private foundations ten years in which to dispose of large holdings of closely held securities. Since a significant portion of the assets of the Foundation consisted of closely held stock in Merchants Terminal Corporation and the Real Estate Holding Company and since their value was in the millions, the Foundation was facing a major dilemma. It did not seem feasible to the directors to gift such large amounts to one or more nonprofits, for by doing so, the Foundation's future income from its remaining assets would be greatly reduced.

As 1979 was approaching, the Foundation was in a quandary. However, being on the board of the Zanvyl and Isabelle Krieger Fund, I was aware that its director, Bob Hiller, had worked with a well-known Washington tax attorney to develop a concept that permitted a donor to create a foundation (known as a "support foundation") whose control would be in the hands of a public foundation (like The Associated) but whose minority members could be appointed by the donor.

The IRS had accepted the concept, and the Krieger Fund was the first of hundreds of such support foundations to be created around the country. I informed the directors of the Hoffberger Foundation of this opportunity that would enable us to set up a support foundation at The Associated to which we could convey the stocks that the Reform Act required us to dispose of.

NEW HOSPITAL GIVEN $100,000

Gift To South Baltimore Is From Hoffberger Unit

A $100,000 gift to the South Baltimore General New Hospital Fund was announced yesterday by hospital officials.

It is the largest contribution to date.

William C. Purnell, hospital fund campaign chairman, and Herman L. Gruehn, president of the hospital's board of trustees, said that the gift was received from the Hoffberger Foundation and the National Brewing Com-

Jerold and me presenting a check to South Baltimore General Hospital on South Charles Street, *The Evening Sun*, Baltimore, n.d.

The directors of the Foundation agreed that such a transaction would be "the best of both worlds." It would allow the Foundation to meet the terms of the Reform Act without "strangers" owning our stock and enable our Family to continue to make grants in the same amount as before, except through two Family Foundations. Thus, the Hoffberger Family Fund Inc. was created in 1979 as a support foundation of The Associated. While the Family members of this Foundation were minority members of the board, their suggested grants have, without exception, been approved.

After "Reds" Charlie passed away in 1997 (Jerold and Morton Hollander having already been deceased), I was the only member of the board of the Hoffberger Foundation from my generation (the second) that had taken over from the original founding members of Hoffberger Brothers in 1941.

For some years now, the third generation of Hoffbergers has taken over. While I am still chairman, I have chosen to play a minor role in the deliberations of the board and its grant-making decisions. However, from time to time, I am asked to briefly relate what the dynamics of the Foundation were in the "old days" and to give my thoughts about how the Foundation can continue to make a difference in the Baltimore Jewish and general community.

What delights me about the third and fourth generations now in control of Hoffberger Philanthropies (our new name) is not only how seriously they have involved themselves in the Foundation's work, but how well they relate to one another and how proud they are to be the "face" of the Family in the Baltimore community. As long as a substantial number of the Family remain in Baltimore, I am confident that the Family's unity will continue from generation to generation. Grandmother Sarah Hoffberger would be pleased to see how well her sons, grandchildren, great-grandchildren and great-great-grandchildren have followed her admonition: "If you stick together, you will succeed."

> As long as a substantial number of the Family remain in Baltimore, I am confident that the Family's unity will continue from generation to generation.

Special Community Projects Which I Created

While The Associated continued to be the major recipient of the Foundation's available resources, I felt strongly that the Foundation should be more proactive in its giving, rather than reactive to requests. I interpreted Dad's injunction to "look around corners" to mean "be creative." My service on the boards of The Associated, Levindale and numerous other nonprofits had given me a good overview of both Jewish and general community needs and where there were gaps in the services available. As a result, I was instrumental in the development of some projects which enabled the Foundation to have a beneficial impact well beyond the amount of money that it was feeding into the philanthropic community of Baltimore.

I will now describe some of the projects that have been especially meaningful to me. In some instances, my involvement in these undertakings came about because of my spontaneous reaction to shocking public events and, in others, to certain social conditions that needed addressing.

Facilitating Integration at Loyola High School, Maryland

Loyola (Blakefield) High School, an excellent private Catholic High School in Towson, was at one time "all white." However, one of its liberal teachers, Father Frank Fisher, convinced its board to allow inner-city boys, who were primarily African American, to attend a "Head Start" summer tutorial program. That program proved to be so successful that Father Fisher felt that a number of the boys could handle the rigorous academic demands of Loyola, as full-time students, with help from the teachers which he and other faculty were willing to provide.

Thus, Father Fisher came to the Foundation for a grant that would enable ten inner-city boys to attend this elite educational institution for four years with all of their tuition paid by the Foundation. He convinced the board of Loyola to accept the African-American students, and I convinced the board of the Foundation to subsidize their education. Through this endeavor, we were able to demonstrate that with voluntary tutoring, most of these boys could navigate the rigorous curriculum of the school with success. Subsequently, Loyola, which until then had only admitted white students, opened its admissions policy to minorities.

> I interpreted Dad's injunction to "look around corners" to mean "be creative."

When, in the late 1980s, there was a national scandal on Wall Street having to do with insider trading and securities fraud by several successful Jewish financiers, including Michael Milken and Ivan Boesky, I was both embarrassed as a Jew and incensed. I clearly recall that I wanted them "hung," but when I articulated my anger to my then wife, Rebecca, she said, "Don't add heat, shed light."

I thought her words were profound, and I began to think about what good could come out of this reprehensible occurrence. Before long, I came to the conclusion that, because the business world was full of complexities that could lead even honest persons to unknowingly engage in activities that gave rise to conflicts of interest and worse, fraud, our universities, particularly business colleges, should teach courses in business and professional ethics. While being knowledgeable about what is or is not ethical does not guarantee that someone will make the right choice, an awareness of what is morally or legally correct will give future professional and business leaders the knowledge needed to intentionally opt to do the right thing.

This thought prompted me to call a friend of mine, Sheldon Caplis, who was the director of development at the University of Baltimore to ask, first, if the University had any courses in business ethics and if not, whether it would be interested in developing such courses if the funding were available. His response was extremely enthusiastic since, coincidentally, the university was already working on a program to include the teaching of ethics in all of its three colleges: the School of Accounting, the School of Business and the Law School. He said he would like to talk to the dean, expedite finishing a conceptual presentation of its intended ethics program and then meet with me.

The three of us met sometime thereafter in my office, and I explained why I thought the Hoffberger Foundation would be interested in funding an ethics program. The dean explained that what she had in mind was not adding one or two separate courses in ethics to the curriculum, but getting each of the schools to incorporate ethics into every course that was being taught. In addition, as background for this program, students would be required to read classic works on ethics.

The emphasis of the program, however, would be on exposing the students to everyday questions of ethics in professions and on bringing in leading practicing business and professional persons to lecture on issues they, themselves, had faced involving questions of conflicts of interest and potential breaches of fiduciary duty.

The three of us met sometime thereafter in my office, and I explained why I thought the Hoffberger Foundation would be interested in funding an ethics program.

Several more meetings were held to finalize the program and to estimate its costs. As I recall, the price tag was around $1 million, payable over a period of five years. The program was presented to the board of the Foundation by the dean and development director and was unanimously approved. Thereafter, the university set up The Hoffberger Center for Business and Professional Ethics in 1987. Since its inception, the Center has been received by the faculty and the students with considerable enthusiasm and has even become the core of an intercollegiate debating event known as the Ethics Bowl, in which teams of students from various universities compete with each other in debating ethical and moral issues confronting society. [42]

Word of the success and popularity of the Hoffberger Center spread beyond the walls of the University of Baltimore. When several of the state's community colleges, having heard about it, asked the university to help install the program in their curriculum, the Center came back to the Foundation for additional funding. This request was received very favorably and was granted.

St. John's College of Annapolis

Back in the fifties, when I was on Levindale's board, one of the regular members of the Residents' Admissions Committee was a man by the name of Victor Frankel. Victor was the president of a large construction firm named Baltimore Contractors. No doubt, Victor's political contacts were instrumental in his getting large public institutional and government-related work. I suspect because he had built a facility for St. John's College and perhaps had made a significant contribution to the college, Victor was made a member of the board. For some reason, Victor liked me and I think, having worked with me, had acquired a respect for my capabilities. He also knew that, as president of the Hoffberger Foundation, I was influential in the determination of where its grants were directed.

One day I got a phone call from Richard Weigel, president of St. John's College, whom I did not know, asking me to come see the campus at Annapolis. I accepted the invitation since I had heard impressive things about the college's Great Books curriculum. After visiting the campus and meeting the chairman of the board, a Mr. Nelson, whose son, Chris, is today president of St. John's, I was asked to join the board.

I was surprised by the invitation, but concluded that the reason was a prelude to a solicitation of the Foundation for a grant. While a request to the Foundation was ultimately made, as I will explain, President Weigel's real hope (as he expressed to me) was that I could also give him entrée

I accepted the invitation since I had heard impressive things about the college's Great Books curriculum.

into the Baltimore philanthropic community. It is hard to believe that such a prestigious college, only forty miles away, could be relatively unknown to Baltimoreans, but that was evidently the case.

When I joined the board, I learned that St. John's had recently established a campus in Santa Fe, New Mexico, which was in serious financial difficulty due to a lack of students. The St. John's academic program and its method of teaching were so foreign to college-age youth living in the West (and to their college guidance counselors) that few of them applied. Many of those who did attend were Easterners who wanted the experience of living in the West.

President Weigel asked me to visit the Sante Fe Campus with him and to meet with some of the members of the board of the Santa Fe Campus. Located along the side of a mountain, the campus was beautiful, with adobe buildings in keeping with the architectural style in that part of the country.

Shortly after that visit, I received a request for a grant by the Hoffberger Foundation to support the Santa Fe Campus. While I was obviously in favor of the idea, I did not think that I would be able to convince the board of the Foundation to approve it as it was outside of the geographic area of our interest – greater Baltimore. With regret, I therefore told President Weigel that the request did not qualify for consideration. However, I was still determined to see if there was a way the Foundation could help provide funding for the Santa Fe Campus.

Whether there was something in the original request that indicated that St. John's had a summer program for teachers desiring to obtain a master's degree, I can't recall. Nevertheless, something sparked an idea in me that would make it possible for the Foundation to participate in funding that program. Perhaps we could get ten or so teachers in the Baltimore inner-city schools to consent to attend three successive summers at the Santa Fe Campus (at the expense of the Hoffberger Foundation) and then agree to continue to teach in the inner city for at least three more years after they completed their studies. Such a proposal would fall within the parameters of the Foundation's guidelines since it involved enhancing the teaching skills of Baltimore teachers who were teaching the city's most problematic students.

I told Dr. Weigel about my idea, and he presented a revised proposal from St. John's to the Foundation. The board agreed to make a grant to St. John's for the purpose of fully funding three or four separate groups of ten teachers each to obtain a master's degree in education at the St. John's Santa Fe Campus.

Nevertheless, something sparked an idea in me that would make it possible for the Foundation to participate in funding that program.

I still have
that admiration
today, so much
so that I believe
St. John's
is the finest
educational
institution in
the country.

I, of course, do not remember the names of any of the teachers who were funded, but I do remember that I received letters from some participants, telling me that they had never dreamed they would have the opportunity to study with such brilliant professors (tutors, as they were called at St. John's) whose teachings had influenced their entire thought process and, in turn, had made them far more capable of performing their jobs back in Baltimore.

I stayed on the St. John's board until 1972 when I decided to take my family to live in London, as previously mentioned in these memoirs. During the ten years or so that I spent on the board, I was exposed to the thinking of different tutors, who sat in on board meetings, as well as to the ideas of the many students whom I met. As a result, I became enamored with the St. John's method of using history's great books to shape the critical thinking of its students.

I still have that admiration today, so much so that I believe St. John's is the finest educational institution in the country. My admiration of the distinctiveness of the graduates' thinking has been confirmed on several occasions when I have met someone new at a party or at a meeting and listened to him/her talking. Halfway through the conversation, I cannot resist asking where he or she went to college. Invariably, the response has been "St. John's College."

Founding of the Maryland Center for Arts and Technology

During the summer of 1996, President Clinton signed the Welfare Reform Act, which radically transformed the nation's welfare system. A provision in the Act known as Temporary Assistance to Needy Families (TANF) limited welfare to a maximum of five years, during which recipients, primarily single mothers, were supposed to be trained to enter the workforce. As the president of the Hoffberger Foundation, I thought there might be an opportunity for private, nonprofit foundations to play a role in developing job training programs for welfare recipients, using both private and public funding.

My wife, Rebecca, had heard of an African-American man in Pittsburgh by the name of Bill Strickland who had created an organization called the Bidwell Center for Arts and Technology. This center had been successful in combining an arts program for at-risk high school students with a job training program. Led by the Heinz catsup company, the Pittsburgh business community had pledged to hire unemployed welfare recipients (primarily thousands of laid-off steel workers), provided they were retrained by the Bidwell Center to have the particular skills the employers needed.

Somehow, Rebecca had become acquainted with Bill, and, through her, I invited him to Baltimore to tell the board of the Hoffberger Foundation what the Bidwell Center was all about and how it had become a success. When I met Bill and talked with him briefly, I could tell that he was a very dynamic person with an intuitive sense of how to get things done. He made a presentation to the board and all of the members were impressed with his story about what he had accomplished at the Center, as well as with his great charisma.

It was, however, evident that the type of welfare recipient Bidwell had been successful in placing with businesses in Pittsburgh was different from the primarily single, long-term welfare mothers we were going to be trying to train in Baltimore. We, therefore, asked Bill to do a comprehensive study of the profile of the welfare recipients we would be dealing with in Baltimore and the local job market – i.e., the type of jobs that employers in Baltimore would be looking to fill, as well as what skills applicants would need to fill them. Bill agreed to undertake the task, and the Foundation hired him as its consultant.

Bill took about two years to complete his study, partly because he was very busy with his own work at Bidwell. To assist in the study by analyzing the potential Baltimore job market, the Foundation hired Patrice Cromwell, a Princeton graduate with experience in doing surveys. Bill's report clearly indicated a need for an organization that would provide start-up support for job training based on the Bidwell model. It also indicated that the typical students would be primarily single welfare mothers with little to no work experience. Patrice's survey revealed that the jobs primarily available were entry-level clerical positions that required certain computer literacy. The businesses in need were those with large clerical pools, such as hospitals and banks.

The Hoffberger Foundation agreed to make a multi-year grant of $250,000 to this undertaking. I then went out and, with Bill at my side, convinced the Krieger Fund, the Strauss Foundation, the Blaustein Foundation, the Weinberg Foundation and a few others to join us in this endeavor. I was also successful in getting the Abell Foundation to lend us $750,000 for working capital to be repaid in five years.

With commitments for $750,000 in capital and $750,000 in a loan, we decided to set up a nonprofit foundation called Maryland Center for Arts and Technology (MCAT) to carry out our mission using the Bidwell concept as our guide. Patrice was hired to recruit employers who would commit to employ those MCAT had trained.

Adrian Bedone, who was a St. John's College graduate, was selected to head MCAT. He was to build a core of capable teachers and develop the

It also indicated that the typical students would be primarily single welfare mothers with little to no work experience.

curriculum that would impart to the students not only the necessary skills, but essential work habits. Our initial location was in Building D at the Bayview Campus of The Johns Hopkins Medical System. Computer teachers were hired, as well as social workers, whose job it was to deal with personal problems that were inherent in the poverty population we were serving. Teaching MCAT students such basic things as showing up on time and dressing properly for work became major challenges.

A vital factor in being able to cover the cost of training was getting adequate funding from the city and state. This consisted of obtaining contracts each semester for the educating of a given number of students. City and state resources being what they were, it was a constant struggle to obtain adequate funding for student enrollment. In fact, public funding was never sufficient to cover the cost of the training, so supplemental funding from the private sources mentioned above and from others was vital to the operation of MCAT.

Nor was it an easy task to come up with enough qualified applicants. Most, of course, were single mothers who had to overcome all sorts of problems in order to enroll. Some way had to be found to take care of their young children while they were being trained at MCAT. Some way had to be found to get children to school and mothers to MCAT, as public transportation was not always adequate, particularly to the area where MCAT was located. Even getting the students appropriate clothes to wear to attend MCAT and subsequently to work in was problematic. But, probably the biggest problem MCAT had to deal with was the lack of motivation of students to persevere.

Since the positions that potential employers needed to fill required some degree of computer competency, our classrooms were (with the funds I had raised) equipped with an array of computers. Although employers were unwilling to bear any of the costs of training, they were willing to work with MCAT in developing the programs needed to train students to perform the tasks that the employers needed.

For example, Hopkins Hospital agreed to employ trainees who had successfully completed a curriculum that they had created for certain computer-oriented positions, primarily the registering of patients. The University of Maryland and Mercy Hospital also came on board. There were several other employers who likewise agreed to hire graduates who met their particular requirements. Naturally, MCAT was not just interested in the initial hiring of its graduates, but in their retention. Thus, it often had to provide follow-up services to deal with issues that arose on the job.

Teaching MCAT students such basic things as showing up on time and dressing properly for work became major challenges.

Nevertheless, with a struggle, the project seemed to be working and even expanding. MCAT, therefore, decided to move to a larger and more convenient location in the 100 block of West Fayette Street. Unfortunately, just about this time, Adrian decided to resign in order to go into his own business. He had been developing a computerized system of tracking the progress of persons employed and felt that there was a great need for this sort of service. He was right, and today he is running a successful business doing just that.

Jan Rivitz, the Hoffberger Foundation's part-time executive director, and Patrice undertook the job of finding a replacement, and after an extensive search, they recommended that a man who managed a large local shopping center be hired to take Adrian's place. In order to get him, however, they were recommending that MCAT pay him a salary of $140,000 plus benefits. This was tough for me to swallow, as Adrian had been making nowhere near that amount of money. However, I had confidence in their judgment, so I recommended that the board hire him.

That decision turned out to be a bad mistake in more than one way and resulted in the ultimate loss of the support of the foundations, including the Hoffberger Foundation that had created MCAT. Not long after becoming director of MCAT, the new executive began to hire a support staff at commercial-level salaries. As if this were not bad enough, unknown to me was the fact that the support people were all members of his church which, when discovered, obviously aroused my suspicions.

As expenses increased and public funding declined, it became evident that our selection of a new director to head MCAT had been a mistake; so I had no choice but to confront him with the fact that MCAT was operating at a substantial deficit which it could not sustain. In addition, I was hearing that there were serious tensions between him and his employees. His explanations concerning these conditions were not plausible and with the agreement of Jan and Patrice, I decided to ask for his resignation. With some resistance, he complied.

MCAT had by then run out of private sector money. We had repaid the $750,000 loan from Abell, which was not renewed. I did not feel that I could go back to the Hoffberger Foundation for more funding and certainly not to the other foundations that had originally supported MCAT. Also, due to the bad economy, we were not getting as many stipends from the city and state for students; so it did not seem possible to continue. Nevertheless, because of the recession, there was now a new and different pool of unemployed persons who needed retraining. I therefore felt there was still a need for an organization like MCAT,

> MCAT had by then run out of private sector money. We had repaid the $750,000 loan from Abell, which was not renewed.

As I look back,
I ask myself
if this venture,
of relatively
short duration,
served a
meaningful
purpose.

but my experience made me aware that public sources alone were not adequate to sustain a meaningful program of retraining. Not knowing where to turn for private sector support for MCAT, I indicated to the board that I thought we should dissolve our operation. To my pleasant surprise, an African-American woman on the board by the name of Catherine Pugh, who was then a member of the City Council and is now a state senator, volunteered to take over.

As I look back, I ask myself if this venture, of relatively short duration, served a meaningful purpose. I think so. MCAT's mission was to provide training for those unskilled, long-term welfare recipients who had to be given a skill that made them employable before their welfare payments stopped. In helping those people, MCAT did a reasonably effective job.

Just one more thought about whether I should feel that this venture was worthwhile. Recently, when I was leaving an appointment at the Johns Hopkins Outpatient Center, an African-American gentleman in a white coat who was seated behind the counter called out, "Hi, Mr. Hoffberger!"

I stopped and looked at him and recognized that he was the same person whom I had seen several times before working in this department and who was originally an MCAT-trained student.

I said, "Hello. Weren't you an MCAT graduate?" He said, "Yes." "How long have you been working here?" I asked. "Ten years," he replied. I then said, "Wow, you must be happy here!" His response was, "Yes, but I'm looking forward to my retirement soon." I further inquired as to whether there were any other MCAT graduates working at Hopkins, and he told me there were several.

As I walked to the garage to get my car, I thought to myself, "Even if I am aware of only one person whom MCAT trained, whose life was turned around as a result of the program I created, I should feel (and do) that I created something worthwhile. In Judaism, there is a saying that 'saving one life is equivalent to saving the whole world.'"

CHAIRMAN OF THE BALTIMORE CITY HOSPITAL COMMISSION

In 1967, Thomas J. D'Alesandro III (Tommy), the newly elected mayor of Baltimore and a friend I had made while participating in the Young Democrats, asked me to become the chairman of the Baltimore City Hospital Commission. I said I would be happy to serve. As I recall, the commission consisted of about five men and an ex-officio member, Fred Hubbard, who was the CEO of the hospital. City Hospital was, for generations, known as the "hospital of last resort" for the indigent of Baltimore. Before the advent of Medicare and Medicaid, such persons were not usually admitted at other hospitals, but were sent for care to City Hospital.

While City Hospital had a large chronic disease facility that housed the indigent, it was mostly an acute hospital staffed by doctors who, while they were paid by the city, were either on the faculty of The Johns Hopkins Medical Institutions or the University of Maryland Medical System. It was also staffed by rotating interns and residents of these institutions who spent part of a year at the hospital. Although many of its buildings were old, its equipment was first-rate.

Unfortunately, the hospital consistently incurred a deficit of around $6–7 million per year, which the city could ill afford. While most cities in the country had already abandoned such hospitals, being unable to afford to update them and to cover revenue shortfalls, Baltimore was still trying to keep the doors of its hospital open to serve its large, medically indigent population.

Thomas J. D'Alesandro III swears me in as chairman of the Baltimore City Hospital Commission, 1967

With this in mind, I tried to involve myself in the budgeting process. The CEO and his staff would prepare the budget each year which would show a break-even operation. However, inevitably, each year some thing or things that were not anticipated would bring about huge deficits. The truth of the matter was that, while I gradually realized that I could not rely on Fred's ability to operate within the budget, I was helpless to know how to prevent these horrendous losses from occurring.

Severely strapped for funds, the city was reluctant to agree to give the hospital any funding that was not included in the hospital's approved budget. Thus, each time additional funding was needed, I, accompanied by Fred Hubbard, would have to go see the mayor and present our case. Requests for increases in doctors' salaries were, in particular, a constant issue. This was so because the hospital's doctors, as city employees, received classifications according to the city's employment system which bore no relationship whatsoever to the competitive salaries for physicians at other hospitals. Fred was convinced that if we didn't find a way to better compensate our doctors, they were going to leave en masse.

Then one day Fred came to me with an idea that I thought had great merit. Medicare and Medicaid, which had become effective in the mid-'60s, permitted doctors to charge fees for service which they did not and could not do as city employees. Fred therefore suggested that we set up a corporation (Chesapeake Physicians) to employ all of the hospital's physicians. Chesapeake's physicians would, in turn, render services to the hospital for which Medicare and Medicaid would reimburse Chesapeake Physicians.

We presented the proposal to the city which, despite some resistance from certain bureaucrats, ultimately approved it. Hopkins, too, had to be convinced that the new arrangement would not upset the dual role that City Hospital's doctors played as associate professors at Hopkins and staff at City. However, I think that it become clear that raising the salaries of the doctors at City to be more in line with their peers was a win-win situation.

For the first time in the history of the hospital, we now had a way to pay competitive salaries to the medical staff, who were no longer city employees. This not only made our then-current dissatisfied medical staff happy, but paved the way for the hospital to attract additional outstanding doctors.[43]

For the first time in the history of the hospital, we now had a way to pay competitive salaries to the medical staff, who were no longer city employees.

Unfortunately, even with the doctors being off of the city's payroll, City Hospital could not maintain a break-even budget. The non-professional employees of the hospital were in the city's union, which was pretty powerful. At one point, Fred told me that the union was demanding a wage increase for its employees and that since this item was not in the budget, we would have to convince the mayor that it was justified, or a strike might ensue. So, once again, off to see the mayor went Fred and I. We explained the situation to him, and although he did not like hearing what we were telling him, he did not want a strike on his hands.

Not knowing what to do, Tommy got on the telephone and called in Peter Marudas, who was his chief of staff. He asked us to tell Peter the problem and then asked Peter for his advice. Feeling that a strike by the city's union was not politically acceptable, Peter told the mayor he thought he should approve the request for the increase. I don't think this pleased the mayor, so he picked up the phone again and called Charlie Benton who was the city's longtime chief financial advisor. The story was repeated for Charlie to hear and ponder. It didn't take him long to tell the mayor that the city could not afford the increase and that there had never been an indication made to the union that this was possible.

At that point, Tommy went over to the far side of his large office and picked up a wooden shepherd's staff that was standing in the corner. He walked back behind his desk and banged the staff on the floor several times. He then said to me, "You see, Roy, he (pointing at Peter) tells me to do it and he (pointing to Charlie) tells me not to do it. We don't know what the f--- we're doing and I'm going on television tonight and tell the people of Baltimore that we don't know what the f--- we're doing!" I burst out laughing even though it was evident that this was no laughing matter to the mayor.

The city was broke, but there were legitimate needs of the hospital for money, so the mayor was beside himself. The combination of the 1968 riots following the assassination of Martin Luther King, which had ravaged certain parts of Baltimore, and the unsolvable fiscal problems facing the city were so distressing to him that Tommy decided not to run for a second term and left active political life for good. It was his sister, Nancy (D'Alesandro) Pelosi, who carried on the family's political tradition.

The city was broke, but there were legitimate needs of the hospital for money, so the mayor was beside himself.

I served as chairman of the hospital commission for about four years, resigning when I left Baltimore for London. During my tenure, I made a number of good friends on the medical staff, one or two of whom I still bump into on occasion. They were excellent doctors, but they had often been treated by their peers at Hopkins and the University of Maryland School of Medicine like "stepchildren," because they were practicing at City Hospital. Notwithstanding, when in 1979–1980 City Hospital was sold to Hopkins, a number of our doctors were transferred to the Broadway campus of Hopkins and within a short time became both full professors in their specialties and chiefs of their respective departments.[44]

MARYLAND INSTITUTE COLLEGE OF ART

My interest in art was expressed at an early age, when in 1935 I began attending a drawing class for elementary school children at the Maryland Institute College of Art (MICA) on Saturday mornings. The class was held from 9 AM to noon, but I always managed to finish by 11:30. Then I would sneak out and slip up to the second floor of the building where there was an adult art class and hopefully a nude woman model! This was my first exposure to MICA, and little did I know that this institution was later to become one of my greatest personal philanthropic interests.

MICA had been in existence since the 1820s, when it was founded by some prominent Baltimoreans as a school of architectural drafting. Although it had survived the Civil War, the historic Great Baltimore Fire in 1904 and other subsequent catastrophic events, in the 1960s its future as an art institution was in serious jeopardy due to a lack of financial resources. In order to deal with this dilemma, Bud Leake, who was president, had embarked on a program to rejuvenate MICA. He invited onto the board some dynamic community businessmen who could understand his vision for the college and help him raise the money needed to renew and expand the campus. Among those he selected was my close friend Irv Blum.

One of the problems facing MICA was its lack of studio and classroom space. Therefore, when the B&O railroad ceased to use Mt. Royal Station and put it up for sale, Bud convinced the board that it should be acquired by MICA and renovated to house the college's sculpture department, provide studio space and expand its library. I believe that the amount needed for this was $6 million, and Irv was put in charge of the campaign. Irv came to me with a request for $250,000 from the Hoffberger Foundation. Unfortunately, I had to tell him that the

> This was my first exposure to MICA, and little did I know that this institution was later to become one of my greatest personal philanthropic interests.

Foundation was really no longer interested in "bricks and mortar" projects, but rather in programming.

Then, Irv came back with an idea that I thought the Foundation would like. He suggested that the Foundation's grant would initially be used to help rehabilitate the B&O Station, but that when sufficient funds were raised for the Station, the Foundation's $250,000 would be restored and transferred to an endowment fund that would be dedicated to the creation of the Hoffberger Graduate School of Painting. I really liked his idea and thought that his proposal should be considered by the board (which at that time consisted of Morton Hollander, "Reds" Charlie Hoffberger, Jerry Hoffberger and me, as its chairman). Irv's proposal was enthusiastically approved and in 1962, the Hoffberger Graduate School of Painting was born.

Fred Lazarus IV and me on the occasion of his retirement as president of MICA. Cocktail party at the Brown Center at MICA, 2013. Photograph by Paula Gately Tillman

After Bud Leake retired and a few of his successors had failed to provide the needed leadership, Fred Lazarus became president of MICA. Fred arrived around 1980 and for over thirty years has continued Bud's vision of making MICA one of the best art colleges in the nation. He, too, had placed on MICA's board community leaders who could help realize his vision and who could give as well as raise money. One of his initial board members was Herbert Fried (who had been the local representative and ultimately the president of the Doner Advertising Agency that handled the marketing of "Natty Boh" beer).

One day I got a telephone call from Herb asking me to meet with him and Fred for lunch. I willingly agreed because of my original involvement with Irv in the creation of the Hoffberger Graduate School of Painting. At the luncheon, Fred asked if I would join the board, and I said I would. That was in about 1980, at a time when MICA was in the midst of a new fundraising campaign. Of course, the Foundation and I were expected to participate.

In 1980, the Hoffberger Graduate School of Painting had as its scholar-in-residence Grace Hartigan, an internationally renowned painter. As a result, the school was attracting a small group of excellent students from around the world to study under Grace. I can't recall whether the Foundation had made any additional contributions to the Hoffberger School of Painting since the original request from Irv, but it was not difficult to convince the board to give an additional $250,000. I can't recall how much I personally contributed, but making a personal contribution was a pattern that I had developed: I would "put my personal money (not in the same amount but a significant contribution for me) where my mouth was" to demonstrate my commitment to any cause that I asked the Foundation to support.

When I came on the board, MICA was still in serious financial difficulty. There were times when we were not sure that the cash flow would be sufficient to pay faculty their salaries. I therefore directed my attention to serving on the finance committee (of which I eventually became chairman) and to fundraising. I recall that shortly before I became chairman of the board, I was asked to chair the largest campaign ever launched by MICA. This involved raising $17 million.

As usual, MICA had engaged a professional firm of consultants from Philadelphia (Ketchum) to organize the campaign and to provide advice along the way. I recall that the consultant's representative told our committee that if we expected to be successful, the board would have to commit 25% to 30% of the goal, roughly $5 million, before the public phase of the campaign could begin. Although we had some very wealthy members on the board (such as George Bunting and Alonso Decker), the board had never previously given amounts that made raising $5 million among them a "sure thing." Nevertheless, I willingly accepted the job of chairing the campaign.

I recall reporting to the board what my expectations were of our overall participation and that whether we reached our goal or not, I expected every member of the board to participate to the best of his/her ability. This, of course, meant that I, personally, and the Hoffberger Foundation would have to make "leadership" commitments. The exact amounts that the Foundation and I pledged to the campaign I don't recall, but I know that my personal gift and the Foundation's grant were something to be proud of (i.e., we both really stretched to fulfill our role).

I was elected chairman of the board in 1990, soon after the successful conclusion of the $17 million campaign. Having reported, as chairman of the finance committee over a number of years, on the improving financial condition of MICA, and having successfully led the college's largest fundraising campaign, I felt that I had gained the full confidence and support of both the board and Fred.

Fred's drive to make MICA the leading art college in America had caught fire with the board and faculty, and there was a united effort to keep improving and adding courses and facilities. This meant that we were going from one campaign to the next, even though the board was concerned about continually returning to the Baltimore community for more support. However, Fred had expanded the board to now include wealthy directors from outside of Maryland and had also interested national foundations in contributing to MICA.

Being aware of the need for additional funds to carry out Fred's ambitious plans, I knew that MICA owned an asset which, if sold, had the potential to substantially enhance the endowment fund. That asset was the Lucas Collection of 19th-century French paintings and prints. These works were on long-term loan to both the Walters Art Museum and the Baltimore Museum of Art (BMA) for no financial consideration. There was always the possibility that this collection could be sold to provide a large sum of money for MICA's endowment.

The Lucas Collection had been given to MICA by the art collector George A. Lucas through a bequest written in language that made it questionable whether Mr. Lucas intended that his collection be kept, permanently, for the "benefit of the citizens of Baltimore" or that MICA had outright ownership with the right to dispose of it. On previous occasions, MICA had considered selling the collection and knowing this would be a very contentious issue with the museums and the public, MICA had obtained the opinions of two very prominent lawyers which supported its right of ownership. Despite these opinions, "discretion being the better part of valor," MICA had never tried to exercise its right to sell.

The Lucas Collection had been appraised for $12 million, an amount which, if realized and added to MICA's endowment, would support additional programming that Fred thought would be in keeping with George Lucas' original intention that his collection be used as "teaching tools." Supporting me was a good friend on the board, Robert Shelton,

Fred's drive to make MICA the leading art college in America had caught fire with the board and faculty, and there was a united effort to keep improving and adding courses and facilities.

a very bright lawyer who was next in line to be chairman and who was totally familiar with the opinions of the lawyers who confirmed MICA's right of ownership.

Armed with Fred Lazarus' and Bob Shelton's support, I began to talk to the board about what I felt was its fiduciary duty to utilize our assets in a way that would serve the best interests of MICA. I was not being unmindful of the great civic pride that existed in having the Lucas Collection remain in Baltimore, available for viewing at the Walters and the BMA; but I told the board, as forcefully as I could, that it owed a duty to MICA that transcended our civic interest. The board ultimately agreed with me and voted to offer the collection for sale to the Walters and the BMA.

Needless to say, both museums were irate as they had had the free use of the collection for so many years that they had come to feel that they owned the works. Efforts to negotiate with them were in vain, leaving litigation as the ultimate recourse for resolving the issue of ownership. As I recall, MICA filed for a declaratory judgment, claiming the right of full ownership. The issue was to be heard by Judge Caplan, who naturally wished to avoid a contentious showdown if he could.

At this point, having served as chairman for about three years, I decided to step down from my position and with the board's approval, have Bob Shelton take over. Bob's knowledge of the history of the Lucas bequest as well as his knowledge of the law made him particularly equipped to pursue MICA's claim. Judge Caplan realized (as did all parties to the suit) that this issue was one best resolved by mediation. The cultural and philanthropic communities had strong emotional feelings about what MICA's board was saying about not only its right to sell, but its duty to do so. A prolonged and costly legal battle was not in the best interest of MICA, but it could not and did not back down.

With Judge Caplan acting as a mediator, the parties grudgingly agreed to a compromise whereby MICA would accept $8 million (instead of the $12 million appraised value) from the BMA and the Walters which would each split the cost. The question was how were the museums going to find the money to make this compromise happen? With the State of Maryland expressing a willingness to put up $4 million and the two other museums reluctantly agreeing to each put up $2 million, the issue was resolved, at least, from a financial perspective.

While the burden of facing harsh feelings from a number of prominent persons close to the two museums was, unfortunately, borne mostly by Bob, rather than by me or Fred, Bob did not regret leading the charge.

Although I felt that I had really initiated the move by MICA to convert the value of the Lucas Collection into endowment, for some undeserved reason, I had escaped the wrath of my friends at the museums. Why, I am not certain.

I have continued to remain on the board of MICA but have ceased playing an active role. Feeling that the board position which I had occupied for forty years should be made available for a younger person, I resigned and was made an emeritus member. Moreover, on May 11, 2012, I was given an honorary Doctorate of Humane Letters at the Commencement ceremony of the Graduate School.

Joan Waltemath, director of the Hoffberger School of Painting, read a proclamation that set forth my accomplishments at MICA that were the basis for my being awarded the honorary doctorate. Fred read the citation and conferred the cape. In response, I read some prepared remarks and added some off-the-cuff comments. Evidently, everyone was moved by the sincerity and poignancy of my speech, and I received kudos from both friends and strangers. Fred was particularly moved by the humorous but meaningful analysis that I had made of the significance of the honor. I will long remember the joy of that day, and how proud Paula, Douglas, Catherine and my grandchildren said they were of me.

Because I am fond of Fred, as a friend and as the force behind MICA's rise to prominence as one of the best (if not the best) art colleges in the country, MICA has become my primary philanthropic interest. After much thought as to how I could best increase the endowment

Receiving an honorary Doctorate of Humane Letters which MICA awarded me in 2012. Photograph by Paula Gately Tillman[45]

for the newly renamed LeRoy E. Hoffberger Graduate School of Painting, I decided to make a $500,000 gift of Davis shares to MICA (which was completed in November 2012) and to bequeath in my will my German Expressionist collection to MICA with instructions to sell it and add the proceeds to the School's endowment.[46]

I thank my mother for having encouraged me to develop an appreciation for the arts, which has so enriched my life. That joy and the desire "to give back" have motivated me to help talented students develop into world-class artists.

FOUNDING MEMBER OF THE INSTITUTE FOR CHRISTIAN AND JEWISH STUDIES

Following the Second Ecumenical Council of the Roman Catholic Church in 1965, conferences were held throughout the U.S. to discuss Pope John Paul XXIII's ecumenical edict concerning the Church's relationship with other religious groups, particularly the Jews. One such conference was held in Baltimore. Among those attending were Charles Obrecht and Rick Berndt, both of whom were interested in having Baltimore play a leading role in seeking to implement those provisions that dealt with the Church's recognition of the legitimacy of Judaism and the prohibition of the Church's effort to proselytize the Jews.

Charlie and Rick then called together leading Catholics, Protestants and Jews, both lay and clerical, in the Baltimore community to see if there was interest in creating an organization, The Institute for Christian and Jewish Studies (ICJS). Its purpose would be to develop educational programs (based on research done primarily by Christian theologians on first-century Christianity) that shed new light on the Gospels and rid them of their historic anti-Jewish interpretation. The idea was also to have the Jewish representatives of the organization enlighten the Christian representatives concerning Hebrew Scripture, the interpretation of which would shed light on certain basic religious concepts that differed from (but in some instances were similar to) Christian beliefs.

Almost from the beginning, I was asked by Charlie and Bernie Manekin to become a founding board member. I was delighted to accept. The board, which consisted of about thirty persons, was equally made up of Catholic, Protestant and Jewish lay and clergy members. In addition to Rick, Charlie and Bernie, I recall that Owen Daley, George Hess, George Bunting, Bishop Frank Murphy, Rabbi Joel Zaiman, Reverend John Roberts, Melvin Sykes and David Hirschhorn

> I thank my mother for encouraging me to develop an appreciation for the arts, which have so enriched my life.

were among those elected to represent their religious denominations.

The Reverend Chris Leighton, who had previously been the chaplain at Gilman School, was chosen to be the executive director, and Roseanne Catalano, PhD, was also on the staff as the scholar-in-residence of the Catholic faith. There was a Protestant clergyman, who served on a voluntary basis; but there was no paid rabbi on staff, initially, due to the fact that it was difficult to find good candidates as well as the funding to support the position. Rabbi Zaiman thus became the volunteer Jewish consultant.

For me, the most interesting aspect of being on the board occurred in the early years when the board was being educated by leading Christian theologians from around the country. They explained how the Gospels had become progressively more anti-Jewish, concluding with John, whose reference to "the Jews" (and not the Romans) in connection with the crucifixion of Jesus had become distorted to mean not only "the Jews" at that time, but also "the Jews" of all times.

Thus, the allegation by the Church that the Jews were guilty of deicide became imbedded in Christian theology. The messages being conveyed by the Christian scholars, who lectured to the ICJS board, were that parish priests, ministers and their congregants must understand the historical context in which the Gospels were written in order to dispel their distortions and to rid them of their anti-Jewish interpretation. Needless to say, I felt privileged to be able to listen to these enlightened scholars lay the historical foundation that may one day free the Gospels of 2,000 years of anti-Semitism.

Coincidentally, not long after I had become a board member of ICJS, the United States Holocaust Memorial Museum, under the leadership of Bud Meyerhoff, a longtime friend, launched a major campaign to fund the cost of constructing a national museum in Washington, DC, and to sponsor related activities. The Hoffberger Foundation was asked by Bud to make a major contribution toward the building. I told Bud that I would have a hard time getting the board to be receptive to his request since "bricks and mortar" were not something the Foundation wished to support. I explained that our interest was in programming, and that I would try to think of a program to be conducted by the Museum which we would underwrite.

Being so moved by what I had learned at the ICJS about the efforts some denominations of Christianity were making to enlighten their laity concerning the Church's role in fostering prejudice through its misinterpretation of the text of the Gospels, and being convinced that years of Christianity's denigration of the Jews had laid the ground for

> Needless to say, I felt privileged to be able to listen to these enlightened scholars lay the historical foundation that may one day free the Gospels of 2,000 years of anti-Semitism.

the Nazi persecution of the Jews leading up to the "final solution," I wanted to see if the United States Holocaust Memorial Museum could develop a program that would shed light on how longstanding Christian anti-Semitism had been a major contributing factor to the Holocaust.

It so happened that Charlie Obrecht's wife, Peggy, was working at the Museum as the Director of the Church Relations Committee. She and I began to shape a program that would underwrite the cost of sending Christian clergy to college campuses and other venues to lecture on the historic connection between the Church's vitriolic attitude toward the Jews and the Holocaust.

When we had agreed on the fundamentals, I brought the program before the Hoffberger Foundation and the Hoffberger Family Fund and asked that we contribute $1 million, payable over five years, to underwrite it. Since this was an extraordinary undertaking both in its nature and in its size, I suggested that our contribution be contingent on a comparable contribution from a Christian source. My rationale was that I wanted to see a "buy-in" by Christians of the importance of making all Americans aware of how historic prejudice plays out in "man's treatment of his fellow man." The boards approved the request.

I'm not sure how, but the Museum (Peggy) got a Mormon to match our $1 million grant. Although I have now lost touch with the current programming for which the Family's funding is being used, I have confidence that the present director of the Museum is continuing an agenda that carries out the purposes for which our grant was made.

After active participation as an ICJS board member for over 25 years, I decided to ask to be made an emeritus member. I attribute my desire to step down to two reasons. One was that having heard my Christian friends speak so knowledgably about their religion, I had developed a strong desire to know more about Judaism and in particular about the Torah. I, therefore, found that I was more interested in devoting my time to a process of self-education by constantly reading, cover to cover, first, the Reform *Chumash* (Five Books of Moses) that Rebecca had given me and then the Orthodox *Chumash* that I had bought.

While this familiarized me with the superficial meaning of the text of the Torah, I realized that I needed rabbinic instruction if I were to grasp its deeper meaning. It was then my good fortune to discover Rabbi David Fohrman, a Biblical scholar, whose lectures Rebecca and I attended at Hopkins. I will tell the story of how I met and became devoted to Rabbi Fohrman's teachings later on, but suffice it to say, I became completely absorbed with the study of Hebrew Scripture, leaving little time for the ICJS.

Secondly, over the years, I became disappointed that the ICJS had not more aggressively sought to take its message to a much broader constituency (i.e., to venues outside of Baltimore). While I realize it has created alliances with religious groups in other cities, particularly in Atlanta, it had not in my opinion adequately used the Internet to carry the Institute's message to a worldwide constituency. Those who had been exposed to what the Institute was teaching were very supportive of its work and were even transformed. What I had hoped was that the ICJS would have, after over thirty years of existence, been an international force to enhance Christian-Jewish relations. I still believe that it has the potential to achieve that objective.

CO-FOUNDING THE AMERICAN VISIONARY ART MUSEUM (AVAM)

While my communal life was quite fulfilling, my personal life was not. After more than twenty years, my marriage to Hilde was coming apart, and in 1987 we divorced. It was during my legal separation from Hilde that I met Rebecca Alban Puharich. She was the development director of an outreach program for the chronically mentally ill sponsored by Sinai Hospital called "People Encouraging People (PEP) Inc."

Since I was legally separated from Hilde, I was free to begin courting Rebecca. Our courtship consisted primarily of my taking Rebecca out to long lunches, in out-of-the-way restaurants, at which we discussed an agenda (actually prepared by her each time we met) of subjects that ranged from religion to art. Rebecca was particularly interested in my comments about my collection of German Expressionist art. I told her how the Expressionist artists were expressing in their art their contempt for pre-World War I German society, which was superficially "living it up" to hide inner feelings of despair. Having heard what motivated much of the Expressionist movement, Rebecca concluded that the mentally ill must also have a genre of art that expressed their innermost feelings and thoughts. Thus began her quest for examples of such art and her ultimate desire to have a place where these works could be shown to the public.

Rebecca must have begun talking to some of the mentally ill patients and others about her interest since the next thing I knew she invited me to see a collection of drawings and paintings by the mentally ill father of someone she had met. The artwork was most impressive (and expressive). The artist used techniques similar to those used by the German Expressionists to reflect his inner feelings. I actually remember remarking that these were works that, if done by a German Expressionist,

Since I was legally separated from Hilde, I was free to begin courting Rebecca.

I would pay $20,000 or $30,000 for, no doubt spurring Rebecca on in her search.

As luck or coincidence would have it, an article appeared in the Sunday *New York Times* about a psychiatrist named Dr. Hans Prinzhorn. In the early part of the 20th century, Dr. Prinzhorn worked in a mental institution in Heidelberg, Germany, called Gugging. There, he encouraged his patients to create art as a part of their normal activities and therapy. Dr. Prinzhorn eventually published a book of some of the best of the artwork by his patients. Upon seeing this publication, the German Expressionists got permission from him to come to the mental institution to study how its patients were expressing their feelings and thoughts. Their experience there evidently had a lasting influence on their own art.

Excited by this information, Rebecca convinced her friend George Ciscle, a Baltimore gallery owner, to do a show featuring "outsider" artists. This term, coined by a British professor and writer named Roger Cardinal, refers to self-taught artists, not only those who are mentally ill, but all those who are out of mainstream society. The exhibition was a roaring success, drawing record crowds and realizing numerous sales. I was one of the buyers, purchasing at least two works. One was by Martin Ramirez, an Hispanic artist who did crayon drawings of bandits on horses (I assume in the image of Pancho Villa). The other was a crayon drawing by an institutionalized German, Adolph Wolflie, who did large elaborate drawings, full of symbolic images, on paper stuck together with glue made from potatoes.[47]

> The Ciscle exhibition awakened both Rebecca and me to the validity of this unbelievably creative, but not officially recognized, genre of art.

The Ciscle exhibition awakened both Rebecca and me to the validity of this unbelievably creative, but not officially recognized, genre of art. Each artist was creating one-of-a-kind art that did not have its origin in some tradition, but was the product solely of the artist's imagination and, in many cases, pain. Rebecca did not like the word "outsider" as she felt that it stigmatized these artists. Rather, she preferred to call these artists "visionaries," a term which has grown in acceptance as the most appropriate name for those who can envision in art form things that others cannot. The works turned out by the mentally ill and others, such as recluses, poor African Americans and extremely religious persons, were usually distorted by their inner angst and often quite unique.

The success of the Ciscle show, combined with Rebecca's discovery that there are museums around the world focusing on this kind of art, gave her the passion to think about how meaningful it would be if a national museum dedicated solely to "visionary" art (of which there were none in the U.S.) could be created in Baltimore.

She was further inspired by a trip we made to the Collection de l'Art Brut, one of the best known of such museums of art by self-taught artists, in Lausanne, Switzerland. This museum houses the collection of the artist Jean Dubuffet who, when he had stopped painting for a number of years, gathered art by untrained artists for inspiration. Along with a friend from California, Donna Matson, who did filming of children's educational programs, we flew to Switzerland to see and film this collection. It was a fascinating experience which exhilarated Rebecca and made her even more determined that Baltimore was going to have an equally remarkable museum.

When she told me this, I told her that this would be an enormous undertaking fraught with all sorts of problems. She was not to be dissuaded so I, now married to her, agreed to support her efforts and to contribute as much of my own time and financial resources to the project as I thought I could afford.

So, off Rebecca and I went to see Mayor Kurt Schmoke. We wanted to tell him what we had in mind and to ask him to have the city contribute one of the many vacant properties in its inventory for conversion to a museum. We both agreed that the closer such a property was to the Inner Harbor, the better the chance a museum would have of attracting visitors.

Rebecca found an abandoned police station on Hamburg Street, located several blocks from the Harbor, which she thought would be perfect. It had a gothic exterior in good condition and was decorated with gargoyles. The interior also had some interesting possibilities, such as several jail cells that Rebecca thought could be turned into a café. This she had already named "Café des Con Artistes."

After some encouragement from Mayor Schmoke, who seemed to like the idea of using the station for a museum, we went about getting some schematic drawings from a local architectural firm and responded to the city's RFP. Unfortunately, one of the competing groups, also interested in acquiring the building, was a nonprofit that had better political ties to the city than we did, and we lost the bid.

Rebecca was heartbroken, and I was frustrated and ready to give up. "No!" she said. "I know that G-d has something better in mind." How could I fight that? She continued the search.

Fortunately, the mayor had been so impressed with Rebecca's proposal that he wanted to see if he could find another suitable site in the Inner Harbor. Soon he called Rebecca and told her that there was a structure, a former paint factory known as the Reeder Building, located

Naturally, the next step was to design a museum which, due to the city's urban renewal requirements, had to retain the exterior of the existing building.

at the foot of Federal Hill on the west side of Key Highway, facing the water. The mayor told Rebecca that the building was being held for an accounting firm located in Tennessee that had indicated a desire to move to Baltimore. Two years had passed, and no decision had been made to move, so the mayor put a short deadline on getting a response from the Tennessee company. When the answer came back in the negative, the mayor gave Rebecca the exclusive development rights to build a museum, subject, of course, to the city's and the nearby neighborhood's approval of the design and her ability to raise the necessary funding. The cost of the property was $1.

Naturally, the next step was to design a museum which, due to the city's urban renewal requirements, had to retain the exterior of the existing building. The building was interesting in that it was shaped like a wedge of pie, but otherwise, there was not one redeeming feature about it. Rebecca felt that the local architectural firm she had used to bid on the Hamburg Street Police Station was not imaginative enough, so she began to search for other local architects.

We were living at Harbor Court Condominiums in Federal Hill so we carpooled for school with two other families in the neighborhood. One of the women with whom we carpooled was Rebecca Swanston. She was an architect whose specialty was the restoration of historic row houses. She was good at that and had won several national awards for her work. Rebecca, my wife, liked her and thought that because of her specialty in the restoration and conversion of residential properties, Rebecca Swanston would be the right architect to help design the museum, in spite of the fact that she had never designed a commercial building, let alone a museum. Fully aware of that fact, my wife realized that Rebecca would need someone experienced in designing museum interiors to work with her.

Through one of her many sources, my wife heard of an architect named Alex Castro, who had been a student of Professor Louis I. Kahn of the University of Pennsylvania, one of the foremost architects of the 20th century and the designer of several museums, including the Yale University Art Gallery. Although Alex was a graduate architect living in Baltimore, he was not licensed in Maryland and had never designed a building. His specialty was designing exhibition space in museums so as to adapt a particular exhibit to the space in which it would be exhibited. Rebecca thought he would be perfect to assist Rebecca Swanston since the Reeder building, being pie-shaped, had the potential for some unique exhibition spaces. Her intuition was on target.

ART OF THE INSANE AND THE ECCENTRIC FINDS A HOME

AS AN ART COLLECTOR, LeRoy E. Hoffberger '47 was drawn to the genius of Egon Schiele, Emile Nolde, Gustav Klimt, Ernst Ludwig Kirchner, and other German Expressionists. Their visual depiction of internal despair and turmoil in pre–World War II Germany had a strong emotional impact on the Baltimore arts patron. And for Hoffberger, emotional impact is a vital measure of any art.

He never suspected that a passion for German Expressionism would one day be superseded by a passion for the work of untrained artists, among them criminals and the mentally ill. It began in 1983 when Rebecca Puharich, who became his wife in 1989, applied for a grant from the Hoffberger Foundation; she hoped to establish an outreach program for the chronically mentally ill, with an ultimate dream of establishing a permanent home for their art, like the one in Switzerland founded by the French artist Jean Dubuffet to display the works of untrained factory workers, farmers, asylum inmates, and prisoners.

As Hoffberger and Puharich became further acquainted, he showed her his collection of Expressionist prints, including the 1909 *Russian Dancer*, by Kirchner and the 1913 *Dancer*, by Nolde. In these pieces, she recognized the same raw, emotional imagery and techniques associated with art by the mentally ill. Not long

The Hoffbergers
PHOTO COURTESY LEROY HOFFBERGER '47

after that, Puharich showed him an article about the German psychiatrist Hans Princehorn, whose studies of art completed by patients in mental institutions were avidly read by the Expressionists.

Hoffberger began to think in new ways about the Expressionist art he so admired. And about the "visionary" art Puharich introduced him to, Hoffberger says, "It was a revelation to discover that there was a body of art that excited me and that I knew nothing about. It was more capable of evoking emotions than any art I had previously seen."

In the past, Hoffberger has poured significant resources into the Maryland Institute, College of Art. Lately, he is lavishing the same attention on the new American Visionary Arts Museum, born of his wife's longtime dream. The museum, which opened last November, has been hailed nationally for its sensitive approach to visionary art (sometimes called "outsider" art) and for its exceptional home overlooking Baltimore's Inner Harbor.

The credibility of the Hoffbergers' pioneering venture was enhanced when Congress passed a resolution in 1992 recognizing the museum as a national repository and educational center for visionary art.

For Hoffberger, formal and informal art are not mutually exclusive. "I don't have any trouble legitimizing the art of untrained persons," he says. "They follow no known school of art; nevertheless they are producing art which evokes substantial emotion. That's what art is supposed to do, make you react."

Today, Hoffberger counts among his friends men and women who have spent their lives interpreting visions and expressing their inner thoughts and spirituality through eccentric works of art rendered from raw materials, junk, paint, and mundane objects such as toothpicks and matches.

Visionary artists are "marvelous human beings," Hoffberger says. "They are what they are, and they like what they are." Befriending such artists as Baltimorean Gerald Hawkes, a man who builds sculptures out of millions of tinted matches, is a privilege for which Hoffberger credits his wife. "Never on my own would I have sought out or gotten to know these people," he says.

***Joy America*, by Eric Holmes, an example of visionary art**
PHOTO BY ALAN GILBERT

The Hoffberger family found fortune in Baltimore through such diverse enterprises as the National Brewing Company, the Pompeian olive oil company, heating oil and refrigeration services, real estate, and the Baltimore Orioles baseball team.

Although Hoffberger received his law degree from the University of Maryland in 1950, he hasn't practiced law in 30 years. Instead, he helps to manage his family's investments, now largely consolidated into the Davis New York Venture Fund, the refrigerator warehousing business, and real estate holdings.

Hoffberger is president of the Hoffberger Foundation and vice-president of the Hoffberger Family Fund. The family's largess is apparent throughout Baltimore, at institutions such as the Hoffberger Center for Professional Ethics at the University of Baltimore; the Hoffberger School of Painting at the Maryland Institute, College of Art; and the Hoffberger research wings of the Johns Hopkins Hospital Children's Center.

The Hoffberger Family Fund has also contributed to Jewish charities in Baltimore and around the world. Hoffberger credits an "overdeveloped sense of responsibility" for his and his family's efforts. Citing a Hebrew adage, *tikkun olam*, which means "to improve the world," Hoffberger says, "I see it as my responsibility, one we all have, to serve our fellow man."

Hoffberger, a devout Jew, recalls that his time at Princeton was a time of silence. As a student in the Woodrow Wilson School in the post–World War II years leading to Israel's statehood, he found no "touchstone" at Princeton for affirming his Jewish identity. There was little discussion of the Holocaust. "I was not aware of there being another Jew at Princeton, and yet I know there were," Hoffberger recalls. Just the same, he says, "I never experienced any anti-Semitism at Princeton."

—Stephanie Shapiro

Princeton Alumni Weekly,
April 17, 1996

Having assembled her team of architects, Rebecca enlisted my help to put together an RFP that included a financial feasibility analysis and was sufficiently impressive and credible to result in the city awarding the building to a nonprofit that we had set up called "The American Visionary Art Museum (AVAM) Inc."

Understandably, there were conditions to the award. Since we were required by the city to fully acquaint the Federal Hill neighborhood with our plans, Rebecca and I attended a special meeting of the neighborhood association where we described our project and presented the drawings. The drawings consisted of three interior floors and a basement as well as a sculpture garden on the roof. Much to our surprise, there was serious objection to the roof garden.

The basis for the objection was that the height of the structure with the outdoor sculpture garden exceeded the height of Federal Hill. While the association actually liked the idea of the garden, it felt strongly that if it approved our violation of what was apparently an existing zoning height restriction, it would set a precedent for others to likewise seek an exception. No matter how hard we tried, the association would not budge.

Since we felt that the sculpture garden was an extremely important element of the project, we were devastated. Then the president of the association said, "Why don't you ask the mayor for the adjoining property which would give you room for the garden?"

I could have strangled him. "That's easy for you to say," I countered, "but why would the mayor give us another lot?" He responded, "I don't know, but it can't hurt to ask." Of course, he was right. At first, we didn't think we had the chutzpah to carry out his suggestion, but in the end we did.

The mayor understood the situation and without much hesitation, he agreed to sell AVAM the adjoining lot (again for $1) which consisted of a warehouse and some vacant land. What luck! The extra space gave us the opportunity to relocate the sculpture garden both within the warehouse, which was a former storage facility that had a height of at least 25 feet, and in the open space adjacent to the warehouse.

The revised plan was approved by the association and submitted to the Baltimore Development Corporation and the city's planning department, both of which approved it. So, on paper we had a magnificent design for a museum. All we needed to do was to have working drawings prepared (which I paid for) and then raise the money needed to construct the museum.

In spite of our confidence in this project, as indicated by our going ahead with expensive drawings, we knew we needed to seriously start a fundraising campaign in order to move ahead.

In spite of our confidence in this project, as indicated by our going ahead with expensive drawings, we knew we needed to seriously start a fundraising campaign in order to move ahead. Rebecca and I prepared an appealing brochure that described the project, showed several conceptual drawings of the buildings and the garden and provided financial information. The amount needed for the construction of the facilities was $7.5 million. The brochure showed this along with the pro-forma projection of annual self-generated revenues of the museum, based on estimated attendance and several other sources of revenue (from the gift shop, restaurant and rental of the Sculpture Barn for events).

To estimate annual attendance for AVAM, we had asked the other museums in Baltimore what their annual attendance figures were, hoping that information would enable us to make an educated guess. To our pleasant surprise, the figures we obtained from the Walters and BMA were in the 300,000 – 500,000 range. So, we finally ended up estimating an attendance of 300,000 visitors annually, increasing by a relatively small percentage in each of the five years of the financial analysis.

Had I known that the figures we had received were highly inflated, since they included counting exits and entrances by employees during their work day, I would not have been so optimistic about AVAM's ability to self-generate most of the money we needed to make it a viable operation. As it was, based on our estimates of attendance and other revenues, there was still a $400,000 shortfall. Since that was not an unreasonable amount to have to raise, annually, by donations, the projections seemed to me to be credible and I thought that others, from whom we were asking for funds, would feel likewise.

The first potential donor that Rebecca and I approached was USF&G, a major insurance company headquartered in Baltimore and headed by a dynamic community leader by the name of Jack Mosley. Jack was very receptive and gave every indication that he could get his board to approve the $250,000 we had requested. As luck would have it, about a month later, we got word from Jack that his request had been approved. Encouraged by that success, we moved on to our next major prospect, Zan Krieger.

Zan had a foundation which was run by a man by the name of Robert Hiller, whom I knew quite well. Rebecca and I acquainted Bob with the AVAM project, and he was fascinated with both the uniqueness of the art to be shown and the life stories of the artists who produced it. As a former social worker, Bob felt that much of the art, with its childlike portrayal of images, would encourage creativity in children.

Feeling that the museum would be a worthy addition to the cultural life of Baltimore, he, primarily, with our assistance, went about trying to convince Zan to contribute $2 million toward the construction of the museum, which we agreed would carry his name. As philanthropic as Zan was, it was not easy to get him to understand how the museum would be more than just a place with interesting art (Zan had little interest in art per se). Bob, Rebecca and I finally got Zan to agree to a $2 million challenge grant, even though I don't think he fully understood why what we were telling him about the museum was so unique and important.

With a commitment from Zan, we were one big step closer to our goal of raising $7.5 million. I therefore felt it was my turn to step up to the plate. I did not have a great deal of cash, and while I had a large amount of Davis stock, I did not wish to dispose of it (which, as it turned out, was a major mistake). What I decided to contribute was a portion of my German Expressionist art collection which contained some very valuable works. I identified four or five graphics and one watercolor which I gave to AVAM with the understanding that they would be auctioned at Christie's in London in a special auction featuring German and Austrian artists.

I had, over a number of years, created a friendship with a young man at Christie's by the name of Simon Theobold, who headed its London print department. Simon told me that my works would be perfect for the first all-German-Expressionist sale that Christie's had ever held. He and a man by the name of Jussi Pylkkanen, who headed Christie's London contemporary painting department, were working together to promote this sale and were actually going around Europe and elsewhere drumming up potential bidders for an array of outstanding German Expressionist paintings, drawings and prints. He estimated that my works would bring at least $1 million net of all fees. I had my fingers crossed.

Rebecca and I flew over for the auction. Needless to say, we were both excited and anxious, fearing that my works might not bring the amount we needed. I can recall that when the five-color lithograph by Emil Nolde titled *South Sea Dancer* came up for sale, we were very nervous since it and the Egon Schiele watercolor titled *Akt gegen farbigen Stoff* were the core of what we were relying on to reach our goal. The bidding on the Nolde was going well in the beginning, but then it stopped momentarily before starting again. That brief halt was unbearable, but when the bidding restarted, it kept going and the work went for a world record price. We hugged and were euphoric.

What I decided to contribute was a portion of my German Expressionist art collection which contained some very valuable works.

Akt gegen farbigen Stoff (Nude Against Colored Fabric), Egon Schiele, 1911. A watercolor given by me to AVAM and sold at auction. © Christie's Images/Corbis

The bidding on the Schiele watercolor was next. Unfortunately, it did not reach the reserve price that I had put on the work so, to our great disappointment, it did not sell. However, following the auction, Jussi informed us that a Swiss bidder had informed him that he would pay $400,000 for the Schiele, a price well over our reserve price and one which Jousi felt was fair. However, his offer was contingent on payment being over ninety days. Jussi said that the man was trustworthy and that we should accept his offer. Since $400,000 was more than we had estimated we would receive, we were pleased to accept it.

Little did I know what value that work would eventually have! Recently, I was told by Jane Kallir, the owner of the Galerie St. Etienne in New York and the expert on Schiele works, that in today's market it would bring over $5 million. The reader can now understand my earlier comment that holding on to my Davis stock rather than my German Expressionist works was not a wise decision!

The Hoffberger Family Philanthropies was our next candidate for a gift. Since by my gift of German Expressionist works, I had contributed over $1 million to the museum, I felt that I could persuade the Family Foundations to make a similar grant. Rebecca made a persuasive presentation to the boards of the Family Foundations and, although knowing of my personal gift, the Family only gave a grant of $250,000 toward the Hoffberger Library to be housed on the third floor of the museum.

Tänzerin (South Sea Dancer), Emile Nolde, 1913. A rare four-color lithograph also given by me to AVAM. Image courtesy of LeRoy E. Hoffberger

Being a voracious reader, Rebecca had read a story about a woman named Anita Roddick, who founded a U.K. company called The Body Shop that produced organic products for the skin and hair.

Being a voracious reader, Rebecca had read a story about a woman named Anita Roddick, who founded a U.K. company called The Body Shop that produced organic products for skin and hair. From a single shop in Brighton, England, she had created a chain of shops around the world, two of them in Baltimore. Rebecca and I visited the one located in the Inner Harbor, and after looking at the array of products, Rebecca engaged one of the store's personnel in conversation. As luck would have it, she discovered that Anita was due to visit the Baltimore stores in several days. She inquired if she could meet her, and the saleswoman said, "Certainly."

As soon as Anita arrived in Baltimore, Rebecca asked her if she would be willing to give an early morning talk to a group of businessmen about her business philosophy. Anita agreed and we arranged with the Harbor Court Hotel, which was part of the condominium complex where I had a condominium, for a meeting room. In about 24 hours, Rebecca had called Baltimore's leading businessmen and women (many of whom were familiar with The Body Shop's success story) to give them a last-minute invitation to hear Anita.

The following morning we met Anita in the small windowless room in the Harbor Court Garage, adjacent to the hotel, which served (rent-free) as Rebecca's office. Almost instantly, Rebecca and Anita were sharing stories, and the basis for a fabulous relationship between the two began. Then, we joined the group at the hotel where more than fifty people had gathered to listen to Anita talk about her unique business philosophy.

Anita began to speak, and in the first five minutes she sounded like she was a Communist. She condemned just about every business practice held sacred to those in the audience, and I was sure most of them were going to leave. However, with further explanation, she began to enlighten the audience about how she did business with a social conscience. She gave examples of how she tied in the purchase of some of her raw materials, which came from some of the Pacific Island countries, with human rights demands for the workers who gathered the materials. Because her company had become of such major importance to the economy of these little countries, she was able to effect significant social and economic improvement in these societies.

At the end of her talk, the audience was on its feet giving Anita thunderous applause. Afterwards, Anita, Rebecca and I went back to Rebecca's cubbyhole office. It was then that Anita said, "What can I do for you?"

Although Rebecca was no doubt hoping that one day in the future there would be an opportunity to "pop the question" concerning a grant, she certainly was not expecting that it would be at this first meeting. I really don't think that Anita had the slightest notion about Rebecca's museum project, but, sensing that Rebecca was a "mover and shaker," she intuited that Rebecca must be doing something worthwhile.

Rebecca walked Anita over to the little model of the museum that had been made for presentations and for the first time began telling Anita of her vision. Anita listened intently and then told Rebecca that she was overwhelmed with her rationale for wanting to create such a museum. She also said that she was interested in making a pledge, but that she had to discuss it with her husband. Naturally, we were elated, but anxious over how her husband, Gordon, whom we had never met, would react.

It was about two weeks before Rebecca heard from Anita, who had returned to her home in England, but the suspense had its reward. Anita said that Gordon was impressed with what Rebecca had accomplished and agreed with his wife that they should be participants in the project. We had no idea of what they were thinking about contributing, so when Anita said that they would be giving AVAM the equivalent of $1 million in pounds sterling, we were flabbergasted. It was then that Rebecca told Anita that she would like to name the Sculpture Barn after her.

Anita said that Gordon was impressed with what Rebecca had accomplished and agreed with his wife that they should be participants in the project.

I asked my British friend and lawyer Victor Stone (my attorney from my Formula 16 undertaking) how the Roddicks should go about making the gift, knowing that, under special circumstances, it could be made in a way that would be tax-beneficial, which is usually not the case under U.K. tax law. Victor formed a British Charitable Trust to which the Roddicks gave their pound sterling gift in two payments. By forming the trust, which was called The American Friends of AVAM, the Roddicks received generous U.K. tax deductions and AVAM received, in addition to their $1 million, an extra payment from the U.K. Treasury equal to the income tax the Roddicks would have paid on their gross income had they not made the gift. What a civilized incentive for charitable giving!

We now had enough funds pledged or in hand to put the project out to bid. There were three bidders: Whiting-Turner, J. Vinton Schafer and Kirby Construction. At the time of the bidding, the real estate market was not good, so we were hoping that the winning bid would come in at the estimate we had received from the architect, which was about $4 million. A month or so later, the bids were returned, and to our great delight the winning bid, which was submitted by Schafer, was under the estimate. We felt that we were off to a good start, but, as with all construction jobs, we were in for a few surprises that threatened to cause the costs to go not only well over budget, but over the actual money that had been raised or pledged.

In fact, before we even broke ground, the first setback occurred. The entire south side of the proposed extension to the existing building was a cylindrical, three-story structure of poured, reinforced concrete. The winning bid for the concrete work was by a minority-owned firm whose participation was important because city and state law required minority contractors to have a portion of the total job. The minority-owned firm bid was several hundred thousand dollars less than the next lowest bid, which was not by a minority firm. However, before the minority-owned sub even set foot on the site, it informed Ron Knowles, the owner of J. Vincent Schafer, that it was bankrupt.

Ron called Rebecca and me and asked for a meeting. At the meeting he acknowledged that replacing the concrete sub was his responsibility, but by having to use the second lowest bid, which was $200,000 higher than the original, he would incur a significant loss on the job. His admission made me believe that Schafer's need for work to keep his organization intact was so great that Ron knowingly took on a risky sub. Despite my conclusion, I did not think that it was a good idea to start the project with Ron and me both knowing he was going to lose money.

After thinking about this for a while, I called Ron and we all met again. I told him that if, when the building was completed, his company was facing a loss, I, personally, would pick up half of it up to $50,000. He was pleasantly surprised and deeply appreciative, as was Rebecca. As it turned out, J. Vinton Schafer did lose money on the job, and I did give AVAM an additional $50,000 to cover a portion of the loss. I am not sure exactly why I was so generous, but I do not regret having been so. Ron and Warren went all out to do a superb award-winning job, perhaps, in part, because I had treated them so fairly.

The concrete sub was replaced, and we began doing the excavation for the basement and the court. Again, misfortune struck! The area south of our building had held some sort of structure which the city had razed when it acquired the property. In doing so, it had failed to remove a large tank, which had been buried in the ground and contained Varsol, a by-product of gasoline that had been used as a paint thinner by the previous owner. Instead, the city bulldozed the area surrounding the tank and in the process had broken it open so that the soil surrounding that area was saturated with a hazardous material. This made it necessary for us to not only remove the tank, but also all of the contaminated soil.

Now, we were facing a major catastrophe. To remove and dispose of the hazardous material was estimated to cost about $300,000. That would take a big chunk (if not all) of the reserve we had set up for contingencies.

> Now, we were facing a major catastrophe. To remove and dispose of the hazardous material was estimated to cost about $300,000.

When a state inspector came around to inspect the site, Rebecca poured her heart out to him. As a consequence, he significantly modified what had to be done by reclassifying certain aspects of the contamination. In addition, he made us aware of a state fund that was available to help cover the cost of remediation. Ultimately, we received over $100,000 from this fund and with that we were able to pay for the less stringent requirements set out by the inspector.

I don't recall that there were any other major setbacks. However, every week we would have a meeting with the contractor and the subs to discuss progress and the growing amount of "extras" resulting from omissions from the drawings. I had gotten Charlie Obrecht, my friend from the ICJS board, who was in the real estate business and had considerable construction experience, to volunteer his services. Charlie was very helpful in our decision making, and with careful scrutiny by Charlie, Rebecca and me, AVAM was able to remain within its construction budget.

After about 18 months, the museum, the Sculpture Barn and the courtyard were substantially finished, and AVAM was ready to move in with its first visionary art show late in 1994. While the construction was still taking place, Rebecca had engaged Roger Manley, who was an authority on American visionary art, to be its first temporary curator. Roger had been working for about a year identifying paintings, drawings, huge sculpture and other art objects to be shown in AVAM's initial exhibition, called *Tree of Life*.

These works were brought to the museum and installed in a relatively short period of time. Rebecca had been successful in getting Mark Ward and Theresa Segreti to leave the Walters Art Museum to come with her (for less money) because they wanted to be a part of this new venture, and they were instrumental in the installation and presentation of the objects. Through funding from Lois Feinblatt and me, of $200,000, Rebecca, Roger and Theresa produced AVAM's first and only catalogue. It was beautifully done and printed on special paper of extraordinary quality. Unfortunately, the museum did not raise enough money to publish a notable catalogue for the following 15 exhibitions.

To do justice to this first exhibition, we held, by invitation only, a formal gala dinner sometime in November 1994, immediately prior to the opening. About fifty or sixty people who had played a role in the launching of AVAM were our guests. I went all out to make the occasion as memorable as possible by breaking out my cache of 1982 Château Mouton Rothschild wine.

To do justice to this first exhibition, we held, by invitation only, a formal gala dinner sometime in November 1994, immediately prior to the opening.

There was a significant contingent from England that included the Roddicks (and I believe one or both of their daughters); Edward Adamson, who had contributed two magnificent works from the Adamson Collection; Lady Helen Vincent (widow of Sir Lacey Vincent, part-owner of the U.K. Grecian Formula franchise) and Victor Stone, AVAM's U.K. legal counsel who had set up the charitable trust through which the Roddicks had made their gift, and his wife, Naomi.
This group, most of whom were wine connoisseurs, was particularly appreciative of my gesture, knowing that 1982 Mouton was considered "the Bordeaux wine of the century."

Senator Barbara Mikulski, who had been instrumental in the unanimous adoption of a resolution by the U.S. Congress that made AVAM the national repository for visionary art, as well as the center for educational programs dealing with such art, also attended.[48]

The day of the opening started off as a mild fall morning, but as evening arrived, storm clouds formed. Just as the event began, the sky exploded with rain, thunder and lightning. As the tour of the exhibition by Rebecca ended and the guests were crossing the yard to the barn to sit down for a lavish dinner, the rain suddenly changed to snow, accompanied by winds of about twenty to thirty miles per hour. This change in weather was so unusual that it is, no doubt, etched in the memory of all who attended. I like to think of it as having been a good omen – that G-d was showing us his great pleasure for what we had accomplished by exhibiting his own display of beautiful natural phenomena.

Rebecca and me in November 1995 at the opening of AVAM's inaugural exhibition, *Tree of Life*. We are standing in front of a sculpture titled *City Under the Sea*, by the Reverend Albert Wagner.

A portion of the third floor of the museum was designated as space for a restaurant which was to be leased to an owner-operator and be a source of revenue for the museum as well as an amenity for visitors. Since I was on the board of the Davis Funds, Rebecca and I went to Santa Fe at least once a year to attend a board meeting. Having done this for several years, we became familiar with the Santa Fe restaurants, our favorite being The Inn at Anasazi. Its cuisine was nouveau western, a type of cooking that several chefs out west had developed. One of those chefs was Peter Zimmer, who was then chief chef at the Inn.

Both Rebecca and I thought that this type of cuisine, which we did not think had yet surfaced in Baltimore, would be perfect for the AVAM restaurant. Having gotten to know Peter, I asked him if he would be interested in coming to Baltimore to be the chef and half-owner of the restaurant. He said that he was interested so we brought him to Baltimore with his lovely wife to show them the restaurant facility and to let them get a feel for Baltimore. They were both impressed, so he accepted my offer. I then went about establishing an LLC and creating a business plan based on Peter's pro-forma projections of revenues and expenses. It, of course, showed that we could make money, provided I could raise $500,000 to adequately capitalize the venture.

Rebecca had been given an oil painting by one of the outsider artists that showed a nude standing in front of an electric chair. Crudely painted at the top of the picture were the words "Joy America." We both thought that would be a great name for the restaurant. A year or so later, Rebecca had the occasion to see the artist at the museum and she asked him why he had named the painting *Joy America*. "That's not the name," he replied. "The name is *Virgin Standing in Front of the Electric Chair.*"

As I recall, I put in $250,000 and raised the other $250,000 from a group of friends. I must admit – I did not want to be in the restaurant business, having heard too many stories about how hard it was to be successful. Actually, I was cautioned by my brother Stanley, who, together with his wife, Judy, had on two occasions tried to make a go of it in Washington, but failed. Nonetheless, the museum needed a restaurant and I thought because we had selected as the chef someone who had a national reputation for the uniqueness of his cooking, we had a chance of succeeding.

Boy, was I wrong! Although the restaurant was popular and everyone raved about the food, Peter turned out to be totally irresponsible. He always had an excuse for why the costs were higher than budgeted and why he was not paying our bills on time. He lasted about four years,

Both Rebecca and I thought that this type of cuisine, which we did not think had yet surfaced in Baltimore, would be perfect for the AVAM restaurant.

I think, and then I got fed up with the losses that were mounting (and I was paying), so I fired him. His wife, with whom Rebecca and I had become somewhat friendly, understood why I had no choice but to terminate our relationship. She was actually present when I fired him and was totally sympathetic. Her husband had taken an exceptional opportunity to make money as half-owner of what could have been a successful operation and had blown it.

It was a sad departure and a costly one. One of the unsophisticated women investors, whose accountant recommended she invest, thought she should get all of her original investment back, so I returned the $25,000 she had invested out of my own pocket. The other investors, who were businessmen, took their losses graciously. I guess I lost upwards of $500,000 since I had been putting in money, along the way, to meet shortfalls in revenues.

Fortunately, some of the chefs that Peter had trained continued to operate the restaurant until two fellows by the name of Spike and Charlie came along. They had another apparently successful restaurant elsewhere in Baltimore and had been recommended to us by one of our board members who owned the shopping center in which Spike and Charlie had their restaurant.

As it turned out, this plan did not work either, and the restaurant space was, for the first time since we opened, empty. This was, in my opinion, a loss of an important amenity not only for patrons of the museum, but for those who wanted to host private parties there. Nevertheless, I did not miss being in the restaurant business.[49]

Before AVAM opened, I had predicted an average annual shortfall in revenue of about $400,000. I, therefore, devised a plan with Rebecca that I would raise $400,000 a year for five years while she built up the endowment and annual giving. I was successful in getting five-year commitments from a number of foundations and individuals, including myself and the Hoffberger Foundations, to provide this vital infusion

AVAM: east view of cantilevered concrete addition to original exterior of Reeder Building, Baltimore, 1996. Photograph by Alan Gilbert

AVAM: Phase I south view of cantilevered concrete addition covered with tile mosaic artwork by most-at-risk students from Southern High School, 2013. Photograph by Paula Gately Tillman

During that five-year period Rebecca still kept trying to find her "knight in shining armor" who would endow the museum for $25 million.

of operating money. With a substantial gift of Davis stock, I kicked off the endowment campaign, but, unfortunately for the most part, Rebecca's attempts to raise more money were not successful. Neither was her effort to develop annual giving to where it was producing a significant and reliable annual sum.

At the end of the five years, AVAM was unfortunately still about $400,000 in the hole each year. While revenues had increased, so had expenses, although it was amazing how Rebecca had been able to keep such talented staff at salaries less than they could have made elsewhere. They were truly committed to AVAM and, more so, to Rebecca.

Nevertheless, I did not think I could again approach the foundations and individuals that I had previously asked to cover AVAM's annual operating shortfalls, so I turned to the Family Foundations and to myself to cover the entire $400,000 annual shortfall for the next five years. While not enthusiastic to again be covering the museum's operating deficits, the Family Foundations, out of respect for me, came through and agreed to join me in providing $2 million to AVAM over the next five years.

During that five-year period Rebecca still kept trying to find her "knight in shining armor" who would endow the museum for $25 million. Why she felt we needed a $25 million endowment, I do not know, but that was her unshakeable goal. She met and wooed some very rich, well-known personalities who included George Soros; John Lewis, the head of Progressive Insurance and the largest contributor to museums in the country; Rosie O'Donnell, the comedian; Frank

Purdue, the chicken king; and other celebrities. But, none of them came through with any money. Thus, at the end of the second five-year period we were no better off than when we had started ten years previously – except for the amount that I had contributed to the endowment fund.

By this time, Rebecca and I had been married for about fifteen years. During the whole of our marriage, our lives had been wrapped around the development of AVAM. I was now in my seventies, and Rebecca was in her forties. It became clear to both of us that we had different needs and priorities going forward, and our marriage gradually fell apart. I will have more to say about this in the personal section of my memoirs, but I mention it now to shed light on what then took place in terms of my lack of further participation in the affairs of AVAM. I felt that, being separated from Rebecca, it would be awkward for me to continue to serve as chairman of the board, so I resigned.

Furthermore, having given AVAM a significant portion of my entire net worth and having raised many millions from others, including the Hoffberger Foundations, not only for the construction of the museum, but for its operation over its first ten years of existence, I felt that "enough was enough," and that it was now up to Rebecca to carry this burden.

Over many years, AVAM has been the largest recipient of my philanthropy, and it is gratifying to have played a major role in its creation and formative years. It has been acclaimed by the media and many art critics to be a mecca for visionary art and a "fun" place to be, especially for children, attracting audiences young and old from all parts of the U.S., Europe and Asia. It was selected by *Travel + Leisure* magazine as one of the ten best museums in the country (ranking third or fourth) and, subsequently, as the best place to take a child of ten or under, even ahead of the Grand Canyon, Yellowstone and the Statue of Liberty.

Over many years, AVAM has been the largest recipient of my philanthropy, and it is gratifying to have played a major role in its creation and formative years.

Paula and me beside the plaque honoring me for my role as co-founder of the American Visionary Art Museum, Baltimore, 2013. Photograph by Jodi Wille

Several years ago AVAM's board was split over Rebecca's role in the future of the museum. Its differences concerned finances and governance. I was asked to resume my involvement with AVAM for the purpose of bringing stability to the board, and this has been accomplished to a great degree. Now, AVAM is back on its feet, and substantial groundwork has been done toward its institutionalization. Rebecca's imprint of creativity and spirituality will always distinguish AVAM, but to survive, the museum must become a viable organization on its own merit.

FOUNDING OF THE HOFFBERGER FOUNDATION FOR TORAH STUDY INC.

After reading a publication about the anticipated demographics of the worldwide Jewish population over the next fifty years and being concerned that the statistics showed no worldwide growth (except in Israel and the U.K. to a minor extent), I began giving thought to the reasons why this was predicted to occur and what significance it had in a world whose overall population was expanding, particularly among other religions.

I was aware, firsthand, of the growing rate of intermarriage and assimilation of Jews in the U.S. into the non-Jewish community. My first wife, Hildegard, was a Christian who had converted to Judaism, at my request, before we married. Our sons, Jack and Douglas, were B'nai Mitzvah, but were not thereafter interested in Judaism. No doubt, this was, in part, because I had not set an example for my sons that demonstrated that being a religious Jew was important to me and should be to them.

Although (as these memoirs demonstrate) I was involved in just about every Jewish activity imaginable, my participation was primarily of a secular nature. Except for attending shul on the High Holy Days, I had not passed on, in a meaningful way, any Jewish tradition to my children.

The statistics show that many other Jewish parents are guilty of the same neglect that I was. No wonder the demographic data that I had read predicted that more Jews were likely, in the next fifty years, to depart from Judaism than to remain in it.

Could anything be done to stem or slow this rate of attrition? Frankly, I did not see how I or the Foundation could play a role in bringing that about. Personally, I knew that I would remain a committed Jew, but I decided I also wanted to be a knowledgeable one, particularly knowledgeable about Torah. Somehow I felt that the study of Torah would set me on a course of becoming more aware of the essence of

> Personally, I knew that I would remain a committed Jew, but I decided I also wanted to be a knowledgeable one, particularly knowledgeable about Torah.

what Judaism had to offer the world and, on a more personal basis, of what I should understand about what G-d expected of me.

One Monday evening in the fall of 1997 while Rebecca and I were having dinner at home, I was looking through my mail and saw a brochure from Hopkins about continuing education courses. I picked it up and began looking through it. The announcement of a course on the Garden of Eden, being taught by a Rabbi David Fohrman (of whom I had never previously heard), caught my eye so I mentioned it to her.

I am sure that the reason it resonated with me was that Rebecca had, several years previously, bought me my first *Chumash* (Five Books of Moses) translated by a Reform Rabbi by the name of Plaut. I had read the Plaut version of the Torah, in English, cover to cover (well over one thousand pages) several times, together with the commentary. I knew the stories in Genesis and Exodus and in the other books, but only superficially. I could repeat the fairytale-like narratives, but I sensed that they had to have a deeper meaning than I was able to extract, even after reading the commentaries.

Now I would have an opportunity to hear a Biblical scholar (I hoped) tell me what I longed to know: why is the Torah so revered when it seems to be filled with archaic fables that are hard to believe and laws that do not appear to be very relevant? Rebecca and I signed up for the course which was scheduled to be taught on Monday nights at Hopkins from 7:30 to 9 PM.

We arrived on campus on the first Monday evening and were joined by about 15 other adults. We did not know whether all of the other students were Jewish, but suspected that some were not. Rabbi Fohrman was a young man of about thirty, clean-shaven and, except for the fact that he wore a *kipot* (yarmulke), his denomination as a Jew was not evident from his appearance. After the first lecture, I still was not sure whether he was a Conservative or Orthodox rabbi. I assumed that, since he was wearing a *kipot*, he was not likely to be Reform.

Rabbi Fohrman's method for having his students understand the text on a deeper level was to have them focus on textual similarities that reveal otherwise undisclosed meaning. He would also ask the class, "What are the 'elephants in the room'?" – the points in the text that are so obvious that, without understanding their significance, you cannot grasp the true meaning of the story. Once the class had identified these, he would then point out that these issues were what the author of the story (and that is the way he put it, not referring to G-d at all) wanted you to reflect on. Often, however, the language is shrouded in mystery that has to be resolved before the full meaning of the *parashah* (the portion of the Torah being studied) may be revealed.

He (Rabbi Fohrman) would also ask the class: "What are the 'elephants in the room'?"

Rebecca and I came away from the first lecture completely enraptured with the way Rabbi Fohrman lectured. Both of us had heard many lectures by well-known scholars and experts on numerous subjects, but none of them had held our attention as had Rabbi Fohrman. After the second lecture, we were both in love with his ability to enlighten his students with his remarkable knowledge of the Bible without being either pedantic or proselytizing. We both determined that we wanted to know him, personally, as well as possible.

After class, which usually went on at least an hour longer than scheduled, we would walk him to his car, asking him more questions about his lecture. After doing this for about three or four times, I finally asked him what he did for a living, in addition to being an adjunct professor at Hopkins. He said that he was working for ArtScroll, the largest printer of Orthodox books in America, translating (along with eight other rabbis) the Talmud from Aramaic to English. I asked him if he liked what he was doing and he responded: "It's a living." Sensing that he was not altogether enamored with what he was doing, I said: "If you had your druthers, what would you really like to do?" He promptly responded, "Teach!" Knowing by then what a remarkable teacher David was, I said, "Let me see if I can make that possible."

My intention was to try to get the Hoffberger Foundations, together with as many other foundations as possible, to create a new foundation that would engage Rabbi Fohrman, as its full-time scholar-in-residence, to lecture in various informal venues to audiences of Jews who wanted to better understand the deeper meaning of Torah. Of course, I realized that to do this I would have to raise several million dollars, but I felt confident I could.

As usual, this meant that I, personally, would have to make a significant contribution to lead the way. This I did, quite willingly, with a $500,000 contribution in Davis stock. I knew that my next essential task was to bring the two Hoffberger Foundations into this undertaking with a major grant. In order to do that, I thought that I should invite David to lunch with the boards of these Foundations to have him give a short version of one of his lectures. I was hoping that he would excite them with his unique method of teaching Torah, and more importantly, make them aware that the project I was suggesting they support had the potential to make Jews realize that the Torah, when understood, had great relevance to their lives both as Jews and as human beings.

However, knowing that there were no members of the Family who were Orthodox, I was concerned that the mere fact that David was an Orthodox rabbi, educated at Ner Israel Talmudical College, would

After class, which usually went on at least an hour longer than scheduled, we would walk him to his car, asking him more questions about his lecture.

be a strike against their wanting to help fund this venture. I had to have a well-articulated story as to why this undertaking was important, beyond just further educating observant Jews about their religion.

I explained to the boards that the demographics of the North American Jewish Community were discouraging and did not augur well for the future of non-Orthodox denominations. I indicated that not only is the total Jewish population projected to be stagnant at best, but the number of non-Orthodox-affiliated Jews (i.e., those Conservative and Reform Jews affiliated with a synagogue) is projected to decline. I said that intermarriage is taking its toll in that most of the children of these marriages are not being raised as Jews. Furthermore, I explained what should be obvious to our Family: younger Jews are assimilating and their interests are increasingly secular in nature. I explained that under those circumstances, the survival of Judaism, its culture and philosophy, in America is in real jeopardy.

My premise for asking for Family support for this venture was based on my belief that Rabbi Fohrman had the unique ability to relate to non-Orthodox audiences the relevance of Torah to their contemporary lives by making them cognizant of its underlying meaning. I felt that while David's explanations were based on traditional interpretations of the text, there was nothing in his teachings that would be offensive or unacceptable to non-Orthodox Jews.

However, Jerold raised the issue of David's presenting only the traditional interpretation of Torah, i.e., the Orthodox interpretation. Thus, it appeared that my efforts to show him (and perhaps other board members) that David's interpretation was universal to all Jews and that there could be little meaningful disagreement with what he was teaching had evidently not succeeded. No matter how hard I argued, the boards wanted the project to also include programming based on the Conservative and Reform interpretations of Torah.

They therefore decided to make a $500,000 grant to what we decided to call "the Orthodox Division" and two additional grants in the amount of $500,000 each to what would be the Conservative and Reform divisions. Although this was not my original plan for Family participation, I was satisfied that this level of involvement would help me get the total funding I needed to underwrite the cost of engaging David as the scholar-in-residence of a new foundation devoted to the study of Torah.

I then went to the Harry and Jeanette Weinberg Foundation for a $500,000 grant to the Orthodox Division, knowing that the strengthening of the Jewish community, both in Baltimore and elsewhere, was a priority of its members. As I had done with

I had to have a well-articulated story as to why this undertaking was important, beyond just further educating observant Jews about their religion.

the Hoffberger Foundations, I had Rabbi Fohrman give a lecture to its board members. They were duly impressed with his teaching skills and subsequently approved the requested grant.

Now, having enough commitments to engage David, I formed the Hoffberger Foundation for Torah Study Inc. (HFFTS) in December 1998. The bylaws proved to be a challenge to draft, since having three separate operations, each with its own funding, required adapting policies that realistically matched the available funding and the likely method by which each division would fulfill the mission of the Foundation. Only the Orthodox Division had enough money to support a full-time person. The other two divisions, having only the funding of the Hoffberger Foundations, were to work with the local synagogues to develop annual events where Torah would be taught primarily by pulpit rabbis and visiting scholars.

During the course of our relationship, I learned that David's stepfather was a billionaire who had come to the U.S. as a survivor of the Holocaust with "just the shirt on his back." He had settled in New York where, through investments in real estate and the stock market, he had made a huge fortune. David suggested to me that I meet him as perhaps he would be interested in our project. Zev Wolfson, David's stepfather, usually used his great wealth to fund Yeshivas which he created and supported all over the world and particularly in Israel. His conviction was that a young Jew would stay committed to Judaism only if he had a thorough Jewish education. In his opinion, that meant providing him with a Yeshiva education.

I traveled to New York to meet Zev at his office in a magnificent high-rise office building that he owned in the financial district. Zev was very cordial and listened as I explained what I thought his son and I could accomplish through David lecturing wherever invited, but, primarily, to adult audiences of Jews of all denominations. After listening for a while, he said, "I know my son is a great teacher, and that he can 'entertain' an audience with his lectures, but without one-on-one follow-up, I don't believe your program will succeed." I asked him what percentage of Jews he thought he could reach with his philosophy and he replied, "About five percent."

I then asked him, "What about the other 95 percent?" – the ones that I thought his son could influence to be better Jews. Whether I had convinced Zev that our approach was worth a try or he wanted to help David get started, I don't know. Nevertheless, he said that he would make a $500,000 contribution to the Foundation, provided his money was used to provide "follow-up." David thought that could be done, so Zev came on board, or at least we thought he had.

During the course of our relationship, I learned that David's stepfather was a billionaire who had come to the U.S. as a survivor of the Holocaust with "just the shirt on his back."

However, Zev put so many conditions on how he wanted his money to be used that David and I ultimately decided to transfer his funds to Etz Chaim, a nonprofit Orthodox educational organization that provided Jewish educational programs for adults. Etz Chaim hired a rabbi to teach students, one-on-one, about Torah using David's methodology. However, after two years or so, the funds were nearly exhausted and Zev decided not to continue to support the program, which was then discontinued.

Trying to manage his monetary gift was not the only way that Zev injected himself into the affairs of HFFTS. He told me that the investment of our funds in the stock market was not producing the returns that he had obtained through his access to major, much sought-after hedge funds. By investing our funds in a certain hedge fund that had produced substantial annual returns for him, he claimed he would produce annual returns of 20%–30%. I told him that I did not think that hedge funds would be a prudent investment for a foundation to make and that I would have to check with our tax lawyer, Thor Halverson, of Covington & Burling. Thor confirmed my position, which I conveyed to Zev. When informed of Thor's opinion, Zev said: "What if I guarantee the Foundation against any loss of its investment?" I asked Thor if that would change his opinion, and he said that it would. Thor then prepared a guaranty agreement which Zev signed.

As it turned out, the hedge fund recommended by Zev did poorly and Zev, on two occasions, had to reimburse the Foundation. What was worse, the hedge fund had made certain off-shore investments that produced "business income" that was taxable to the Foundation.

Two years of losses were enough, and I told Zev we were withdrawing our investment in the hedge fund. He could hardly object and, as a matter of fact, he withdrew his own funds. I then decided that the burden of investing the funds was something I did not want, so knowing that the Consolidated Investment Fund (CIF) of The Associated Jewish Community Federation of Baltimore had a good long-term track record, I turned our entire endowment over to it. That turned out to be a wise decision. After about ten years of having been invested in the CIF, the market value of the Foundation's total assets is in excess of the original amounts committed by the donors. This was after having withdrawn five percent a year as income for operations since the Foundation's inception in 1999.

In addition, in order to cover the expenses of the Orthodox Division, which exceeded the income that the bylaws permitted to be withdrawn from the endowment, I agreed that to the extent of any shortfall in the

As it turned out, the hedge fund recommended by Zev did poorly and Zev, on two occasions, had to reimburse the Foundation.

annual income of the Orthodox Division of the Foundation, I would allow the Foundation to invade the corpus of my endowment fund (which then substantially exceeded my initial contribution of $500,000) to cover the excess. We were paying David about $100,000 per year, including his health coverage for his family, and the Foundation was earning about $70,000, so the withdrawal from my endowment was an annual event. As of December 31, 2010, the market value of my endowment just exceeded $500,000. Therefore, I feel good that I managed to cover these annual shortfalls without invading the amount of the original grant that I had made.

So much for the ups and downs of the financing of Rabbi Fohrman's tenure as the scholar-in-residence of the Orthodox Division, which ultimately became known as the Hoffberger Institute to avoid distinguishing it as "Orthodox." From 1999 to 2010, David lectured primarily in Baltimore, but on occasion elsewhere as his reputation grew. Many of his local lectures were held in the basement of Rebecca's and my home, where thirty to forty adults would come on Monday evenings. His fascinating lectures covered mostly portions of Genesis and Exodus, but also included the story of Samuel, the prophet, and the kingship of Saul, the first king of Israel, and his downfall. David spent a full year lecturing on the Book of Job, probing with us its hard-to-fathom meaning. I took copious notes of each lecture, as I had learned to do in law school, and never once dozed off!

David also created a website for the Foundation on which he put the lectures he had recorded at my home and elsewhere. Since all of the topics David covered usually required more than one lecture, he would serialize the lectures in a manner where in one lecture he would raise an issue concerning the text that was problematic, help his audience discover the solution and in doing so, identify yet another mystery that arose in the text – the solution of which would be presented in the following week's lecture. He also presented the material in a way that the series constituted a course for which he had an outline and source material. The material could be downloaded and the outline obtained by the listener if a fee was paid to HFFTS through PayPal. Since the fee was very reasonable, the Foundation did not receive much revenue from this venture, but the program was nevertheless successful in sustaining the interest of a large number of web viewers.

There was no doubt that David's material and his method of teaching the meaning of the text of the Torah were having an impact on a broad audience that were viewing and listening to our website. David was also reaching high school students by lecturing in Orthodox Jewish day schools. More importantly, he was lecturing at teacher seminars where

From 1999 to 2010, David lectured primarily in Baltimore, but on occasion elsewhere as his reputation grew.

he was able to educate master teachers how to do what he did if they followed his outline and used his teaching technique. This was a full load for David to handle and, as requests for his appearance increased, the demands on his time became overwhelming. Therefore, we had to decide in what venues and forms David's talents would have the most lasting effect and reach the greatest number of Jews in the long term.

The conclusion we came to was that teaching over the Web gave the Foundation access to a very broad audience around the world. Also, instead of teaching individual students and adults, educating teachers to teach like he did would have a tremendous rippling effect. The third thing we concluded was that, by writing books that replicated his lectures, David would leave a lasting legacy of his mastery of discovering and conveying the hidden meaning of the text of the Torah.

David had already been working on his first book, *The Beast that Crouches at the Door,* which dealt with the stories of the Garden of Eden and Cain and Abel and their relationship. Where better to start his career as an author than in the beginning of Genesis? It took a while for David to be able to express himself in writing like he did verbally. Once he achieved this, his first book read just like you were attending one of his lectures. Each chapter presented a facet of the Biblical text that needed interpretation which David so ably provided, while at the same time exposing another aspect of the text that had to be probed in the next chapter. By the end of each of the Biblical stories, David had woven together the numerous subplots and their explanations to reveal to the reader a message of profound significance.

When the manuscript was ready for publication, David and I had to make a decision concerning the appropriate publisher of the book. The decision was not an easy one because, as David explained to me, each publisher of Jewish books had a reputation that would make a book published by it acceptable to one type of Jewish audience and not another. If the book were published by ArtScroll, for instance, it would be read by the Orthodox, but not by other Jewish denominations, nor by the general public. Other publishers were likewise problematic in that they might have the reputation of publishing books that were not considered scholarly. David wanted a publisher that he felt was not tainted with any of these ideological biases.

Somewhere, he heard of an Israeli publishing company by the name of Simcha Publishing Company, owned by a man named Yaacov Peterseil. Simcha Publishing seemed to be accepted as a publisher of scholarly books that, while "kosher," would not be read by just Orthodox Jews but by Jews of other denominations and by the general public. I

The conclusion we came to was that teaching over the Web gave the Foundation access to a very broad audience around the world.

engaged Covington & Burling to prepare the contract, since dealing with intellectual rights can be complicated. I wanted to be sure that the Foundation's copyrights to the books were fully protected and that David's rights as the author were, too.

The first order of the book consisted of 3,000 copies, which may not seem like many books, but is considered an optimistic number for an unknown Jewish author. Unfortunately, Simcha did not have the distribution channels that it claimed it did, and this became an impediment from the beginning. Despite this, David's book got such rave reviews by recognized Jewish book reviewers that sales took off beyond our expectations. After several years, the 3,000 copies were sold out so the Foundation placed an order for a second printing of 3,000 books.

Again, Simcha became a problem. We were supposed to get reports on sales on a regular basis, but this did not happen. Worse, when we got the reports, they had obviously understated the sales. But, the last straw was Simcha's failure to pay the Foundation the royalties that had been agreed to. I was livid and made several threatening calls to Yaacov, stating that suit was imminent. I got nowhere, so I hired Laurie Self, the Covington lawyer who had negotiated the contract, to also threaten him – again to no avail. It soon became obvious to me that Simcha was in serious financial trouble and on the verge of bankruptcy.

By this time, it was determined that 4,400 books had been sold. That left 1,600 books that should be in Simcha's possession. After several calls to Yaacov, I was able to get him to agree to send me the 1,600 remaining books in full settlement of all unpaid royalties, which I think amounted to about $15,000. Yaacov kept his word (almost) and shipped the Foundation 1,500 books, asking that he be allowed to retain 100 to be able to fill some orders. While we had all of the books in print, we did not have the capability to distribute them to bookstores when they ran out. In order to have some books on hand as he received requests, David would acquire several boxes at a time from HFFTS at an agreed-upon price.

While from a financial point of view the Foundation did not do too well on the sale of David's book, I took great pride in the fact that David's first book had achieved literary acclaim. It was a finalist for the National Book Council's "Jewish Book of the Year" award, the first scholarly book on Torah to ever have that distinction. When the news reached me that *The Beast that Crouches at the Door* was the runner-up, and David had informed his family of the book's success, I received a telephone call from his mother, for whom I have always had great respect and with whom I had excellent rapport.

> While from a financial point of view the Foundation did not do too well on the sale of David's book, I took great pride in the fact that David's first book had achieved literary acclaim.

I will never forget that call. With great emotion and sincerity, she told me that she attributed her son's success to my having faith in him and making it possible for him to have the financial resources and moral support to enable him to spend time writing. I thanked her for her expression of gratitude and inquired how Zev felt about David's accomplishment. She put him on the phone, and I asked him. When he said "proud," I felt that I had won a real victory as there was no one more skeptical than Zev of what we were trying to achieve.

The recognition given to David's book (which as I have explained was a written form of his lectures) by the National Book Council validated the impact that his method of teaching had. In addition, David received hundreds of emails from all over the world, praising him for having shed new light on the interpretation of these two stories that obviously resonated with both Jews and non-Jews. The fact that Christians also reacted favorably to David's interpretation of these stories showed me the universality of their meaning.

In 2008, David had been the scholar-in-residence of HFFTS for about ten years, a part of which he had spent in Israel with his family on loan to the Ministry of Education to revise the teaching of Torah and Talmud in the Orthodox school system there, using his methodology. When he returned, he decided that it would be best for his family to live in the New York area since some of his children required special education not available in Baltimore. Thus, he had to resign as an employee of HFFTS. While this was a tremendous setback for the Foundation, I had no intention of letting David cease having a relationship with me personally and with HFFTS.

Fortunately for David, his brother Aaron was a member of a newly formed nonprofit foundation called Arevim, whose mission was to further the Jewish learning of young Jews who had participated in "Birthright Israel," which sponsored a several-week study tour of Israel for young Jewish leaders. As a matter of fact, those persons who were funding the Birthright endeavor were the core members of this new foundation. With resources of $100 million, it could afford to hire David at a much higher salary, thereby enabling him to cover his much higher expense of living in Woodmere, Long Island, where he rented (now owns) a home.

The great literary success of *The Beast that Crouches at the Door* reinforced both David's and my belief that his legacy would be the books he would write. With this in mind, David was encouraged to promptly start on his second book. The subject that David said he had chosen for his next book was the story of Joseph and his brothers which, in lecture

> The great literary success of *The Beast that Crouches at the Door* reinforced both David's and my belief that his legacy would be the books he would write.

form, was an intriguing story dealing with sibling rivalry and Joseph's (as well as our) ability to forgive when a grave wrong had been done to him (us).

However, as it turned out, David put that book on hold, for he had developed a more passionate interest in delving into the Book of Esther, for surprising reasons that the new book reveals. While at the Foundation, he had done a series of lectures on this subject that unraveled a story where miraculous coincidences (G-d's name is not mentioned in the entire story) turned what was intended to be the tragic end of the Jewish people, as plotted by the villainous Haman, into a glorious victory, due to the intervention of Queen Esther with King Ahashuvarus, at the risk of her life. The story reads like a fairytale, but when the nuances of the story are explained by David, it takes on a new meaning. Thus, he titled the book *The Queen You Thought You Knew.*[50]

When I asked David why he had switched his interest in writing from Joseph to Esther, he told me that the Book of Esther, while a separate story, is closely tied in with the story of Joseph and his brothers. He added that there will be a third book about the story of Joseph, creating a trilogy.

> Distance sometimes has a negative effect on relationships, but David and I believe we have a bond that makes us inseparable.

Distance sometimes has a negative effect on relationships, but David and I believe we have a bond that makes us inseparable. We stay in touch and explore ways in which HFFTS can continue to avail itself of his talents. For example, the board of HFFTS approved a grant that enables David to produce state-of-the-art videos for the Internet to be used by master teachers (using his methodology) for teaching a course on Genesis to Advanced Placement students. Following their successful completion of this course (in which David will participate directly in the classroom and remotely via other videos he has produced for the Internet) students will receive three college credits at many colleges.

In concluding this story on my founding of the Hoffberger Foundation for Torah Study, I want to share what has been for me the most important personal aspect of this undertaking. My initial motivation for creating the Foundation was to enable as many Jews as possible to be exposed to David's meaningful interpretation of Biblical text. It was my (and the Foundation's) hope that this would motivate them to become more committed Jews. To be completely honest, my own interest was initially more intellectual than religious. However, after I attended a number of David's lectures (usually held at Rebecca's and my home, as I have previously said), the religious aspect of what David was explaining became more and more significant to me.

One evening, when David was lecturing on the portion of Genesis in which Moses, after being asked by G-d to lead the Jews out of Egypt, asks G-d, "Who shall I say sent me?" David explained the meaning of all of the names G-d reveals he is known as. I was so awestruck by his explanation that I had an epiphany – the nature of which was that G-d does (unquestionably) exist and that he authored the Torah on Mt. Sinai.

I would not describe myself as an agnostic prior to that moment. I just had not given G-d much thought. I felt that during my adult life, I was doing what I had been told as a child – primarily by my parents – were the right things to do. Furthermore, I was giving back to my community in numerous ways, as Grandmother Sarah Hoffberger had instructed my father and his brothers to do. That there were religious reasons for my acts of kindness, let alone that I was pursuing G-d's commandments, had not been foremost in my mind; common sense told me that to be a decent and responsible person one did those things.

But, from that moment on, I had no doubt in my mind and heart that the G-d of Abraham, Isaac and Jacob, who created heaven and earth, and man in his likeness, existed and that he had given the Jewish people the Torah. It was from David's explanation of that portion of Genesis and from his explanations of numerous other *parashot* (portions) of the Torah that my belief in G-d became ingrained.

Yes, I have become a much more observant Jew. But, it is not the fact that I now attend shul (synagogue) nearly every Shabbos and observe many of the Jewish holidays that gives me a feeling of indebtedness to David. Rather, it is his having given me a profound belief in G-d. David did not intentionally seek to make an observant Jew of me, but by enlightening me about the meaning of Torah, through his brilliant analysis of the text, he gave me an abiding faith in my Creator. The peace that I now have as a result of his teachings is immeasurable.[51]

ALZHEIMER'S DISEASE THREATENS

I Bring Hopkins and The Associated Together to Tackle the Problem

My last recollection, and my most recent project, involves once again my ongoing connection with The Associated. It concerns what I believe may turn out to be a significant contribution to the well-being of not only the Baltimore Jewish Community, but of all communities in the U.S. and elsewhere. While this may sound a bit grandiose, the ramifications of what I am about to articulate could truly affect the lives of millions of persons, primarily in the "boomer generation" of America (those born after World War II up until about 1964).

The first of the "boomers" reached 65 in 2011, and the rise of dementia in epidemic proportions, primarily in the form of Alzheimer's disease, had begun. At age 65, one in ten persons will contract Alzheimer's disease; at age 75, three in ten will have the disease; and at age 90, one in two will have some form of dementia. There are estimated to be ninety million "boomers." That means that, at the time I am writing this, hundreds of thousands of our aging population have the onset of Alzheimer's disease.

It is estimated that only 30% of these persons will end up in some sort of assisted living or nursing facility and that 70% will remain in the community to be taken care of by family members or by paid professional caregivers. Little or no Medicare or Medicaid is available to help finance this care. To date, no community in America has developed a comprehensive, state-of-the-art model of care with which community-based agencies may help those with Alzheimer's disease to maximize the period of time they can remain in the community, safely and with dignity. Having become aware of this, I decided that I wanted to play a role in seeking a solution to this horrendous problem.

Having become aware of this, I decided that I wanted to play a role in seeking a solution to this horrendous problem.

As it happened, I learned that The Johns Hopkins Medical Institutions, Department of Geriatric Psychiatry and Memory Center, located on the Bayview Campus, had developed a comprehensive model of care for Alzheimer's patients who were residents of a facility known as Copper Ridge Nursing Home, an Episcopal-sponsored undertaking. The model has been scientifically proven to be effective in slowing the progression of cognitive loss and in improving the care given at Copper Ridge. The plan had been developed by a medical research team led by Dr. Constantine Lyketsos, the chief of psychiatry at the Bayview Campus of The Johns Hopkins Medical Institutions and a friend.

Dr. Lyketsos had been my psychiatrist almost since Dr. Schnaper stopped seeing private patients, and I have established a very good relationship with him. It was this relationship that serendipitously gave rise to our cooperating in a scientific study called MIND@HOME The goal of the study was to determine how much longer Alzheimer's patients could stay in the community if they periodically used community-based agencies whose personnel were trained by Hopkins to provide state-of-the-art care. While I was aware that Dr. Lyketsos' specialty was in geriatric psychiatry, I did not know about his expertise in Alzheimer's care. Nor did he know of my fifty years of lay interest and activity in care for the elderly.

It was only as a result of a casual conversation with the man who had sold Rebecca and me his home that I found out about the model of institutional care for Alzheimer's patients that Dr. Lyketsos had developed.

The person with whom I was speaking was on the board of the Copper Ridge Institute, which is a joint venture between the local Episcopal Church's nonprofit medical research organization and Hopkins, specifically created to sponsor Dr. Lyketsos' work.

The next time that I had the occasion to see Dr. Lyketsos, I informed him of my lifetime interest in care for the elderly and mentioned that I would like to visit Copper Ridge and learn more about what he described as the coming "epidemic" of Alzheimer's disease. Accordingly, we set a date for me to tour Copper Ridge, which is in Sykesville, Maryland.

I was greatly impressed both with the facility, which had a home-like environment, and with the quality of the care and personal attention provided by the nursing staff for the residents, who were all in various stages of the disease.

Soon thereafter, I met with Dr. Lyketsos and his staff, as well as the administrator of the facility. Dr. Lyketsos asked me if I would be willing to get involved in raising money for the Institute; I immediately consented. What I had in mind was for the Institute to franchise nursing homes throughout the country and to permit licensed facilities to use the Hopkins name (like the Good Housekeeping Seal of Approval) if they adopted the Hopkins model of care. Hopkins had already selected several regional nursing homes as "testing grounds" for its program and was distributing DVDs and manuals to various nursing homes around the country. I began to meet with the Hopkins development personnel to flesh out how Hopkins should further pursue this endeavor.

However, as sometimes happens, as you learn more about a problem, you realize that your attention has been focused on only one aspect of the issue, in this case on nursing home care, which though important, is dwarfed by the magnitude of the need for community-based care. What Hopkins had accomplished at Copper Ridge was certainly noteworthy, but why had it not also directed its attention to developing a plan for the 70% of those with Alzheimer's disease who will remain in the community?

When I asked Dr. Lyketsos this very question, he replied that, in order for the development of a community-based model of care to be of interest to Hopkins, it would have to be scientifically valid so that it could be replicated throughout the country. He said that demographic data would have to be obtained on a significant portion of the

What I had in mind was for the Institute to franchise nursing homes throughout the country and to permit licensed facilities to use the Hopkins name (like the Good Housekeeping Seal of Approval) if they adopted the Hopkins model of care.

population to be studied and that, unfortunately, the existing U.S. census does not contain the information he would need. Furthermore, he added, the government had clearly indicated that it did not have the funds for Hopkins to do a special demographic study on a large segment of the population. Thus, he concluded that, unless private funding could be obtained to gather that information, which would cost millions, such a study could not be undertaken.

Out of curiosity, I asked him what kind of demographic data he needed. He listed a number of items ranging from medical to socioeconomic information. In a very matter-of-fact way that I knew would startle him, I responded: "I can obtain that information on the Jewish Community of Baltimore." "How is that?" he asked.

I then began to explain that every major Jewish community in North America (including Canada) does a scientifically valid sampling of its Jewish population every ten years and that The Associated had that information on the ninety thousand Jews in Baltimore. Needless to say, being Greek Orthodox, he had no idea that the Jews of North America deemed that such information is so important to our well-being as a community that we would spend millions of dollars to obtain it.

Naturally, Dr. Lyketsos was quite excited, and he asked if I could put him in touch with the right people at The Associated to see if it would share that information with him. More importantly, he asked me whether I thought The Associated might be interested in having its agencies that dealt with the elderly participate in a study (that would be the first of its kind as far as he knew) that would seek to determine whether, through a joint effort between The Associated and Hopkins, a community-based model of care could be developed and tested that would scientifically determine if such a model would prolong the period persons with Alzheimer's disease could remain in the community. I answered "yes" to both questions.

I called Marc Terrill, the president of The Associated, and told him what Dr. Lyketsos would like to propose. Marc was interested, and shortly thereafter, a meeting was arranged between Dr. Lyketsos and some of the professionals of The Associated's agencies that render various kinds of services to the Jewish elderly. It was obvious from the beginning that The Associated and Hopkins had a compelling common purpose in joining forces. However, one important element of the study was missing: i.e., how much would the study cost and where would the money come from to do it?

Having played a major role in bringing these two institutions together to deal with a disease that was about to plague America's elderly, I could not resist volunteering to undertake the fundraising responsibility, provided the cost of the study was not prohibitive. I asked Dr. Lyketsos to do a detailed analysis of what would be required to accomplish our goal and then to estimate what the cost of the project would be.

As I recall, it took about two months to produce the first draft of the plan and its cost. I could not, of course, judge the adequacy of the plan, but when I saw the cost, I told him frankly that I did not think that I could raise the amount he believed was needed – over $4 million. He agreed to reexamine the plan and when he did, he found that there were redundancies that, when eliminated, would significantly reduce the estimate. Consequently, he reworked the plan and came up with a two-phase project, estimated at about $2.25 million, payable over the five-year period of the project.

When I learned of the revised number, my "gut" told me I could do it, and I am not speaking figuratively. It may sound strange, but during my entire fundraising career, whenever I literally get a certain pleasant feeling in my stomach, I feel confident that the cause is right and that I can convince others to join me in financially backing the endeavor I fervently believe in.

Out of pride, I decided that I would limit, if possible and feasible, my solicitation to the Jewish Community. The Baltimore Jewish Federation would then not only make it possible for our Baltimore Jewish Community to be the first in North America to have developed a viable plan to provide community-wide care for its Alzheimer's victims, but this plan could also become the model for other communities, Jewish and non-Jewish.

I first approached the Hoffberger Foundation and Hoffberger Family Fund to join forces with me, personally, to make a significant commitment to the funding of Phase I of the study. In Phase I, Hopkins was to do some preliminary testing of the concept with The Associated, as a result of which it could establish the protocols for the full-blown study to be done in Phase II. The Family committed about $150,000 to this initial part of the five-year study. I then obtained additional funding from The Lois and Irving Blum Foundation which, together with my personal contribution, was sufficient to cover the cost of Phase I.

Phase I began in 2006 and took about 12 to 18 months to complete. Its findings were totally supportive of proceeding with Phase II. I then went to the Harry and Jeanette Weinberg Foundation for a challenge grant to enable me to raise the approximately $2 million needed to fund the clinical testing. Since care for the elderly is one of its main interests, the

Out of pride, I decided that I would limit, if possible and feasible, my solicitation to the Jewish Community.

professional staff of the Weinberg Foundation crafted a commitment that amounted to a contingent $600,000 grant, payable over three years, provided I was successful in meeting certain annual dollar hurdles. Armed with this pledge, I then set out to solicit other Jewish foundations that I had previously gotten to participate in cooperative projects.

To my great disappointment, the two foundations that I felt would certainly be interested turned me down, saying that research was not their mission. While this was a setback, I was by no means discouraged. I then went to The David and Barbara B. Hirshhorn Foundation, The Leonard and Helen Stulman Charitable Foundation, The Joseph and Harvey Meyerhoff Family Charitable Funds and The Henry and Ruth Rosenberg Foundation, all of which agreed to participate.

At this point, with commitments for about $1.1 million, I could have continued to seek more participation from other Jewish foundations and individuals. However, it dawned on me that ultimately public participation at the state and federal levels would certainly be necessary to implement the model of care that would evolve from the study. I realized that if I could get some state and local governmental support for the study, the more likely it would be that subsequent grant money to implement the plan would be forthcoming from the federal government.

Alas, the economy had just tanked, big time, and governmental jurisdictions were suffering from budget shortages. Nevertheless, Baltimore County, where much of the Jewish population in the Greater Baltimore area is currently located, was not in as bad shape as the State and Baltimore City. Furthermore, the Baltimore County Commission on Aging, under the chairmanship of Arnold Eppel, had already been participating on the advisory committee of the study, and Arnold had indicated that he strongly agreed with my conclusions about the advantage of government (public) participation in the project.

Arnold offered to talk to Jim Smith, the then-county executive, about the project and to request that Jim put $200,000 into his budget to support it. He set up a meeting for Dr. Lyketsos and me to explain to Jim why county participation was important. Jim agreed with our rationale and agreed to put an item in his budget for $100,000. With the support of Kevin Kamenetz, the head of the County Council, the $100,000 grant to the Commission on Aging was approved and was actually forthcoming.

Although I tried to get the governor to include the final $200,000 needed to complete the funding of the project in the state budget, I never had any indication that the legislature ever considered it. How sad that the state missed an opportunity to access federal research

I realized that if I could get some state and local governmental support for the study, the more likely it would be that subsequent grant money to implement the plan would be forthcoming from the federal government.

funding by leveraging off of the private sector's major contribution toward establishing a plan to deal with the coming epidemic of Alzheimer's disease!

Due to the difficulty Hopkins was having in obtaining the three hundred participants needed for the study, Phase II of the project was delayed. Thus, I had more time in which to raise the final $285,000 needed to obtain the third installment of the Weinberg grant. I now launched a campaign directed at those remaining foundations and philanthropic funds of The Associated that I had not solicited.

Although I sought donations from every source I could think of, I was unable to raise the final $200,000 needed for completion of the study.

Although I sought donations from every source I could think of, I was unable to raise the final $200,000 needed for completion of the study. Needless to say, I was not going to see this project founder, so I willingly stepped up to the plate and contributed a total of $212,000 even though I had to borrow a portion from the bank.

Phase II of the MIND@HOME Project was concluded at the end of 2011, as scheduled, and the final report was submitted. When I read the findings of the study, I was, in one important instance, unable to reconcile what the report found to be of substantial significance with what my initial expectations were.

The report revealed that of "significant" importance was the finding that the difference in the period of time that a person with Alzheimer's disease, who had received the benefits of the Hopkins intervention, remained in his/her home was 51 days. When Dr. Lyketsos and I originally discussed the project, we were thinking in terms of six months or more. Thus, I wrote to Dr. Lyketsos, expressing my feeling that the study was groundbreaking but also asking him to explain why the finding that I have just alluded to was so significant. I also asked him whether the "in-home" period might have been longer if the study had been longer (as was originally intended).

In response, he pointed out that a 51-day difference has significant financial implications when the average cost of a day in a nursing

Dr. Constantine Lyketsos, Chief of Psychiatry, Bayview Campus, presenting me with the 2009 Ambassador Award for my leadership in supporting the Johns Hopkins MIND@HOME Alzheimer's research project. Photograph by Paula Gately Tillman

home for Alzheimer's patients is $200–250. The importance of this is certainly true on an individual basis, but will be much more so to the government as millions of "boomers" contract the disease and look to the government to carry the cost of care. Dr. Lyketsos also picked up on my question concerning whether there is a correlation between the length of time of the study and the length of time that the study showed a person with Alzheimer's disease could (with community agencies' intervention) safely and with dignity remain at home. He definitely felt that there was a likely correlation and that hopefully the hiring by Hopkins of one of the care coordinators involved in Phase II for an additional year would shed more clinical light on this. This indication pleased me and I suspected it would likewise please the other donors to this project. The money needed to pay for the care coordinator was provided by the Hoffberger Foundation.

Not to be overlooked is an anecdotal finding gleaned from conversations with the one hundred-plus participants, who received the Hopkins intervention. Not only were they able to remain at home longer, but they had a better quality of life, which contributed significantly to their dignity and sense of well-being.

It is now 2012, and the additional information collected from the data developed by the care coordinator, who continued to see patients during the year extension of her involvement, showed that the group receiving the Hopkins intervention could remain in the community well over one hundred additional days. Thus, after six years of research and cooperation between The Associated and Hopkins, a scientifically valid (and replicable) quantification of the positive effect of a community-based model of care has evolved. Its ramifications should garner the attention of the federal government and result in grants to help implement the findings of this highly significant study.

SERVICE ON THE BOARDS OF OTHER NONPROFITS

The above recollections do not complete the story of my communal career, but they do set forth in considerable detail those organizations where my participation did, in my opinion, make a difference. There were other boards on which I served that I think I should mention. These include: The University of Maryland Medical System, The University of Maryland Graduate School of Social Work, The University of Maryland School of Law, The Baltimore Community Foundation, The Maryland School for the Blind, The Gilman School, The Zanvyl

> Not only were they able to remain at home longer, but they had a better quality of life, which contributed significantly to their dignity and sense of well-being.

and Isabelle Krieger Fund (the first support foundation), The Gil Fox Foundation and The Kolker Foundation.

I am sure there are other events in my communal life that I cannot at this moment call to mind. Not discussed in these memoirs are a myriad of occasions where I have helped friends and persons unknown to me (before they asked for help). Usually the help requested was financial, but not always. I feel no further need to test my ability to recall or reveal further acts of service and "loving-kindness."

SUMMARY OF MY COMMUNAL AND PHILANTHROPIC LIFE

As I review the episodes of communal and philanthropic activity that I have chosen to recount, I am mindful of the great variety of causes that became the focus of my interest and to which, in most instances, I became passionately committed. Some were religious and some secular; some were long-standing, and some I founded. Suffice it to say that apparently where I sensed that my participation in helping to meet a need could make a difference, I did not hesitate to devote my time, energy and money to try to make it happen.

What I have set forth gives me great comfort and a feeling of satisfaction that I have helped make my community, and perhaps the world, a better place in which to live. Notwithstanding, I look forward to remaining active in some of the undertakings that I have described above and to finding new ways in which I can contribute to the well-being of my community and humanity in general.

> What I have set forth gives me great comfort and a feeling of satisfaction that I have helped make my community, and perhaps the world, a better place in which to live.

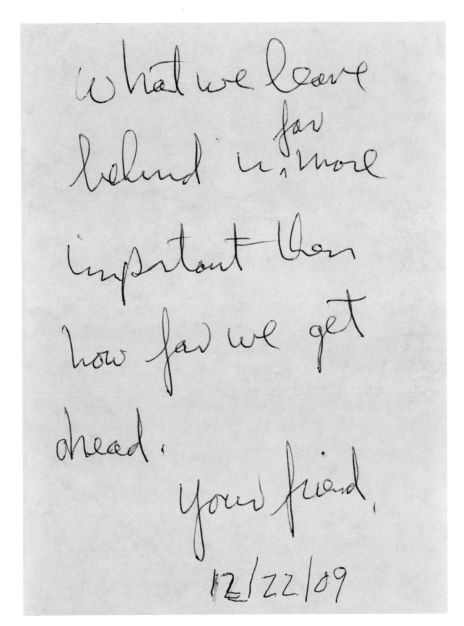

What we leave behind is far more important than how far we get ahead.

Your friend,

12/22/09

A proverb of mine

MY PERSONAL LIFE

5

INTRODUCTION

Except for the beginning of these memoirs where I have traced my childhood, reviewed my educational and military experiences and dealt with my chronic depression, I have occupied myself with detailing episodes and events in my business/professional and communal life. In dealing with my personal life, I am going to discuss relationships and personal interests as well as speculate about the meaning of my life.

MY PROLONGED BACHELORHOOD

When I returned from Princeton to go to the University of Maryland Law School in 1947, I spent most of my time either working part-time for Uncle Sam or studying. However, on the weekends, I tried to relax and have fun, which meant joining a group of four or five other bachelor friends, ages 21 to 22, to do some bar hopping.

The group consisted of Irv Tarlow, who had served in the infantry in Europe and was working (unhappily) for his father in the fur business; Leonard Sachs, who had served in the Air Force in Europe and was working (unhappily) for his father in the wholesale women's clothing business; Norman Bear, who had served in the Engineers Corps in Europe and was working (unhappily) for his uncle in managing several movie theaters; Buddy Marcus, who had been in the Army Air Corps and was working (unhappily) in his family's coat manufacturing business; and me, who had served in the V-12 Navy Officer's Program and was going to law school (because I was asked to do so, not because I wanted to).

I guess there were two things we had in common. We were all, in varying degrees, not very fulfilled with what we were doing, and none of us had a serious girlfriend. Hanging out at our favorite bars gave us the opportunity to have some laughs together, and getting high let us forget the boredom of the work we were doing during the week. And if we were really lucky, it gave us the opportunity to meet some girls.

There were three or four places, most of which were located on North Charles Street, north of the Washington Monument, that became our favorite watering holes and dining spots. A few of the bars were nightclubs (Club Charles) with shows that featured up-and-coming great comedians like Dean Martin and Jerry Lewis and Buddy Hackett, as well as old-timers like Milton Berle and Sophie Tucker. However, most of the spots we frequented (Chesapeake Restaurant, Harvey House,

> Hanging out at our favorite bars gave us the opportunity to have some laughs together, and getting high let us forget the boredom of the work we were doing during the week.

Eager House, the Owl Room at the Belvedere) were where many of the "young Jewish singles" met to eat, drink and have fun.

But where our male group would hang out was most often determined by where a bartender by the name of Phil Burke was working. Phil stuttered terribly, but he turned his stuttering into a comic routine known as "double-talk." When he couldn't pronounce a word, he would make up a word that sounded like it might have meaning, but which really didn't. He combined his "double-talk" with an outrageous sense of humor that kept our group and others, who knew of his talents, falling off of our bar stools with laughter. As Phil changed jobs (usually going to bars/restaurants which we already frequented), his new place of employment became our number one hang-out.

The great Louis Armstrong and me during a break in his jazz performance at a DC nightclub, 1950. Photograph by Irv Tarlow

Phil was more than just a fun guy to be around; because of his winning personality, he was someone you wanted as a friend. Phil's parents were Irish-American, working-class people who were devout Catholics. They had four children, three boys and one girl. All were educated in Catholic schools and, like their parents, were devoutly Catholic – that is, except Phil. While proud of his younger brother, Bill, who became a priest (and then a Monsignor) and his sister, Mary, who became a nun, Phil's Catholic upbringing had much less influence on how he chose to live his life. It was rather the environment outside of his home and church, the War and his speech impediment (most assuredly) that shaped Phil's personality and character.

First, the fact that the Burkes chose to live in the almost entirely Jewish neighborhood of Park Circle (lower Park Heights Avenue) had a marked effect on Phil's thinking about the "other." As a Gentile living among Orthodox Jews, Phil grew up hearing Yiddish (some of which he picked up) and seeing how his Orthodox neighbors observed their religion. At the request of his Orthodox neighbors, Phil, as a youngster, would do the chores for them that Orthodox Jews cannot do on the Sabbath, as work is forbidden on that day.

Second, most of Phil's young friends were Jewish kids who lived in the neighborhood. As described by Phil, each one of them was a character whom Phil could mimic and would incorporate into his comic routines. They must have all been free thinkers whose lifestyle suited Phil more than the conventional wisdom of parents, teachers and clergy.

When Phil turned 18, he enlisted in the Navy not so much for patriotic reasons, I suspect, but because seeing the world outside of Park Circle must have had great appeal. Phil served for several years and wherever he was, I am sure his "double talk" routines made him popular with his fellow "swabs" and officers.

Phil Burke – comedian,
bartender and friend, 1950

While stationed on the Bainbridge Naval Base outside of Baltimore in Harford County, he met a character by the name of Jackie Edelstein from Philadelphia, who had returned to the U.S. from serving overseas on an aircraft carrier as a Navy aerial photographer. One night at The Harvey House, where Phil was tending bar, he excitedly yelled to me (pointing to a nice-looking, somewhat balding fellow about my age): "Roy, Roy! This is the guy I have been telling you about, who was in the Navy with me." He then introduced me to Jackie. This was the beginning of a long friendship and a period in my bachelorhood where I spent time every weekend in Philadelphia during the winter and in Ocean City, New Jersey, during the summer.

Phil and I developed a great friendship that lasted for many years until his death. He taught me how to "lighten up," even though his own life was full of problems, usually financial. We both realized that being a bartender had no long-term future for him. Then one day he told me that he had an opportunity to lease a defunct bar on Maryland Avenue, not far from where our gang usually hung out. He, of course, had no money to buy the liquor license or to make the improvements needed to meet city code requirements. As I recall, the cost was about $30,000.

I told Phil that I would help him and that I would see if some of the other fellows would do likewise. As it ended up, Buddy Marcus, my brother Stanley and I each put up $10,000. Phil was, of course, elated, and soon he was behind the bar in a place of his own. Because of his notoriety, Phil's Bar became a success overnight. While it was pretty run-down, everyone in town wanted to see and hear Phil do his stuff. So, on the weekends, there was usually a line outside waiting to get in. Phil had to hire other bartenders to help out while he entertained the crowd. Therein was the beginning of his downfall.

Phil put in a jukebox with all of the latest rock and roll records, and despite there being little space to move, much less dance, people began dancing to the records. This was a "no-no," as it constituted "entertainment" under the liquor laws, which therefore required Phil to have a different type of license and to pay an "Entertainment Tax." Knowing this, Phil tried to put a damper on the dancing, but to little effect.

Phil's Bar was the place to be and it appeared he was going to be a financial success. However, as the adage goes, "appearances are often deceiving," and this was unfortunately true in Phil's case. First, the Liquor Inspectors charged Phil with operating a bar with entertainment and assessed a large tax against him. While he challenged the allegation, he did not succeed and, unfortunately, he did not have the money to pay the tax. Not being a businessman, Phil's records were not good, and his accountant finally determined that he was insolvent.

All that success and Phil was broke? As it turned out, when he hired assistant bartenders, he forgot to tell them that they were not his partners. In other words, it turned out that they were "dipping into the till" to such an extent that there was little left after Phil was taking out what he wanted. Phil had no choice but to close and go into bankruptcy. Needless to say, I was quite unhappy for Phil since it meant he would have to go back to bartending for others to make a living.

There was, nevertheless, a bright spot in all of this. Phil had been dating a nice woman from West Virginia who, although not well-educated, had good common sense. She had been trying to bring more order into Phil's life, and although unsuccessful, had tried to give Phil a heads-up about what she had suspected was going on as a result of him not watching the cash register. Phil ultimately married Jeannie, and it was a turning point in his life. This pleased me greatly and gave me hope that Phil would do something more substantial with his life.

As it turned out, Phil got an opportunity to work as the maître d' at the Sheraton Hotel in Ocean City, Maryland. The owner was one of Phil's many admirers. Phil and Jeannie bought a home in Ocean City where they lived happily until Jeannie died of cancer. As I recall, Phil stayed on in the house until his demise some few years later. I attended both of their funerals and grieved for some time thereafter, knowing I had lost two genuine friends with whom I had spent many years feeling good, just being around them. It is interesting that, despite our totally different backgrounds, we were able to bond so closely.

Phil ultimately married Jeannie, and it was a turning point in his life.

PHILADELPHIA WEEKENDS AND SUMMERS ON THE MAGOTHY RIVER

As I have mentioned, Jack Edelstein and I became friends almost from the very first time we met at The Harvey House. As a result, he began to invite me to come to Philly on the weekends and stay at his parents' home where he was still living. I believe what attracted me to Jack was his wild sense of humor and equally unorthodox conduct. These were the days when I was not yet on medication that kept my "Black Dog" at bay, and being around Jack provided another opportunity for me to get my mind off of myself and be with someone who, though quite out of control when drunk, was otherwise fun to be with.

A typical weekend in Philly consisted primarily of going with Jack to the Warwick Hotel (the place in Philadelphia where young Jewish Society gathered on Saturday night) to hang out with his friends. These consisted of many of the established and up-and-coming young men in town. While his friends were mostly Jewish, Jack had other friends who were not. I recall that he was quite friendly with the Kelly family, particularly Jack Kelly, who was the single scull Olympic Gold Medalist. He was also close to the Kelly sisters, including Grace.

Grace Kelly's sisters and me with a friend at the Warwick Hotel, Philadelphia, 1960

Sailing on the Magothy River in my Oxford 400, c. 1960s

Most of the crowd were unmarried, and there were plenty of single, beautiful, young women for me to meet. I dated several, including one of the Kelly girls, but Riva Schapiro was the one young gal that I really took a liking to and she to me. She was intelligent and had a good sense of humor.

Since a weekend in Philly gave me little opportunity to have any private time with Riva, I began inviting her to Baltimore. Buddy Marcus, Leonard Sachs and I had rented a summer cabin on the Magothy River, and it was there that I romanced her. I showed off my water skiing skills and sailed with her in my Oxford 400 on the Chesapeake Bay.[52] We were quite smitten with one another to the point where she wanted me to meet her parents, and I wanted her to meet mine. I went with her up to her parents' home in New Jersey to meet her folks who were lovely, and I could tell that they liked me. I believe she also met my father and mother, although I have no recollection of that occasion.[53]

HILDEGARD VOSS BECOMES THE FOCUS OF MY AFFECTIONS

Then, something happened that brought my relationship with Riva to a sudden halt. That "something" was my meeting Hildegard Voss while in Germany visiting Irv Tarlow. She lived in Bad Hamburg, a spa town outside of Frankfurt.

Ten years younger than I, Hilde was one of the most beautiful women I had ever seen, and I began a long-distance pursuit of her affections. Since she seemed to also have an interest in me, my trips to see her became more frequent. As we became more serious about each other, I decided to invite her to come to New York to live and work (after she obtained a "green card"). I filled out all of the immigration papers and assured the immigration authorities and the government that I would be her sponsor/guarantor and that she would not become a ward of the state.

At that time, I was still living at my parents' home so there was no way Hilde and I could live together unless I moved out. Moreover, while my parents were aware of my dating Hilde, they would not have liked the idea of my seriously courting her since she was not Jewish. The marriage, a number of years earlier, of my brother Bert to a non-Jewish woman had been a hard pill for them to swallow, even though his wife and grandchildren had ultimately gained their affection.

Hildegard Voss Hoffberger in our home at 16 E. Mt. Vernon Place

To temporarily avoid repeating a similarly stressful situation for all parties, I thought that New York seemed the logical place for Hilde to live and work until we decided whether to marry. The Real Estate Holding Company had acquired through George Englar an interest in The Beaux Arts Hotel, a residential hotel located in Manhattan. George, who was friendly with the controlling shareholders and managers, the Wolfe brothers (Charles and Morton), recommended that they put me on the board of the hotel. Then Morton, who was the managing director, arranged for me to rent a one-bedroom furnished suite for Hilde. During the week, Hilde worked in the garment district as a fashion model, and when she was not in Baltimore for the weekend, I would come to New York to stay with her.

While this arrangement seemed to work for me, Hilde wanted more of a commitment – i.e., wanted to know when we were going to get married. At the time, as previously mentioned, my father was terminally ill, and my mind was focused not only on his condition, but on my mother who relied on me for support and care more than on my brothers, who were married.

My father passed away in 1963, as I have already stated. Also, as previously mentioned, the trauma of the event caused a dislocated disc, that had previously been problematic for me, to rupture on the very first night the Family was sitting Shiva. In the morning, I was hospitalized at Johns Hopkins and went through a ten-day procedure of being hooked up to weights that were attached to my legs in order to try to stretch my vertebrae and relieve the pressure on the ruptured disc. When this treatment didn't work, I had to be operated on by Dr. Otenasek, who was a world-renowned neurosurgeon.

> I loved Hilde, and I believe she loved me; so at 42, I decided we should marry.

I have previously described the tense scene that occurred when I came out of the recovery room which led to my mother wanting to know what my intentions were concerning Hilde. I loved Hilde, and I believe she loved me; so at 42, I decided we should marry. As I reflect, the timing of that decision was precipitated by my mother's comment, while I was recovering in the hospital, about my intentions and her inquiry, "What is going to happen to me?" This made me realize that, with my father gone, Mother was going to be much more dependent on me.

I remember being somewhat angry when she asked this question, feeling that she was being manipulative. So, in response to her question, I said that I was going to marry Hilde, but that I was not going to neglect her. Although I had recently moved into an apartment that I had renovated in a stately Georgian house that I had bought at 16 East Mt. Vernon Place, it was conceivable that Mother might have thought it more appropriate for me to move in with her in the new condominium she had acquired when my father became ill. After all, even though I was then 42 years old, I had lived with my parents most of my life, so continuing to live with my mother was probably not considered by her to be abnormal.

LIFE AT 16 EAST MT. VERNON PLACE

After we married, Hilde and I moved into my one-bedroom apartment at 16 East (as we affectionately referred to it). However, it soon became apparent that, even without children, it was far too small. It sufficed for several years, but when Hilde became pregnant, I decided we needed to not only occupy the first floor of this four-story house, but the second floor and basement as well. While extensive renovations were taking place, Hilde and I moved to a carriage house that Bert had bought behind 16 East on Lovegrove Alley. Bert, who was in the process of divorcing his wife, Terry, had acquired this white brick, two-floor building, but for some reason, which I do not recall, he was not yet living there. Since it was available for us to occupy, I rented it for about nine months while the renovations to 16 East were taking place.

Jack was born on May 27, 1969, right before we were ready to move back into 16 East. It was an exciting day. He had been born on the day that I was being honored by The Associated Jewish Charities upon the completion of a successful annual campaign that I had chaired. In my comments I recall starting off announcing Jack's birth, which was received enthusiastically by those attending. Being a first-time father at age 45 was quite a thrill. Although not obsessed with the idea while single that I might not have an heir, I now felt that my life was much more complete. Unfortunately, at Hilde's insistence, we did not have a bris, and Jack was circumcised by a doctor at Greater Baltimore Medical Center (GBMC) at the time of his birth. Her conversion had not resulted in her trusting a mohel (usually a rabbi trained to do circumcisions) to do the job.

When Jack was born, I explained to Hilde that it was traditional in Judaism to name the first-born son after a deceased relative, and if one's father were deceased, then preferably after him. My father's first name was Jacob, although he was always called "Jack," so she agreed to name our first-born son "Jack." When I told her that the name "Jack" is a nickname for "Jacob" and that this name would appear on his birth record, she balked; so I agreed that Jack's name on his birth certificate would be "Jack."

Then, when we began to select a middle name, I said it was her turn to choose a name. Since her deceased father's name in German was "Wilhelm," she said that she would like his middle name to be "Wilhelm." Now I put my foot down. I said that if she objected to using the name "Jacob" on his birth certificate, then it was only fair that she should agree on using the English translation of her father's German name, which would be "William." We agreed, and the naming process was over.

Not too long after Jack was born, we moved out of the cramped Lovegrove Alley carriage house and back into the spacious, refurbished 16 East apartment. There were three bedrooms on the second floor. The front one facing Mt. Vernon Square was Hilde's and my bedroom, but the bathroom and dressing room were hers; the middle bedroom, next to ours, became Jack's; and the back bed and bath rooms became my dressing room and bathroom.

The first floor contained the living room, which faced Mt. Vernon Square, as well as a library with a working fireplace. In the middle of the first floor was a spiral staircase, next to which there was a powder room. Beyond the stairs was the dining room, at the back of the first floor,

Being a first-time father at age 45 was quite a thrill. Although not obsessed with the idea while single that I might not have an heir, I now felt that my life was much more complete.

overlooking the walled-in patio-garden below, and adjoined by a long narrow kitchen. The spiral stairs continued down to the ground level where there were a recreation/playroom, another kitchen for use when we used the patio for dining or parties, a sauna and a large wine cellar. Also on this level was the separate cellar that contained the HVAC system and a large storage area.

We employed an African-American cook/house cleaner, whose name was Matilda, and an African-American janitor who had worked for my father, whose name was Eddie. When Matilda left, we hired a woman whose name was Alice and, subsequently, a woman named Mary. Eddie stayed with us until he died. My memory of him is quite vivid because he was totally reliable, when sober, and loyal.

I also remember Eddie because he was the innocent victim of an incident that was quite humorous. As I mentioned in the memoirs of my business career, while Hilde and I were living in London in the '70s, we became friends with Avril and Anthony (Tony) Gordon. After we returned to Baltimore, the Gordons came to visit us, with some hesitation on the part of Avril, who thought that America was primitive and that just about every man she passed was a dangerous criminal.

Now, Eddie came to our house pretty early in the morning to start cleaning the hallway that led to the upper floors of 16 East and the outside sidewalk in front of the house. We had a set of solid oak doors in the front at the top of several granite stairs, and these doors were left unlocked. The next door, which was about six feet inside the first set, was a large glass door with an iron grill covering the glass. It was kept

Me with my sons Jack and Douglas, 1971

locked, but we could open it when a guest wanted to come in by pressing a buzzer. It was not uncommon for a drunken vagrant or two to spend a cold winter night in the areaway in between the doors. I believe I had told Avril that, probably just to tease her.

Well, on one of the days the Gordons were in town, they came to the house somewhat early in the morning. Maybe we had planned a trip to Annapolis or Washington. They opened the double oak doors to ring the doorbell and, fortunately, there were no drunks in the areaway. Then, they buzzed, and we released the lock on the glass door. They entered the long hall, which led to our apartment door. The hall contained a console and two old large Jacobean chairs separated by a console. When Avril approached the second chair, there was Eddie, whom she had not known about, asleep.

Believing she was about to be attacked, she let out a scream that would "wake the dead," as the saying goes. It certainly woke Eddie. We quickly opened the door of our apartment to see Tony comforting her and Eddie on his feet with a look of fear on his face. I had to make a quick explanation to both Avril and Eddie of what had happened. That was the last time the Gordons ever came to Baltimore and, while I have not been in touch with them for a long time, I'm sure they remember the incident and the "uncivilized" area where we lived.

When Jack was still an infant, Hilde became pregnant for the second time. One day, about seven or eight months into her pregnancy, I saw her quickly run into the powder room. She came out about ten minutes later and said, "My water has broken." We called her obstetrician who said he would meet us at the Hospital (GBMC). It only took us about twenty minutes to get to GBMC, but to no avail. About an hour later, the doctor came out to tell me that Hilde was all right, but that she had lost the baby.

I was heartbroken about the baby. I stayed with Hilde at the hospital for a while and then drove downtown to my office. I clearly remember that the first person I wanted to relate this tragedy to was Irv Blum. I went into Irv's office and told him what had happened. As soon as I did, I burst into tears, letting all of the sadness I felt come out. I recall that he uttered the word "Aah," and stood up and put his arms around me. His expression of sympathy and deep concern was of great comfort.

Soon after Hilde returned home, she said that she wanted to get pregnant again. That took a little while to happen since Douglas was not born until April 18, 1972, almost three years after Jack. Douglas' birth went well, but still no bris. This time, the naming process was devoid of any negotiations. Both of us liked the name "Douglas" and

When Jack was still an infant, Hilde became pregnant for the second time.

while I am not sure why it appealed to her, I chose it because I wanted to name him after my friend Douglas Fairbanks Jr. Hilde also agreed to Douglas' middle name of "Millard." I liked it because I wanted him to carry the male form of my mother's name, "Mildred"; Hilde thought it was elegant.

Douglas, Jack, Hilde and me poolside, c. 1970s

ENGLISH HABITS ARE HARD TO BREAK

Nanny Zephyr Stewart-Miles Joins Our Family

In the previous section of these memoirs on my Business and Professional Career, under the title of "The Opportunity to Return to London was Irresistible," I recalled how I took Hilde and the children to London to live for about two years. Coming back to Baltimore, although necessary for the reasons set forth in that story, was not an easy adjustment. While living in London, we had become accustomed to having a full-time English nanny look after the boys. Hilde (in particular) and I had gotten used to being able to spend time, whenever we wanted, with friends without worrying whether Jack and Douglas were being properly cared for. All of our English friends likewise had nannies, and this did not seem to be a privileged way of life, let alone have a potential downside for the children. (Actually, many years later, I discovered from Jack that Nanny Hobbs, whom we thought was perfect, had been abusive to him, but fearing her, he never said a word to me about it at the time.)

So when, back in Baltimore, an opportunity presented itself for us to obtain a real English nanny, we were ecstatic. Some friends of ours, who lived nearby, had two boys about the same age as Jack and Douglas, who were being raised by an English woman by the name of Zephyr Stewart-Miles. Nanny Stewart-Miles was in her fifties and was a proper (fully certified) English nanny, as described in books and shown in films. She looked like everyone's grandmother – a little plump with a pleasant face, always ready to smile or chuckle. She had been a nurse in WWII, in which her fiancé had been killed. She had never married.

Zephyr Stewart-Miles, Jack's and Douglas' nanny and my friend for nearly thirty years, 1990

Unfortunately, our friends had fallen on hard times and had to let Nanny go. But, knowing that I was an Anglophile and that I would no doubt be interested in hiring Zephyr (by which name I never addressed her), they informed us of her availability. Before long, Nanny had moved into 16 East on the third floor, where I had given her a nice one-room flat overlooking the Square. Douglas was still not in nursery school, but was approaching four. Jack was ready for the first grade at Gilman.

Before long, Nanny was a member of the Family. Both Douglas and Jack seemed to like her and from their experience in London, were respectful of her authority. Nanny liked them too and looked after them with real affection. The truth of the matter was that she was a "G-dsend," an anchor of stability which they needed, as Hilde and I had begun to quarrel and have difficulties. The one thing that both of us could always agree on was that Nanny was welcome to stay at 16 East long after her services were no longer needed.

Up in years, Nanny finally moved down the street to an independent living facility for the elderly at North Charles and Center Streets. Every Christmas, for many years, Jack and Douglas would look forward to visiting Nanny, who always had her deep window sills decorated with English country Christmas scenes and her kitchen filled with a large assortment of Christmas delicacies.

This reunion went on for years (even after Hilde and I had divorced) until Nanny became ill, both physically and mentally. I stayed close to Nanny right up until the end, when she died at Union Memorial Hospital. I can recall attending her funeral at the Lutheran Church on St. Paul Street just north of North Avenue where she had become a member the last years of her life. When she died, Nanny's body was cremated and her ashes given to one of her younger friends, for she had no family left in England. Since she has now been gone at least ten years, reviving memories of our fond relationship has truly warmed my heart.

My Collection Also Serves Other Purposes

After I had acquired 16 East, and while I was still a bachelor, I realized
that I needed to decorate the walls of my newly remodeled first-floor
apartment with tasteful art, but I knew little about building an art
collection. I had randomly bought some oil paintings by unknown
artists, which appealed to me. However, after living with them for
a while, I began to realize the haphazard way in which I was collecting.
This did not make me very happy, as it became apparent that I was
spending my money on art that I knew nothing about, and which
I doubted would ever be noteworthy.

It happened that my close friend Alvin Aisenberg was an avid collector
of posters by the famous French artist Henri de Toulouse-Lautrec. He
also had a broad general knowledge of art and knew what was currently
in vogue. So, I asked Alvin to come over to look at what I had
bought and to give me a sense of direction about how to put together a
respectable collection that would not only look good on my walls, but
would be in a genre that he felt was worthwhile owning.

Alvin came over and immediately agreed with my suspicion that what
I was buying had little redeeming value and, in his words, that I
"should stop acquiring such crap." "What about my collecting French
Impressionist posters?" I then asked.

He replied that this market had gotten too high since the good posters
were getting sought after by too many people. He suggested, however,
that I consider collecting German Expressionist graphics which, while
not cheap, were not as popular as French Impressionist posters.

I confessed that I had no idea what German Expressionist art looked
like but that I would like to see some examples of it. We got in Alvin's
sports car and drove not too far from 16 East to a storefront building
on Saratoga Street that housed an art gallery owned by a German-Jewish
refugee whose name was Ferdinand Roten. Mr. Roten's gallery walls
were covered with black and white – as well as colored – graphics and
some pencil or ink drawings by German Expressionist artists, none of
whose names were familiar. A few of the graphics were French.

> He suggested,
> however,
> that I consider
> collecting
> German
> Expressionist
> graphics which,
> while not
> cheap, were
> not as popular
> as French
> Impressionist
> posters.

As I examined the prints, I soon realized that the German Expressionists were trying to express their deep feelings about nature and German society in the period prior to WWI in a curious and somewhat distorted way that created a sense of unease or tension within the viewer. Some of the works on paper – mostly the pencil and ink drawings – had a more normal look in terms of the shape of human figures and the depiction of other subject matter. However, others, mainly graphics, either by the angular shapes of the subjects depicted or the unusual coloring of the scenes, gave rise to a ponderous mood.

For the most part, it was difficult for me to focus on a particular print that I thought I would like to own. However, there was a black-and-white woodcut of a nude woman by an artist named Karl Schmidt-Rottluff called *Girl with Loose Hair* and a pencil drawing by an artist, George Grosz, that caught my attention. I asked Mr. Roten what his asking price was for each and he said: "Four hundred dollars for the woodcut and $150 for the Grosz drawing."

In 1962, that sounded like a lot of money for these relatively small works so I told him I would think about it. After having spent a few hours in Mr. Roten's store, Alvin and I left. Once outside I said to Alvin that I was not sure that German Expressionist art was what I wanted to collect since many of the works I had seen were a bit too grotesque. However, I told him that I was interested in the Schmidt-Rottluff woodcut and the Grosz pencil drawing of the rear view of a nude. Having not really made up my mind, I told Alvin I would think about buying them and let him know my decision.

About two weeks later, Alvin called me at my office and asked if I had decided to buy the works we had talked about. I told him, "No, I haven't." "You dumb SOB!" Alvin screamed into the phone. "Get your ass down to Roten's and buy them!" Respecting Alvin's taste in art and noting how vehement he was about what I should do, I wrote out a check for both works, and the next day I bought them.

That was the beginning of my German Expressionist collection. I am not sure where I took these graphics to be framed, but I am sure it was to the wrong framer. As I recall, I had the Schmidt-Rottluff set in a simple black wooden frame surrounded by a white paper cardboard mat and covered with a plain piece of glass. The Grosz drawing seemed to be more problematic since the nude drawing was off to the left side of the paper which, when framed, would cause the figure to be not in the middle of the frame. The framer's suggestion to cure that problem was to trim the page, which is what I told him to do.

That was the beginning of my German Expressionist collection.

Little did I realize that in both instances I had committed a series of unpardonable mistakes. The mat that surrounded the Schmidt-Rottluff was made of acidic paper that would ultimately damage the print and the glass was not treated to block the ultraviolet rays of the sun which would fade the work. The most devastating mistake made was letting the framer trim the rectangular paper that contained the Grosz drawing, since that destroyed the value of the work forever. Thus, the beginning of my career as a collector of German Expressionist graphics was inauspicious, to say the least.

<blockquote>Having said that, it is clear to me that it was my inexperience that was the problem, and not my taste.</blockquote>

Having said that, it is clear to me that it was my inexperience that was the problem, and not my taste. I evidently had a "good eye." The Grosz drawing was a fine work, and the Schmidt-Rottluff woodcut, I ultimately learned, was a classic example of German Expressionism at its best, and often appears in art books. Today, its value is over $30,000. Ultimately, when I realized the mistakes that I had made in framing it, I had it reframed with the proper mat and ultraviolet-resistant glass by a highly professional framer, Jim Pierce, who did work for the local art museums. Fortunately, I learned of my errors early on, so they were not repeated.

My choice of the Schmidt-Rottluff woodcut I attribute partly to the pressure Alvin Aisenberg put on me once I indicated that I liked it, but also to an intuitive emotional response to the way the artist portrayed the nude figure. The nude woman with her uncombed loose hair was not erotic, but due to the angular shapes used to portray her body and hair, she appeared to be anguished. Why that moved me, I do not know. Evidently I was sensing that the German Expressionists were trying to express their uneasiness with and rejection of German society which, while inwardly suffering from the great depression and hyperinflation that were ravaging their country, were outwardly "living it up" to sublimate their anxiety.

After I made my first acquisitions, I began to order as many catalogues as I could from auction houses in the U.S. and Europe which handled German Expressionist graphics and drawings. In the '60s there were quite a few: Christie's and Sotheby's in the U.S. and London, Hausewedell and Nolte in Hamburg, Kornfeld and Klipstein in Bern and Ketterer in Munich. The brother of the Munich-based Ketterer, whose name was Norbert Ketterer, had a gallery in a small town called Campione, Italy, which was not far from Lugano, where George Englar lived. Norbert Ketterer, who had left Germany because the tax authorities were after him for evasion of income taxes, had managed to take with him a fabulous collection of oil paintings and works on paper from the estate of Ernst Kirchner who, in my opinion, is the best of the Expressionists.

Each time I went to visit George and Margot in Lugano, I made an appointment to visit Mr. Ketterer's gallery in Campione. However, he was only interested in showing me the oils and not the graphics, which is what I was collecting. The oils were unbelievably beautiful, and I was tempted to buy one or two that I liked; but I still was not an expert on German Expressionism, so I could not judge the quality or the value of the works he was showing me. The prices of these oils ranged from $30,000 to $100,000 and this was, obviously, off-putting. Little did I realize that twenty years later, these works would be worth multimillions.

Since he never showed me the hundreds of prints that the estate owned, I stopped going to visit his gallery. This was no doubt a mistake, but I did get on his mailing list for the catalogue of his annual summer auction, and as a matter of fact, I bid on and acquired an Edvard Munch colored woodcut of a woman called *The Girl with Red Hair,* or *The Sinner* (one of the artist's well-known works).

Each of the other auction houses I mentioned had a major annual auction, usually in May or June of each year, and Christie's and Sotheby's had perhaps three or four. Their major auctions of German Expressionist works were in the spring. Once I received a catalogue, I would peruse it carefully to determine which, if any, of the hundreds of prints being auctioned in those days (1962–1990) I thought I would like to have in my collection. During that period I read extensively about the German Expressionists and about which of their graphic works were considered classics. Obviously, the classics were much sought-after by other collectors, so the estimated auction prices shown in the catalogues became a factor in my decision making.

Nevertheless, over the years that I was actively collecting German Expressionist works on paper, I acquired a number of outstanding and rare prints and other extraordinary works. Among them: Erich Heckel's *Self Portrait* (1919); Ernst Kirchner's *The Russian Dancers* (1909) and *The Muim Institut* (1911); Gustav Klimt's *Standing Lovers,* or *The Kiss* (1907); Edvard Munch's *The Girl with Red Hair,* or *The Sinner* (1902); Emil Nolde's *South Sea Dancer* (1913), *The Russian Women* (1913) and *The Young Couple* (1915); and Egon Schiele's *Act Against Colored Material* (1911).

Although on occasion I would discover a work I liked at one of the New York galleries specializing in German Expressionism, I bought most of my collection at auctions. Some of these I attended and some I did not, instead bidding by a written offer on the works as shown and described in a catalogue. Unquestionably for me, attending an

Although on occasion I would discover a work I liked at one of the New York galleries specializing in German Expressionism, I bought most of my collection at auctions.

auction was preferable, but in many instances since the best of the German Expressionist works on paper were being offered at auctions in London, Munich, Hamburg and Bern, I could not always take the time to be there. When I did attend, the excitement of the bidding process exhilarated me to the point where, in some instances, I kept bidding beyond the amount I had mentally set as a limit. When I was determined to own the work, its price almost didn't matter.

Such was the case when, in 1970, I attended a Sotheby's auction at which there were four Egon Schiele works being auctioned. I had previously received a catalogue from Sotheby's showing these works and indicating the estimated prices that they were expected to bring. Having acquired considerable knowledge about Schiele and admiring his amazing artistic ability (he being a protégé of Gustav Klimt), I felt that the estimated prices were low. I called my mentor, Alvin Aisenberg, and told him that I wanted to attend the auction and bid on one or two of the Schiele works. Knowing he would love to join me, and wanting his advice during the bidding, I offered to pay for his trip if he would join me. He, of course, accepted.

The Schiele works were offered in succession. The first watercolor drawing was a very erotic pencil and watercolor drawing of two female nudes making love. The second was a self-portrait of Schiele with an anguished face and distorted fingers. The third was a watercolor of a kneeling, naked woman. Although the first was the most beautiful, I could not see it hanging on my wall (fool that I was). I did not like the second, so I did not bid. The third was the one that I really liked, so I went all out to get it. The bidding was very heated in the beginning, but when it reached about 7,000 pounds sterling there were only two bidders left, another person and me. The bidding continued in 200-pound-sterling increments. When it reached 8,500 pounds, I decided to quit, as my opponent seemed to be determined to continue his bidding. With his next bid of 8,700 pounds, he was the high bidder.

That left the fourth and final work, a beautiful watercolor and pencil drawing of a young nude girl lying on a multicolored blanket. Although not my favorite, as I have previously indicated, I remember telling Alvin that I was not going home without it. Once again, the bidding was brisk up to about 6,000 pounds, but thereafter, the bidding again boiled down to two of us. This time I did not quit, and when the price reached 6,700 pounds, the auctioneer indicated the bidding was over and that I was the high bidder.

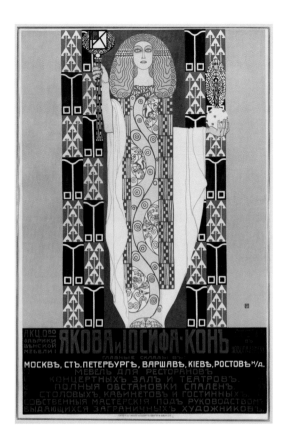

Color lithograph poster
for the furniture company
Jacob and Joseph
Kohn, by Austrian artist
Koloman Moser, 1904.
Photograph by Dan Meyers

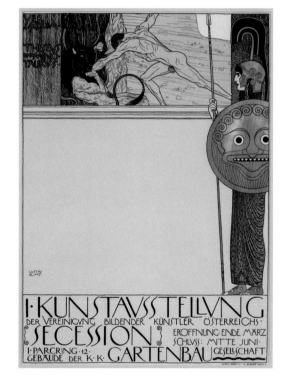

Theseus and Minotaurus,
Color lithograph poster
by Austrian artist
Gustav Klimt. Made for
the first Secessionist
Exhibition in 1898.
This is the censored
first edition. Photograph
by Dan Meyers

Muim Institut,
color woodcut
poster by German
artist Ernst Ludwig Kirchner,
1911.
Photograph by
Dan Meyers

Girl with Loose Hair,
woodcut by German
artist Karl Schmidt-Rottluff,
1913. Photograph by
Dan Meyers

Then, there was some sort of complaint by the other bidder, and my heart sank as I thought the bidding was going to resume. However, the auctioneer ruled that the bidding had, in fact, ended and that I was entitled to the work. I was excited beyond words even though I had no idea at the time how valuable this work would be 35 years hence (i.e., over $5 million). My success was obviously cause for celebration, so Alvin and I went out that evening to a great London restaurant where I treated us to a bottle of good champagne, followed by a sumptuous dinner and a bottle of a great vintage French Bordeaux.

The other interesting acquisition that I made was Emil Nolde's *Tänzerin* (*South Sea Dancer*), which is a rare five-color lithograph. As I recall, I was on my way to visit Irv Tarlow at his beach home on the Isle of Sylt in the North Sea. I had flown to Hamburg, Germany, where I was to meet Irv and some friends and where an auction house called Hausewedell and Nolte, which specialized in German Expressionist works, was located. I went to Hausewedell where I saw the lithograph.

It was spectacular and I wanted it. The only problem was that the auction was the next day and I was leaving that day for the Isle of Sylt. I decided to leave a written bid. Whatever the estimated price was, I doubled it and then left for Sylt as planned, wondering what would take place that afternoon at the auction. The next day I bought a German newspaper that contained an article about the Hausewedell sale. The good news was that I had submitted the highest bid. The bad news was that I had paid a world-record price for a Nolde graphic work on paper.

I continued to collect primarily German Expressionist graphics. Over about thirty years I built up a very respectable collection that I would still have had today – except for two occasions on which I (involuntarily in one case and voluntarily in the other) disposed of some of the best of my collection. The first was when I divorced Hilde in 1986 and, as part of the settlement, I gave her the right to select half of my German Expressionist collection. Several of the works she owns today are outstanding and very valuable examples of the Expressionists. I do not know what motivated Hilde in her choices, but fortunately I was able to retain the works that I liked best.

On the second occasion, I willingly donated five or six of the best and most valuable works that I had retained to the American Visionary Art Museum to help fund its construction, about which I have written in a prior section of my memoirs. At an auction held at Christie's in 1995, these works brought slightly over a net, after commissions, of $1 million that went to AVAM.

Despite the fact that I am no longer married to Rebecca, I do not have any regrets about having given these works to AVAM. I am satisfied that the sale of some of my finest Expressionist works was crucial to launching the construction of AVAM's facilities and that, without the contribution of my time, energy, thought, influence and the best part of my collection, AVAM would not have come to fruition.

The remaining portion of my collection of German Expressionist works and my more recent collection of Austrian Secessionist art adorn the walls of the living room and dining room of our home and are for better or worse often out on loan to museums. Although not as valuable as the works that my first wife selected at the time of our divorce or the works that I willingly gave to AVAM, they are fine examples of the graphics and drawings of the best artists (Klimt, Schiele, Moser, Kirchner, Heckel, Schmidt-Rottluff, Corinth and others) of these schools of art. Several are shown here on the previous pages.

As previously mentioned, I have bequeathed my German Expressionist collection to the Maryland Institute College of Art (MICA). Also, after having several meetings with Doreen Bolger and Jay Fisher, who are, respectively, the director and deputy director of curatorial affairs of the Baltimore Museum of Art, I have decided to bequeath my Austrian Secession collection and several Dutch Jugendstil posters to this museum, which presently lacks any examples of Art Nouveau posters from these countries in its Department of Decorative Arts. Fred Lazarus is quite willing to have the BMA receive these works, and thus, to my satisfaction, I am able to provide support for two major art institutions in Baltimore in a way that best serves their needs.

As previously mentioned, I have bequeathed my German Expressionist collection to the Maryland Institute College of Art.

MY RELATIONSHIP WITH MY MOTHER
FOLLOWING MY FATHER'S PASSING

After my father died, my mother moved into a condominium apartment she had purchased at 3900 North Charles Street, originally believing that my father would recover and occupy it with her. Her apartment was not too far from where I was then living at 16 East. As I recall, she liked her apartment, although needless to say, she did not enjoy living alone. I was a frequent visitor, making sure that Hilde and I were there almost every Friday night for Shabbos dinner. Mother also joined Hilde and me (and after our divorce, Rebecca and me) at Bernie and Lynn Kapiloff's home for very lively Shabbos dinners.

The birth of Jack and Douglas elated Mother. While she never got over my not marrying a Jewish woman (in spite of Hilde's conversion in accordance with Reform Jewish practice), she cherished her grand-children and doted on them. It became routine for Mother to take Jack and/or Douglas to her apartment on Friday or Saturday nights where she gave them bubble baths, prepared their favorite meals and played cards and other games with them. Both Jack and Douglas remember those days with fondness.

Jack, Mom and
Douglas, 1977

As the boys grew up and Mother grew older, she began to feel isolated in her apartment, even though I tried to visit her as much as possible and maintain my routine of Shabbos dinners with her either at my residence or at the Kapiloffs'. She had one or two lovely widow friends with whom she would get together, particularly a woman named Rose Harris who had quite an entertaining personality and who was very fond of Mother. But, when Rose passed away and Mother could no longer volunteer at Sinai Hospital, where she had amassed thousands of hours of service, she spent more and more time in her apartment attended by her maid, Marilee Williams, who had become her caregiver.

As Mother's health began to deteriorate, I decided that it was in both her and my best interest to have her acquire a condominium in the same building (Harbor Court Condominiums) where I was living with my then new wife, Rebecca, and her two daughters, Athena and Belina, and where Jack and Douglas also had a condo. Mother's condo was on the eighth floor and mine was on the eleventh, so it was much easier for me to visit her each day or have her come for dinner.

While this arrangement was satisfactory and convenient for me, it evidently was quite burdensome to Rebecca and particularly Athena (Belina being off to college by then), who, unbeknownst to me, resented being obligated to spend time with Mother when I took them with me to visit her.

By degrees, Mother lost her will to live and voluntarily became bedridden most of the time, being attended to by Marilee and a round of professional caregivers. This went on for some years until Mother reached 93. Then, on Valentine's Day in 1992, when Rebecca and I were having dinner with John Maizels, a friend from England, and his daughter, the caregiver on duty came up to my condominium to announce that Mother had just died. I hurried down to her apartment and entered her bedroom where she lay peacefully in bed.

On her bedside table stood my father's picture with a message on the frame: "The apple of my eye." I now have that picture.

MY SONS – JACK AND DOUGLAS

In previous stories, I have touched on the birth of both of my sons and on their two years in London with their mother and me, as well as their privileged childhood following our return to Baltimore. In the story titled, "English Habits Are Hard To Break," I have related how Nanny Zephyr Stewart-Miles joined our family to take care of Jack and Douglas at 16 East Mt. Vernon. They were then six and three years old, respectively. Jack was ready for the first grade and Douglas for pre-kindergarten. We were fortunate to get Jack into Gilman, through the good offices of Dawson Farber, who was an icon there. We also did not have any difficulty getting Douglas into a pre-kindergarten at one of the good nurseries run by churches in our neighborhood.

Douglas and Jack
Hoffberger, c. 1970s

Jack spent his entire primary, middle and high school days at Gilman and then went on to Washington College on the Eastern Shore, where he spent his freshman, sophomore and junior years. He then decided to transfer to the University of Maryland where some of his Gilman friends were enrolled. However, after one year there, he returned to Washington College, from which he graduated.

Douglas was admitted to Gilman in kindergarten and continued there until he graduated from middle school in about 1985. Instead of proceeding into the upper school, Douglas said that he wanted to go to Peddie. His professed reason was that he wanted to go to a school that was coeducational, which Peddie had become. I, of course, was delighted that he had chosen to attend Peddie, even if the reason sounded a little frivolous to me. However, now and probably then, I believe that his real reason for wanting to leave Gilman was that the quarrelling between his mother and me at home was really disturbing to him. He was having frequent headaches and nervous twitches for which he was seeing a psychiatrist.

Attending Peddie was a marvelous change for Douglas. His migraine headaches and twitches disappeared and, while his constant mischievous behavior was a source of weekly complaints from the headmaster, he seemed to be quite happy. After four years, he graduated from Peddie, surprisingly with good grades.

Like his older brother, he also chose to go to Washington College, where he spent four fun-filled years. There he met his future wife, Catherine van Ogtrop, who was attending the University of Delaware.

While Jack and Douglas were at Gilman, they both took Hebrew lessons and were B'nai Mitzvah. I was very proud of how well they recited their

Maftir and *Haftarah*, and I was equally thankful for the opportunity their taking Hebrew lessons afforded me to get to know their Hebrew teacher, Solomon Manischevitz. Mr. Manischevitz (as I always called him) was a Holocaust survivor from Poland who had been a teacher of Hebrew all of his adult life, both in Poland and in the U.S. While in a Displaced Persons (DP) Camp in Frankfurt, Germany, he taught the survivors, waiting to be resettled in Israel, how to speak and read modern Hebrew.

When I first learned of Mr. Manischevitz, he was teaching at the Beth T'iloh Hebrew Day School where he was revered by both his students and his fellow teachers. In order to make some extra money and because he was dedicated to teaching Hebrew to young children, he gave Hebrew lessons to Jack and Douglas and many others at his home. He was the first adult that I believe made an impression on my sons, not so much because he was an outstanding teacher, but because he was such a loving and compassionate person – a real mensch. He adored both the boys, and his wife did too. She would prepare cookies for them each time they came for lessons. Long after they had stopped coming for lessons (and I had begun my own Hebrew lessons), Mr. Manischevitz would ask how each of them was and what they were doing.

After graduating from college, Jack got a job with Legg Mason, a regional investment banking firm located in Baltimore, as a stock analyst and then as an investment advisor with Smith Barney that had merged with Legg. He was given the portfolios of the Family's two charitable foundations (having assets of about $35 million) to manage. Although Jack's knowledge of the stock market was superb, his heart was not in this line of work and he eventually moved on to something more creative.

Interested in panoramic digital photography, Jack set about teaching himself how to perfect the art. Through observing the works of leading panoramic photographers online, and reading extensively about this art form, he became highly skilled at its technological aspects and developed a wonderful eye for scenic beauty, his primary interest. His works are posted on "flickr," under the name JHoffberger.

Jack likes being an artist, and, while it is not an easy way to make a living, some artists/photographers do quite well. I and others believe Jack has the talent to join this group.

Another skill that he developed (in perfecting his panoramic digital photography) is an amazing proficiency in computer technology. He understands not only how to access all of the capabilities of the computer, but also the technology involved in creating these proficiencies. As a

Although Jack's knowledge of the stock market was superb, his heart was not in this line of work and he eventually moved on to something more creative.

result, he has the ability to build computers that have new capabilities. For example, Jack wanted a computer that could rapidly digest all of the data in the numerous photos he takes to produce a composite panoramic scene. He developed (from scratch) a liquid-cooled computer with that capability. This achievement won him second prize in a national contest conducted by one of the large computer manufacturers.

Jack has perfected other talents, too. He is, for example, a gifted musician and composer. Wanting to share my own love of music, I exposed both of my sons to music when they were very young. Living at 16 East, which was across the street from the Peabody Conservatory of Music, a world-renowned music school, Jack had easy access to a variety of piano teachers and for several years studied classical piano.

Then, tired of playing classical piano, he became interested in playing the guitar, the lead instrument in rock music (Jack's then-all-consuming pastime). He became quite a good guitarist and joined with friends to form a small rock band that included Douglas, who had followed in my footsteps by becoming a drummer. Jack also became very skilled at recording his music and is able to record songs, which he has written, on various individual tracks that can be overlaid to produce a record in which he sings several-part harmony, while playing both guitar and keyboard. "Anything I am truly interested in, I will perfect." These are Jack's words, and I am hopeful this drive will always give his life meaning.

After Douglas graduated from Washington College in 1994, I asked him if he would join my office, which then consisted of me, a bookkeeper and the CPA for all of the companies, partnerships, trusts and the Hoffberger Foundation. I was then 69 years old and fully aware that it would be tremendously helpful to the Family and me to have someone to whom I could turn over the management of the Family trusts, real estate and other entities that I was currently handling. It was my belief that Douglas could "fill my shoes," and "look around corners" like I had learned to do.

Now, almost 18 years later, I know that Douglas was the right person for the job, not because he is my son, but because I have observed how he has grown into the job (which has itself evolved significantly in its scope). Along the way, he entered the graduate business school at Johns Hopkins where he earned a master's degree in real estate administration and, upon completion of his thesis, will receive a second master's in real estate finance.

His excellent business and management skills have proven to be invaluable to the Family. Of equal importance is his recognition of the

It was my belief that Douglas could "fill my shoes," and "look around corners" like I had learned to do.

need to substantially increase communication between the trustees and beneficiaries of the trusts. In making this a priority, he has developed a warm rapport with both groups.

I feel gratified that my efforts, as a father, to pass along some of my passionate beliefs seem to have taken root in Douglas. Since community service played a major role in my life, I am quite proud to see how active Douglas has been on the board of the Hoffberger Foundation as well as on the boards of other nonprofit organizations of his choice (i.e., The Garrett Foundation, a large foundation supporting Hopkins Hospital; the Seed School, a private school providing educational opportunities for underprivileged children; SquashWise, an organization that interests inner-city kids in playing squash as a carrot for spurring their academic interests; and Teach For America, an organization that encourages college graduates to spend several years after graduation teaching in inner-city schools). He has a sincere passion for good causes, and I hear from people in the community that his participation has made a difference. Doing community service is a character trait that is acquired, and in my opinion, not something that one does naturally. I like to believe that his awareness of the importance to me of my community activities did have an influence on him.

Jack, Douglas and me, 2009. Photograph by Paula Gately Tillman

As I try to understand my relationship with my sons, what first comes to mind is the fact that I recall being very demanding about their behavior in general and, more specifically, about their performance in school. My tendency to seek perfection in them (as I unfortunately do in myself) could have been interpreted by them as a vote of no confidence or, worse, as belittling them, rather than as an effort to urge them to improve and to achieve their potential. Thus, while I do not put myself in the class of a tyrant, I see, on reflection, the possibility of lingering resentfulness on their part for my tendency to be critical. But if, at times, I did seem critical, in my heart I was proud of them.

I remember, for example, one time when Douglas was in a swimming meet at Suburban Country Club where, before they went off to camp Winnebago, Hilde would take them to swim and play with the other kids. Toward the end of each summer, the club would have a weekend of swimming matches. Hilde insisted that each of the boys compete in his respective age group, although neither wanted to do so. I did not object to her persistence, but I felt that neither was likely to win. Neither did, and Jack, after losing for several summers, stopped competing. Douglas, however, hung in there.

He was an excellent swimmer, but there was one kid at the club who was bigger and stronger. After one of the events in which Douglas competed against him (and others) and lost to him, he seemed particularly upset when the trophies were awarded. The next day I went to a store that handled trophies and I asked if they would inscribe on one: "To Douglas – To me, you are always a winner. Dad." I gave him that cup which seemed to please him. I believe he still has it. And I believe to this day that both of my sons are, in different ways, "winners." [54]

There are certain things that I wish I could have given Jack and Douglas that they did not have. The first, and perhaps the one on which the others rest, is that they did not have a solid, stable family life. They witnessed and felt the tensions between their mother and me, and their lives were shaken when Hilde and I divorced. How much of a factor that is in our present relationship I am not sure. However, I have been told by my daughter-in-law, Catherine, that Douglas (who was only 13 at the time) felt abandoned and that, unfortunately, he still bears the pain of this wound.

Second, when I now watch Douglas with his children, I long to have given both him and Jack the time and energy that Olivia, Charlotte and Henry are receiving from their father. Like my own father, I was driven by my work, which consumed me most of the time. My father's image, I see now, was somewhat shaped in my eyes by my mother, who worshiped him. I think I intuited that he was attending to us by working so hard for the good of the Family. Jack and Douglas may have felt that I was just not around enough.

In this struggle that I am going through now to assess my own performance as a father, I just realized that there is something that I have overlooked and that is my own relationship with my parents as a young man. Until my father became terminally ill and my mother, in her declining years, became dependent on me to be her caregiver, I

…I just realized that there is something that I have overlooked, and that is my own relationship with my parents as a young man.

was not as attentive and outwardly loving to them as I should have been. While I have previously written that my father was my one and only hero and how indebted I am to him for having so positively impacted my life, I do not believe that he was fully aware of my devotion to him. I must admit missing opportunities to be more demonstrative in expressing my love for my parents.

I know that my father silently longed for more of an outward expression of affection than I gave him. One evening, while still living at home with my parents, I was on my way out to meet my friends downtown. As was my custom, I would always say goodbye to both of them, kissing my mother on the cheek and shaking hands with my father. For some reason, instead of extending my hand, I bent over and kissed my father. That sort of confused me (as that was not the routine) and I sort of apologized. As I fumbled around for the right words to say, my father said: "You know, it wouldn't be such a bad idea if you did that more often."

At the time, I did not realize how revealing and meaningful that statement was and how it affected my life ever afterwards. Not until years later, when my father became ill, did the thought that I had failed to show him the love that I felt for him haunt me. When he was in Sinai Hospital, having suffered a massive stroke that rendered him aphasic, I would come into his room and ask him if he knew who I was, to which he would respond with a wink. I would then bend over and kiss him on the forehead and although he could not verbally express his appreciation for each kiss, I know how much they meant to him. Of equal importance is what those kisses meant to me. They were an effort to make up for all the kisses I could have given him while he was well.

Perhaps my sons will realize that I too, like my father, long for more outward affection from them. Recent contact with them encourages me that this is a real possibility, even a likelihood.

> I know that my father silently longed for more of an outward expression of affection than I gave him.

Douglas and Jack with me on my 89th birthday. Center Club, Baltimore, 2014. Photograph by Paula Gately Tillman

MY GRANDCHILDREN – OLIVIA, CHARLOTTE AND HENRY

I have three lovely grandchildren who are the children of Catherine and Douglas. Olivia van Ogtrop Hoffberger was born on May 5, 1999; Charlotte van Ogtrop Hoffberger was born on March 7, 2001; and Henry van Ogtrop Hoffberger was born on January 20, 2005.

They all attend excellent private schools, with Olivia being a student at Roland Park Country, Charlotte at Bryn Mawr and Henry at Gilman. Like their parents, who are "jocks," they all seem to be interested in every sport imaginable and just about every minute they are not studying is spent practicing or playing one game or another. Needless to say, they are encouraged to do so by their parents.

Although I understand how full the lives of my son and daughter-in-law are, as well as the problems inherent in having three sets of grandparents, I long for more opportunities to be with my grandchildren.

Fortunately, there have been a couple of occasions when Paula and I have really felt a bonding between my grandchildren and me (us). One particularly memorable time was on the last night of Chanukah in 2011 when Paula and I had Douglas, Catherine and the children over for the lighting of the candles. After a dinner prepared by Paula, we, at my suggestion, decided to play the game where someone whispers a few words in the next person's ear and then that person does the same until the whispering goes all round the table and the words are revealed

Douglas and Catherine with their children at The Homestead in Virginia, 2010

Olivia, Pop-Pop, Charlotte and Henry, second night Seder, 2014. Photograph by Paula Gately Tillman

to the originator of the phrase. What the last person whispers is seldom what the original words were, so it is fun to hear just how much the original phrase has deviated. Everyone seemed to be enjoying the game, so it continued around the table.

It came to be Henry's turn to whisper some words. He did so and around the table the whispering continued until the person next to him, one of his sisters, told him what he had said. When he heard how distorted the words he had spoken were, he blurted out, "No, that isn't what I said. I said, 'I think Paula and Pop-Pop are the nicest people in the world and they are smart too.'"

MY BROTHERS – BERT AND STANLEY

In the beginning of these memoirs, I have mentioned how as a child I related to my brothers, Bert and Stanley.[55] In essence, as a youth, I was very competitive with Bert and engaged in a contentious game of sibling rivalry. He was three years older than I, but I wanted to participate with him and his friend from across the street in whatever adventures they were having. He was willing to permit me to do so, but saw to it that whatever role I was to play was quite subordinate to his. He would be the president and I was responsible for handling the trash!

When I was about seven and Bert ten, our rivalry was mostly in the academic arena, with me trying to do as well in school or better than Bert. This desire was not influenced by any sort of competition that my parents fostered between us but was totally self-motivated. Bert did quite well, but so did I. However, for some reason, I grew to look upon Bert as being a better student than I. That did not bother me, but rather gave me an added incentive to achieve.

Stanley, who was four years younger than I and seven years younger than Bert, never entered into the sibling rivalry equation since he was an infant while Bert and I were fighting it out. I can still see him watching Bert and me do battle, but he was never brought into the fray. As Stanley got a little older, he too had a friend from across the street on Springdale Avenue, whose name was Bobbie Smelkinson. Frankly, the age difference between each of my brothers and me meant that throughout our childhood we each had our own friends away from home; and at home (once the fighting with Bert ended), we each seemed to do our own thing.

While Bert was attending Duke University we, for the first time, developed a meaningful friendship when he came home for each summer. This actually enabled us to confide in one another, with Bert

In essence, as a youth, I was very competitive with Bert and engaged in a contentious game of sibling rivalry.

doing most of the confiding. I can remember that my father had given him a Chevrolet convertible to take to college. When he came home at the end of his freshman term, we would go for rides in the Greenspring Valley on particularly hot nights with the top down to cool off. This was, of course, before the era of home or auto air conditioning. It was on those drives that I got to know my brother as a young man with ambitions (he talked of becoming a doctor), but also with lingering resentments.

One of these resentments concerned his chagrin at not having gotten into Dartmouth College. Since his academic achievements in high school qualified him to be admitted, he concluded that his rejection was truly "unfair." He would say, "There is no word 'fair' in the dictionary." I think another resentment stemmed from his loneliness – i.e., his lack of a girlfriend. He seemed to feel that being short and having scars on his face from severe acne in his teens were a fate that had been "unfairly" inflicted on him, and it seemed that he was angry at G-d for having done so. Later in life, I think he became an atheist and, if not, an agnostic Jew who questioned the need for prayer, saying, "Do you think that G-d really needs us to praise him and is influenced by prayer?"

After Bert graduated from Duke in 1941, he immediately went into the Coast Guard and attended the Academy to train to be a deck officer. When he would return home on leave from the Academy, we would hang out together, again taking rides in the valley, during which he would tell me about his training and where he might be stationed after his graduation. By the time that I entered Peddie in 1943, he had

> After Bert graduated from Duke in 1941, he immediately went into the Coast Guard and attended the Academy to train to be a deck officer.

Me with my brothers, Stanley and Bert, 1981

been assigned to a cutter that was escorting "Victory Ships" (freighters) through the North Atlantic to England and Russia. His letters told of how rugged it was, not only hunting for German U-boats, but chipping ice off of the riggings in sub-zero weather in order to keep the boat from capsizing.

When I graduated from Peddie, I immediately went into the Navy V-12 Program at Columbia and from Columbia to the University of Pennsylvania. Although I returned home with some frequency from both of my stations, Stan was usually away at Peddie, so for the two-plus years that I was in the Navy, we did not see each other very much, nor did we correspond.

Upon my discharge from active duty, I matriculated at Princeton as a junior (as I have already related). Stan was then a junior at Peddie (which is located only 15 miles from Princeton), but having no car, I did not visit him except on one occasion when a dance band that several of us had formed at Princeton got a gig at Peddie for the senior prom.

When WWII ended, Bert was stationed in Boston. While still in the service, he told my parents that he had been seeing a woman whose name was Terry Thibodaux and that he intended to marry her as soon as he was discharged. Terry was not Jewish, and my parents did not receive this news with enthusiasm. My father grew more accepting of the idea than my mother, who really was upset. Their efforts to dissuade Bert were not successful and, as I recall, Bert and Terry were soon married in Boston in a civil ceremony.

Time heals most wounds, and so before too long it was agreed by my parents and Bert that he and Terry would move to Baltimore and that Bert would work in the Family's interstate trucking companies (Motor Freight Express and Baltimore Transfer) under the tutelage of my Uncle Saul, who was the president of Merchants Terminal Corporation that owned these companies.

Soon after they came to Baltimore, Bert and Terry began raising a family. My niece, Sandy, was born a year or so after they married and two years later my niece, Laurie, was born. The birth of grandchildren changed what was a cordial relationship between my mother and Terry into a welcoming one, and regular weekly visits, usually on Friday night for dinner, began to occur. By then, I was home, at first going to law school and then working for Uncle Sam, so I usually joined them for dinner. However, soon after dinner I was off with my bachelor friends for a night on the town. When I wasn't going out, I usually fell asleep on a very comfortable leather chair in the library so, sad to

Me with Sandy and Laurie, my nieces, 2013. Photograph by Paula Gately Tillman

say, Bert and I had little real conversation, except for brief talks about business.

Stanley went from Peddie to Princeton, following my path. After he graduated in 1951, he went into the Army Intelligence Corp and was stationed first in California and then in Frankfurt, Germany, where he monitored Russian broadcasts from Moscow at the height of the Cold War. After my freshman year at the University of Maryland Law School, a few friends and I took a car trip out to Monterey, California, and while there, we visited him. It had been a long time since we had been together, and I recall that the visit was particularly meaningful to me as well as great fun.

> Stanley went from Peddie to Princeton, following my path.

When Stan received his discharge, he returned to Baltimore, as expected by my father, in order to go to work in one of the Family businesses. At first, he worked for Uncle Saul at Merchants Terminal in the refrigerated warehousing operation and, then, when my father closed the ice division, he went with him to the Pompeian Olive Oil Company. When my father died in 1963, Stanley became president of Pompeian and its subsidiaries.

It was not long after Stanley's discharge from the Army that he began courting the sister of his best friend, Henry Rosenberg. Her name was Judy, and she was a lovely young lady. They were married in February, 1955, at Judy's palatial home in the Greenspring Valley and I, proudly, was Stan's best man.

Stan and Judy lived in Baltimore for a brief time only. Judy's relationship with her then-widowed mother was a tense one. Her mother was quite domineering and apparently had often been critical of Judy during her childhood, particularly about her weight. Judy's solution was to move away from Baltimore to put some distance between them. Unfortunately, her other solution was to stop eating enough to sustain her body, resulting in a lifelong eating disorder that destroyed her kidneys.

Since Stan was working for the Family in Baltimore, the move could not be too far away. Thus, they settled on living in Bethesda on Bradley Boulevard. There, over a period of 15 or so years, they raised their two boys, Jeffrey and Russell. They opened, ran and eventually sold two tennis clubs and two French restaurants in Washington, DC, and, in general, had a happy life. However, sadly, Judy's eating disorder became increasingly debilitating.

While Bethesda was only thirty miles from Baltimore, my busy professional, communal and social life kept me more than fully occupied and, regretfully, my visits to them were few and far between. I know this hurt them, and was perhaps inexcusable.

After having resided in Bethesda for about fifteen years, they moved to Aspen, Colorado, and then to Houston, Texas. This succession of moves was in part due to Judy's worsening health, which caused her to want to be closer to her therapist, and the Houston hospital where she practiced. Loving Aspen, Colorado, which was not too far from Houston, they built a fabulous log cabin home, just outside of the town. By this time, Judy's kidneys had failed and she was on dialysis. The house, therefore, had a room that contained the medical equipment that Stan had learned to use to regularly dialyze her. This arrangement continued until Judy finally received a compatible kidney.

Despite the difficulties inherent in dialysis, they thoroughly enjoyed living in Aspen, and after her successful kidney transplant, they continued to partake of all aspects of life in their fairytale community. Nevertheless, her condition required frequent visits to Houston, so

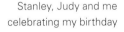

Stanley, Judy and me celebrating my birthday

they maintained a condominium there where she could be near her hospital-based physicians.

Kidney transplants do not last forever, so after being off of dialysis for a good number of years, Judy's kidney replacement failed, requiring her to go back on dialysis. With both Stan and Judy being older and frailer, they realized that continuing to live in Aspen was not practical. They closed the house and moved permanently to their Houston condo. Being determined to have a more normal life, Judy again sought to have a new kidney, although she was in her late 70s. After another period on dialysis, she received her second kidney. While it functioned well enough to keep her from needing dialysis, she was quite weak and homebound most of the time.

Their having "gone West" made it more difficult for me to spend very much time with them and my relationship with Stan was reduced largely to long telephone calls every now and then. I did get out to Aspen on two occasions, one being Stan's seventieth birthday. However, I found that the altitude made it difficult for me to sleep, as my heart would begin beating rapidly to pump more oxygen through my body, causing me to feel very anxious.

I also traveled to Houston on three occasions, one of them being on one of Stan's important birthdays – probably his eightieth. Another occasion was a trip for me to introduce Judy and Stan to Paula, who was then my companion and is now my wife. We had a wonderful time with them as Judy was feeling well enough to go out and show Paula her favorite stores and restaurants. Then, in August 2012, Paula and I flew to Houston to attend Judy's eightieth birthday. While quite frail and obviously failing, she came to the dinner table for what turned out to be a rather lively and fun-filled occasion. However, when we left the next day, Paula and I both felt that we had seen Judy alive for the last time.

Not long after that, on Yom Kippur, September 26, 2012, Judy succumbed to the effects of her debilitating illness and died at home, as she had requested.[56] She and Stan had been married for almost 57 years and were devoted to each other throughout. Judy was cremated, and her ashes were placed on the grounds of the log cabin she loved in Aspen. A memorial service was held in Baltimore.

Bert and his wife, Terry, lived together in Baltimore with their two daughters, Sandy and Laurie, for about twenty years. Practically every Friday night, they all came to my parents' house for Shabbos dinner, and my nieces would usually spend the weekends at our home. It was only recently that I learned how meaningful that was to them. Both Sandy and Laurie reiterated to me how free of angst they felt staying with their grandparents, since they had become fearful of their parents' arguing and fighting. After Bert and Terry divorced, Terry remained in the house where she and Bert had previously lived. Her daughters lived with her for a while and then moved to be with Bert until they left for college. When they did, Bert sold the carriage house on Lovegrove Alley and moved to New York City, from where he continued to run Motor Freight Express.

Getting out of Baltimore was a move that I believe Bert had contemplated for some time. In Baltimore he felt that he was "anonymous." Friends of my father would say to him as they did to me, "Are you Jack's son?" This infuriated Bert, who felt he had no identity of his own. He wanted to be recognized in his own right and in Baltimore that was a challenge, not only for Bert but for all of my generation. Bert wanted to be somewhere where the name "Hoffberger" had little, if any, significance.

Then Bert met Erna, a German friend of Hilde's, at a cocktail party at the home of Marilyn Meyerhoff. After a rather fast courtship, they married. I believe it was in Bert's apartment in New York and I recall Hilde and I being there. Erna had been living and working in New York, so being in the "Big City" was quite appealing to both of them.

As I recounted in the previous chapter on Motor Freight Express, Bert resigned in anger when he was turned down by the Family in his request to buy an additional trucking company. However, soon after he quit he was employed by a wealthy business tycoon to be the CEO of his trucking company, called "Jones Transfer." I know very little about Bert's two-year stint running "Jones," but I believe he did so quite successfully and, according to Bert, was paid a substantial salary and bonus.

Exactly why he decided not to continue to run this trucking company but instead to retire I don't know, but being a Francophile, he decided to go to live in a small town near Grasse, France, called Clavier. He purchased an old, quite lovely house with an adjacent olive grove and became an avid farmer, tending to his olive trees and harvesting the olives which he then sold to the local olive oil co-op.

On one occasion, Rebecca, my second wife, and I visited Erna and Bert in Clavier. He seemed very content and quite committed to his new lifestyle, as did Erna. He proudly showed us his two-hundred-year-old olive trees, which he had very neatly pruned, and introduced us to some of his French farmer friends. Life in the quiet rural village of Clavier certainly seemed to agree with him, and he was the most peaceful that I had ever seen him.

He wanted to be recognized in his own right and in Baltimore that was a challenge, not only for Bert but for all of my generation.

His sojourn in Clavier continued for three or four years and would have probably continued much longer, but, tragically, he severely injured his lower spine by dislocating one or two discs while he was tending his olive trees. Instead of seeking medical attention either in France or returning home, he decided to "tough it out," in his words. Although in terrible pain, with his legs getting quite numb from the discs pressing on nerves, he continued with his somewhat rigorous activities.

Finally, when the pain and numbness did not go away, as he had hoped would be the case, but got worse, he and Erna closed the house and arranged for his most trusted friend to tend his trees. Upon returning to New York he promptly saw a neurosurgeon who told him he should immediately have back surgery to relieve the pressure the discs were putting on the nerves in both legs The operation was performed, and the condition that was the cause of his pain and numbness was alleviated. However, while much of the pain dissipated, the numbness did not abate and Bert, having lost most of the feeling in his legs, was rendered a paraplegic.

I recall visiting him in a hospital in New York after the operation and just after he had been told that he would not regain the feeling in his legs. He told me that with physical therapy (particularly swimming) and the use of braces, he would still be able to get around. Needless to say, he was not very cheerful about this outcome, particularly since it meant he would have to give up returning to his home in Clavier.

However, Bert had no intention of resettling in Baltimore. Living in the country had become his preferred way of life, and he and Erna found that the horse country of northern Virginia was where they felt comfortable. He purchased about one hundred acres of land in Middleburg on which he built a beautiful French-style, one-story home that contained an indoor lap pool. Middleburg is not far from Leesburg, a small well-known village of high-end small retail stores and excellent restaurants where the wealthy people owning nearby horse farms come to shop and eat. Bert and Erna soon made friends with the "horsey set" and once again seemed to be quite happy in their new environment.

Middleburg is only about a two-hour drive from Baltimore and, while I visited Bert and Erna during the construction of their home and a few times afterwards, he and I were still not on good terms. He continued to feel that I had, unjustifiably, been unsupportive of him and had not taken a stand against any of Jerry's activities. I deeply regret our

> Perhaps our sibling rivalry still existed beneath the surface, and I was too proud to say, "Forgive me. I'm sorry."

prolonged disagreement. Perhaps our sibling rivalry still existed beneath the surface, and I was too proud to say, "Forgive me. I'm sorry."

Bert and I finally did make up and I did visit him and Erna in Middleburg several times thereafter. Sadly, however, when Bert was not quite 75 years old his health began to fail and in 1997 he died of some sort of liver failure. I attended his funeral with my then-wife, Rebecca, along with Jack and Douglas. Bert was cremated in accordance with his wishes and pursuant to his request, Erna, several years later, took his ashes to the village of Clavier where she spread them over the ground, perhaps over his olive grove.

Despite the impression that my recounting of my relationship with my brothers may have on the reader (that my feeling for my brothers was not all that strong since I did not spend that much time with either of them), I know that I had and still have great love and affection and a deep sense of caring for both of them. I do regret that I didn't physically spend more time in their presence and that I have not been close to their children. Perhaps some of my priorities, as herein related, were not wisely chosen. Still, I do feel that my deceased brother, Bert, knew, and that Stanley surely knows, that I have truly loved them with all my heart.

BELINA AND ATHENA

Rebecca's Children Whom I Raised As Daughters

When I married Rebecca, she had two young daughters – Belina, who was about 16, and Athena, who was about 7 or 8. Both of them were estranged from their biological fathers. In fact, Athena's first request of her mother when we married was that I agree to legally allow her to use the name Hoffberger as her last name. Although I did not adopt either one of Rebecca's two girls, we formed a strong bond.

At the time of my marriage to Rebecca, Belina was in the 12th grade and, the following year, entered Rensselaer Polytechnic Institute in upstate New York. Upon her graduation, she went off to England to obtain an MBA from Cranfield University. Thereafter, she settled in England, outside of London, to pursue a career of teaching corporate executives and others to use improvisation as a technique for problem solving. I would see her on my annual trips to London and when she came back to Baltimore to visit her mother. I know that Belina values my insight and experience and often wants my opinion on some professional project she is about to undertake. I also know that she enjoys my company, as I do hers, so spending time together on occasion, usually in London, is appreciated by both of us.

Athena and Belina with me, 1980s. Photograph by Rebecca Alban Hoffberger

Belina was well into her formative years when I came into her life so her character traits were already ingrained, mostly attributable to her mother. Like her mother, she is a free spirit and adventuresome. Both her choice of a career and of where she has decided to live were no doubt influenced by Rebecca's lifestyle and sense of independence. I believe that my role in her life has been a supportive one, particularly when she has been confronted with personal and career issues. In this sense, I have acted as a father, giving her as much guidance as I can and financial help when needed.

On the other hand, Athena was still a child when Rebecca and I married and, as she has expressed it, I am the only father she has known. She also told me that what first endeared me to her was my ability to wiggle my ears.

Unlike Belina, who went away to college soon after my marriage to her mother, Athena lived with Rebecca and me from her childhood until she was in her late teens. We got along quite well, and although Rebecca and I had an understanding that I would not discipline her children and she would not discipline mine, Athena was seldom a problem in that she had great respect for what I had to say about how she should conduct herself and about what things in life are important.

Of course, she was not perfect. I recall on one occasion, when Rebecca and I returned home from a weekend in New York, we found shards of glass on the living room floor and splattered eggs on the cathedral ceiling. According to Athena, she had invited a few friends over to the house for a party. Things got out of hand and what was supposed to be a "little party" turned out to be a "big brawl," with her having to call the police to remove uninvited guests.

The biggest problem Athena presented to both her mother and me was her disinterest in school. She attended the Friends middle school but decided, before entering high school, that she wanted to leave. For some reason, perhaps because it was near our new home in Stevenson, we decided to let her try St. Paul's School for Girls. As I recall, Athena could not identify with her classmates, and upon entering the 12th grade, she steadfastly refused to continue.

I let Rebecca make the decision as to whether she would permit Athena to drop out, although I felt strongly that she should complete high school and, hopefully, college. Rebecca, having never completed high school herself (but having gone off to Paris to become Marcel Marceau's first American mime apprentice), felt that finishing a formal education was not the end-all in preparing oneself for life. Therefore, she decided to let Athena quit school, provided she would take a test which I think is referred to as a "GED Equivalent." Athena agreed to this and scored in the 90th percentile. With this certification, she was admitted to the University of Arizona, which she attended for a year or two.

Athena's path through life has been more circuitous than her sister's. She has many different interests, and with her warm and engaging personality has been successful at a variety of jobs.[57] It is a delight to me that she now lives in Baltimore, and we see each other regularly.

Both Belina and Athena have always openly expressed their affection for me and have confided their personal concerns and problems to me. Although no longer even my stepdaughters, I treat them as if they are my daughters, and I derive a great deal of satisfaction from the fact that I have an adult relationship with both of them. I love them and know they love me in return.

Belina and Athena with me in December 2013. Photograph by Paula Gately Tillman

I CHANGE MY SYNAGOGUE AND ACQUIRE NEW FRIENDS

When I decided that Reform Judaism was not fulfilling my desire to become a more committed Jew, I told the newly arrived rabbi of Baltimore Hebrew Congregation (whom I, as a member of the ad hoc committee appointed by its board, had played a role in selecting) that I was going to leave the Congregation and become a Conservative Jew. This was apparently a shock to him, and he felt the community would interpret my leaving Baltimore Hebrew Congregation, after being a member for decades, as my personal disapproval of him having been selected as the new rabbi.[58]

While this was far from the truth, I understood his concern. Realizing, after a long talk, that I had made up my mind to pray in a more traditional environment, he suggested that I remain a member of Baltimore Hebrew for at least a year with the understanding that I could pray where I pleased.

I believe I had told him that I was joining Chizuk Amuno Congregation, which was the leading Conservative synagogue in Baltimore and one of the most important in the entire country. Its rabbi was Rabbi Joel Zaiman, a well-known and well-liked leader in the Conservative movement, and someone whom I knew from our serving together on several charitable boards. We got along well and had mutual respect for one another. Furthermore, a number of Hoffbergers were longtime members of his shul, where there was a beautiful Hoffberger Chapel created by the descendants of Harry and Molly Hoffberger. I also had a few other friends, mostly from my communal life, who were prominent members of the congregation.

As I recall, when I first started to attend services, my two seats (one being for Rebecca) were in the rear of the sanctuary, way over on the left. The other Hoffbergers, having been prominent members of the shul for many years, were down front on the right side of the sanctuary. For some reason, perhaps recalling my father's adage ("better to be in the rear and discovered…"), I preferred to be somewhat anonymous and not "be up front and found out."

Not too long after I joined Chizuk Amuno, Rebecca and I separated and divorced. By that time, I was attending Shabbos services on a regular basis, so I was sitting by myself. Frankly, I didn't mind, as I was still groping my way through the Siddur (the prayer book), trying to familiarize myself with the Hebrew. As I have mentioned in another section of these memoirs, I was studying Hebrew with Mr. Manischevitz

> For some reason, perhaps recalling my father's adage ("better to be in the rear and discovered…"), I preferred to be somewhat anonymous and not "be up front and found out."

who, on occasion, would come to services and sit with me. Nevertheless, solitude was something that I sought as part of devoting my thoughts to prayer.

However, before long Bernie Manekin, who sat with his family to the right and somewhat in front of where I sat, began inviting me to sit with his family.[59] At first I resisted, but gradually I began joining him more frequently as my grasp of Hebrew improved. Like Bernie, I was among the first, if not the first, in shul on Saturday morning, so it gave me the opportunity, before services began, to "schmooze" (engage in small talk) with the group of men who sat around where Bernie sat. Thus, I began to acquire new "shul buddies" whom I looked forward to seeing every Shabbos.

Included in this group are Bernie's two sons, Richard and Robert, as well as Dr. Jerry Buxbaum, a semi-retired dentist and a former president of the Congregation. Another member of the group is Dr. David Roffman, who is chief of the department of pharmacology at the University of Maryland School of Medicine. The final participant is the head of the Congregation's religious school, Rabbi Paul Schneider. Each of the men I have named has a wife who joins our section of the sanctuary at various times during the service.

Being surrounded by my shul buddies made me feel that I had found a new religious home and that I was a real part of the Chizuk Amuno community. Added to that was the joy I experienced listening to Dr. Roffman and Rabbi Schneider, who blend their beautiful voices in harmony with the cantor. As my familiarity with the melodies grew, I, too, tried to use what voice I have to join my buddies in chanting the prayers.

Since attendance at synagogue on the Sabbath does not fill a lot of the seats in the sanctuary, the new chief rabbi, Rabbi Ron Shulman, requested that we all sit up front, closer to the *bemah* (the elevated rostrum where the rabbis and officers of the congregation sit, near the "Aron Kodesh," the ark where the Torahs are kept). He thinks that when members of the congregation sit next to one another, this creates more of a feeling of "community." Some of my shul buddies have now adhered to the rabbi's wishes and are no longer part of our long-standing group that huddled in the rear. In fact, only Jerry Buxbaum and I (and

Nevertheless, solitude was something that I sought as part of devoting my thoughts to prayer.

sometimes Dr. Roffman) have "remained put." I have not remained in this section out of stubbornness. The truth is that if I moved to satisfy the rabbi, I would be sitting among relative strangers, and I would not feel at home.

Now that Paula and I are married and she (having converted to Judaism) accompanies me to synagogue, we sit next to Jerry. And since Rabbi Shulman's effort to get attendees to sit closer to the front of the sanctuary does not seem to be working, I am once again surrounded by my shul buddies. However, now that I am 89, getting to shul early, before services start, is difficult. Paula has convinced me to let my body be my guide (as to when in the morning I feel sufficiently rested to leave home), so I am less often able to schmooze with my shul buddies.

MY MENTORS: THEY HELPED ME PLAY THE CARDS I WAS DEALT

My Father

My father, Jack Hoffberger

It should be clear from the very beginning of these memoirs that I bonded with my father as a child and continued to revere him as father, mentor and friend until the time of his passing. I have already described the lessons I learned from him about humility, hard work and commitment. While my religious beliefs and philosophy evolved largely from my own thoughts and experiences, and my acquired tastes in music and art were facilitated by my mother, in most other ways, I was strongly guided by the way my father lived his life. There is no doubt that his example had a far-reaching influence on how I have conducted mine.

Like my father, I consider myself to be a deeply caring and highly responsible person, as the previous stories disclose. Moreover, although from experience, I had reason to be dubious about trusting others, my father's strong belief in giving the other fellow the benefit of the doubt has made me hesitant to mistrust all of mankind. There have been no others whose friendship I cherished more, and whose character I wished to emulate more, than my father's. That is not to say, however, that the following persons with whom I also bonded did not also have a strong influence on my life.

Dr. Nathan Schnaper

Foremost among these men was Dr. Nathan Schnaper, whose professional know-how as a psychiatrist and compassion as a human being figuratively (and maybe, literally) saved my life. The section of these memoirs on my "Black Dog" documents in detail what he did to restore my confidence when I had lost most, if not all, of my ability to function.

Natty's prodding me to take chances enabled me to be the person I so desperately wanted to be and gave me the courage to reach my potential. But, beyond my benefiting from his professional expertise, Natty and I ultimately bonded as devoted friends. We would lunch together on occasion and exchange thoughts about our personal lives. Whenever we met we would kiss on the lips (it was a habit of his that I had no objection to) and whenever we finished a telephone conversation we would tell each other, "I love you." Unfortunately, at the age of 92 he died, but, as with my father, I am infinitely better for having had him in my life.

At his funeral, I took note of the fact that he was buried in a very plain pine coffin. It reminded me of the fact that, while Natty was religious (although not fully observant), he did not believe in an afterlife. Nevertheless (perhaps because of his Orthodox upbringing), he had as his final act adhered to the traditional belief that the body should be permitted to return to the earth (from which it was formed by G-d) as rapidly as possible. More sturdy mahogany coffins delay this process. That reminded me that, although I have the same belief, I had been persuaded by Levinson's Funeral Home not to be buried in a pine coffin, as I preferred, but rather in a more expensive mahogany one with some sort of outer protective liner. Even after his death, I am taking Natty's advice, and I intend to change my coffin back to a plain pine one, similar to his.[60]

Morton Hollander, Esq.

Another person in my life to whom I am indebted not only for his having mentored me as a young lawyer, but for his unwavering encouragement and support when I became depressed, was Morton Hollander. Morty, who was a Harvard Law School graduate, was a good lawyer, but not as one would normally think of a good lawyer, in the sense of being expert in the law or arguing cases. He was a "problem solver" for the Family, both in business and in the personal lives of Family members. It was from him that I learned that skill.

But, in addition to his professional abilities, Morty was a compassionate man. He would come into my office when he could see that I was depressed and, after listening to my complaining that I did not feel that I could live up to what was expected of me, he would tell me that it was ridiculous for me to seek perfection. I can hear him now telling me,

"We all make mistakes," and, "Don't be so hard on yourself." I always felt good around Morty as his reassurances were very comforting.

Morton loved his cigars and was seldom without one in his hand. It was not unusual in the office for Morton to unknowingly set his wastepaper basket on fire, either with an unextinguished ash or match. His clothes also gave evidence of his constant smoking, since one could often see little burned spots on his jackets or shirts. It was all part of what made him so lovable.

His death from lung cancer was a real blow to me. Morty wanted to be buried in a cemetery in Boston next to his wife, who had died several years before, so, in the late stage of his illness, he was picked up at the office by one of his two daughters (both of whom lived in the Boston area) to be driven to her home. As we stood on the sidewalk in front of the Garrett Building (where our office was located), we did not say very much to each other, but our eyes were filled with tears. I kissed him as he got into the car, and off he went.

Morton Hollander

While I spoke to him once more on the telephone, I never saw him again. Although I asked him to let me come to Boston, he refused. I did get to Boston one time several years after his private funeral, and his daughters took me to the cemetery where he and Louise, his wife, are buried. As I write this, I am choked with emotion. Morty was such a mensch and mentor that I still feel a void without him. Particularly now, I would appreciate his wisdom and advice on my retirement and on this stage of my life.

George Englar

As previous sections of my memoirs have indicated, George Englar was my first non-Hoffberger client, a self-made and very creative person who gave birth to "Grecian Formula 16." My relationship with him started when I was just out of law school and continued for many years until his demise. It was George who taught me the basics of the commercial real estate business and gave me the "know-how" and confidence to undertake the real estate projects about which I have already written. His talents as a negotiator also left their impression on me.

Although George was considerably older than I and his background as a Christian quite different from mine as a Jew, we bonded almost from the beginning. George was easy to get along with, not because he did not have strong opinions and beliefs, but because he would listen to reason and his ego did not get in his way. George had worked his way up in Baltimore society through his business acumen and social graces. He felt proud of his accomplishments and of his stature in the community.

Therefore, when he disclosed to me his love affair with Margot and his plan to marry her and live in Lugano, Switzerland, I realized that I had become his confidant. To my knowledge, no one else (other than perhaps his daughter, Betsy) knew of this secret. He obviously trusted me and wanted me to know his most intimate thoughts.

Once George was divorced, remarried to Margot and ensconced in Lugano, I regularly visited him, at least once a year, to bring him up to date on Grecian Formula and other matters and also to just relax with the two of them. I could see how happy he was living a very simple life, and I envied the ease with which he had given up an active and prominent life in both Baltimore and on Gibson Island.

Sometime after George had remarried and moved to Lugano, his son Brud, who was living in Puerto Rico, fell over a cliff near his home to his death. Brud was a geologist by profession, but after giving gold mining "a go," he had opted to settle in Puerto Rico and not do much of anything. This had greatly disappointed George, and his relationship with Brud was somewhat strained.

When he got the news of Brud's death, he called me and asked me to assist his daughter, Betsy, by going with her to Puerto Rico to arrange for Brud's funeral, collect his possessions and, thereafter, handle his estate. I willingly complied with his requests and kept George informed concerning the settlement of the estate. On one of my visits to Lugano, George reminisced with me about Brud's life and about what his hopes had been for Brud. At the conclusion of his sad reminiscence, he said to me: "Roy, I feel that you are the son that I wish I had had." I was obviously quite moved and, as I recall, I kissed him on the forehead.

George's departure from my life also left a void. No longer did I have the delight of being in the company of such a lovable gentleman full of joie de vivre. As I am writing this, I can see him with his beautiful smile and twinkling eyes. He was truly one of the shining lights in my life.

Irving Blum

Another person who had a profound influence on my life was Irving Blum. Irv was a mentor extraordinaire, and it was from him that I learned many of my leadership skills. But, beyond that, he and I were close friends and it was to him I also turned when I needed advice. I greatly admired his thinking and ability to reason, and I know he likewise respected mine, particularly when it came to real estate. We

> To my knowledge, no one else (other than perhaps his daughter, Betsy) knew of this secret. He obviously trusted me and wanted me to know his most intimate thoughts.

were an awesome team in negotiations, and we could anticipate where each other was going in his thinking process. It was exciting and fun to achieve the objectives which each of us intuitively perceived were essential to the successful consummation of a transaction. His office was on the eighth floor of the Garrett Building, and mine was on the ninth. He had a wooden sign on his office wall that read "Honest Lawyer One Flight Up." I loved that.

Irv was a leader in every sense of the word. He was in the forefront of every worthwhile cause that the Jewish and non-Jewish communities faced. His fervor and dynamism, as well as his eloquence, made his impassioned speeches for Israel and for the civil rights movement moving and memorable, and his vision as to what was possible for society to achieve for the good of man was inspiring. I have tried throughout my career to emulate him to the best of my ability.

Tragically, as I have mentioned before, Irv died from nephritis in his early fifties. His death occurred in the middle of protracted negotiations he and I were having with Fair Lanes concerning the merger of BTR and the real estate subsidiary of Fair Lanes into BTR Realty. I know that, had Irv been around, the tensions that evolved along the way to our becoming a REIT, stemming from the paranoia of the majority shareholder (who believed the Hoffberger Family was trying to take control of the company), would have been kept under control. But, nevertheless, I persevered, eventually becoming chairman of a REIT that ultimately became quite a successful developer and owner of strip shopping centers in the Mid-Atlantic states, called "MART." After ten years of being a public REIT, MART was sold for over $680 million. Irv would have been proud of both his and my role in the origination and maturation of this venture.

It is now more than forty years since Irv's death, but I can still hear him calling me "Reg," his affectionate way of recognizing my love of the British way of life. I can also still feel him shaking me at three o'clock in the morning in a hotel in London believing he was having a heart attack (since his heart was pounding like a hammer due to the brandy he had consumed in the far too many crepe suzettes he had eaten); and I can still hear him making the most passionate pleas for contributions to Israel at a Federation meeting immediately following the outbreak of the Six-Day War. He was a most unique individual.

Solomon Manischevitz

On my journey to becoming a religious Jew, I (and my former wife Rebecca) decided to take Hebrew lessons at our home on Sunday

He was then in his eighties, but he had the spirit and energy of a fifty- or sixty-year-old man.

mornings. Mr. Manischevitz, who taught Hebrew to Jack and Douglas, would drive to our house, and for about one and a half hours, first Rebecca and then I would study Hebrew. This went on until Rebecca and I divorced, after which I then went to Mr. Manischevitz's condo, every Sunday morning, for many more years. During that time, he and I became very good friends.

We thoroughly enjoyed each other's company, and I became his closest confidante. I had his will prepared by GFRH&H and advised him on his investments, which were mostly CDs from reparations he had received as a Holocaust survivor. He was then in his eighties, but he had the spirit and energy of a fifty- or sixty-year-old man. Most of our time was spent not on my learning Hebrew, but on our discussing current events, or my listening to the personal matters that concerned him.

When his wife died, after a long period as an agoraphobic, Mr. Manischevitz became increasingly depressed. He had longed to visit Israel with her, but her fear of leaving home had made that impossible. While periodic visits to his daughter and her family at their home in the Washington, DC, suburbs and to Phoenix, Arizona, where they had had a second home, lifted his spirits, the loneliness he endured most of the time was taking its toll. His health and hearing were also declining. When I was reciting portions of the Siddur, it was obvious he was not able to hear me (which I didn't mind as it meant he was not catching all of my mispronunciations). There also came a point when our eyesight was mutually so bad, we shared a large magnifying glass that he kept handy. In spite of these impediments, I cherished each opportunity to learn from him.

When he died I was deeply saddened, but I knew he was ready to go. He was truly an amazing man, who had gone through "hell" serving in the Jewish Polish underground, and seeing the Russians murder his father, as well as learning that his mother and all other members of his family had been murdered by the Nazis. Nevertheless, he had so much love for humanity, particularly children. There must be literally thousands of Baltimore men and women whom he taught who, like I, will never forget him.

Rabbi David Fohrman

All of the above men with whom I bonded and who helped shape my life have departed from this world, but not, as I have related, without leaving their imprint on me. So, as a result, I had in many respects become a teacher and mentor to those less seasoned than I – i.e., the younger generation of Hoffbergers and others. Then, as mentioned previously,

Rabbi David Fohrman, c. 2010

I met Rabbi David Fohrman, and I was once again a student eager to learn what he had to say about the Torah (Hebrew Bible).

I have already described how Rabbi Fohrman came into my life and how, through the support of the HFFTS, I enabled him to become a scholar, teacher and author of books on Torah and the Tanach (entire Bible). I believe that by doing so I have helped him on his path to becoming a renowned Biblical scholar and original thinker in regard to interpreting Biblical text. I know he is deeply appreciative of that and feels sincerely grateful to me for what I have done for him.

Likewise, I am equally, if not more, appreciative and indebted to him for his having exposed me to his brilliant interpretation of Torah text and its relevance to the way I live my life. His teachings have not only made me a better person, but a fervent believer in G-d and the holiness of his Torah.

My relationship with David, today, goes well beyond that of teacher and student and has evolved into a bonding of friends. Having worked with him for over 15 years, while he was the scholar-in-residence at the HFFTS, I feel that he likes and uses some of my feedback to judge the clarity and effectiveness of his unique thinking on Biblical text. The feeling that I have provided the means for David to thrive as a scholar and teacher, and the knowledge that we have become good friends along the way are most rewarding.

PAULA GATELY TILLMAN AND I FIND HAPPINESS TOGETHER

Paula Gately Tillman Hoffberger in wedding attire at the Baltimore Museum of Art, Antioch Court, 2013. Photograph by Susan Daboll

After my divorce from Rebecca, I dated mostly women whom I had known earlier in life who were widows or divorcees. However, I was unable to connect with any of them in a meaningful way. Then, in about 2006, I got a telephone call from Ellen Aisenberg, the widow of my friend Alvin (of blessed memory), asking if I would like to join her and a girlfriend for dinner at the City Café. The two of them had met while Paula was working in Visitor Services at the Walters Art Museum. I happily accepted and met Ellen with her friend, Paula Gately Tillman, at the restaurant. Little did I know it was *beshert*. We got along nicely, discussing any number of mundane things, including what we had been doing and where we were in our respective lives. The one topic of considerable interest to the three of us was art. It turned out that Paula had been a freelance photographer for many years, primarily in Atlanta but also in New York, in the 1980s. [61]

Ellen Aisenberg, the friend who introduced Paula and me, 2004. Photograph by Paula Gately Tillman

To cap off the evening, I invited both Paula and Ellen to my new flat at Spinnaker Bay to see my collection of German Expressionist and Austrian Secessionist art and to try a little vintage port. They willingly accepted my invitation and we spent several more hours looking at the collection, talking art and enjoying the port. They left around midnight, but not before I got Paula's cell phone number.

It took me about two weeks before I got around to calling Paula. I invited her to an afternoon cook-out and wine party that friends of my son Jack were having in celebration of his birthday. She agreed to come and actually showed up with her girlfriend, Heather, a nurse who held an executive position at Ghilcrist Hospice. A great time was had by all and, having consumed a good bit of fabulous wine, Paula and I kissed. Although I invited her and Heather to my apartment at Spinnaker Bay, they drove off in Heather's car and did not show up.

Despite that, I suspected that there was "good chemistry" between Paula and me, and I knew that I enjoyed her company. Unquestionably, I was interested in getting to know her better so I called her, again, for a date. She accepted and we began to establish a more serious relationship. We dated quite often, thereafter, and realized that we were rather fond of one another. Paula was then 60 years of age and I 81. I told her that having been through two marriages and up in years, I did not intend to get married again. She also had two marriages, one of which had just ended, so she was likewise reluctant to remarry.

> Despite that, I suspected that there was "good chemistry" between Paula and me and I knew that I enjoyed her company.

Thus, realizing that we cared about one another, we decided to try living together in my apartment at Spinnaker Bay, although Paula kept her studio apartment in Hampden where, with some regularity, she spent time pursuing her interest in photography. This relationship seemed to be working to the satisfaction of both of us. I was still going down to the office each day, primarily to write these memoirs, and Paula was working at Johns Hopkins Hospital as a guest services coordinator on the elite third floor of the Marburg Pavilion.

We would meet in the evening for dinner, either going out to some restaurant in the neighborhood or staying in and sharing the cooking responsibilities. She would usually stay over, but leave early in the morning to begin her shift. Although she worked at least one weekend a month, we would just hang out on the other weekends, going to the movies or, on occasion, to a party of either her friends or mine. Going to Europe at least once a year had, as these memoirs indicate, become routine for me, but at 81, I no longer cared to travel alone nor felt that it was wise to do so, even though I had friends in most of the countries that I visited. The problem was that Paula only had a limited number of vacation days, so we had to work our trips to Europe around her schedule.

In 2008, I decided to leave Spinnaker Bay Apartments and buy a condo at The Colonnade on Canterbury Road near the Hopkins Homewood campus. Paula liked the idea and went to work helping me decorate my two-bedroom unit. The unit was ready for occupancy in about March of 2009 and, with the help of Athena, we moved in. Paula was then on leave from her job due to the fact that her father, who was about 86, was in bad health and she had become his primary caregiver. This situation gave us more time to spend together, so Paula's primary residence had become my new condo.

Paula had by now become my companion or, what is more politically correct, my "Significant Other." Our relationship had blossomed into a loving and caring one and we had become truly devoted to each other. She had also become my confidant with whom I discuss practically all of my personal non-business concerns.

We referred to each other as "partner," a term used in the cowboy films which we like to watch, or "pal." While these terms may seem to be less than expressions of endearment, we had established a loving friendship of six years.

Then something happened that significantly deepened my affection for Paula. We were in London, attending the theater with British friends, the Stones, on June 24, 2011, when I had a near-death experience. In between the first and second act of the play, I lost consciousness twice, once while talking to Dr. Naomi Stone and then while talking to Paula. With Paula's help I was able to walk from the balcony to the lobby where she waited with me until the ambulance came to take me to a nearby hospital.

In the emergency room, it was determined that my heart rate was below forty beats per minute, and the blood was not getting to my brain. The resident at the emergency room bluntly told me how serious this was and that I might die. This was confirmed to Paula by Dr. Stone. Fortunately, he was able to stabilize my condition and sent me to the ICU to stay overnight. Paula stayed at the hospital, sleeping in a room where surgeons on night duty would normally sleep.

In the morning the resident returned with the chief cardiologist of the hospital to tell me that I would need a pacemaker to permanently increase my heart rate. I was sent to another hospital where the procedure was performed immediately – that is, after I put up 15,000 pounds sterling (by charging the same on my VISA card) and agreeing to pay another 5,000 pounds before I checked out.

Throughout this ordeal, Paula cared for me; I do not know what I would have done without her loving attention and assistance. I began to realize that I was becoming more and more dependent on her to "take care of me" or at least to be nearby in case something serious occurred. Our bond continued to deepen, and marriage became a possibility.

Six months later, on December 30, 2011, Paula and I eloped to New York and were married at the New York Palace Hotel on Madison Avenue. The only people we told were my son Douglas and Paula's brother, Bruce. Paula wore an elegant navy dress and held a bouquet of a dozen off-white roses that I had bought at a florist shop across the street from the hotel. The ceremony was a civil one, performed by a former New York State judge whom I knew, Susan R. Shimer.[62] She and her husband, Zack, were the only ones present, other than a photographer. We celebrated with a bottle of champagne, followed by a lovely dinner at the Palace Hotel, where we stayed through the New Year.

Notices were sent to members of the Hoffberger Family and to our friends announcing our marriage. They were elated, and showered us with their good wishes. In that notice we enclosed a small card indicating that we intended to marry in a religious ceremony at Chizuk Amuno sometime in the near future. That event occurred on August 23 at four o'clock in the afternoon before about one hundred family members and friends.

In the months between our civil ceremony and our religious ceremony, Paula studied Judaism with Dr. Shualy, a learned and compassionate official at Chizuk Amuno. Her study proved to be very rewarding for her as she began to understand the uniqueness of Judaism and how loving a religion it is. Before our religious ceremony, she converted to Judaism, bathing in a mikvah, a ritual that is required in traditional conversions. Her reason for converting was to more completely be a part of my life, since my religion is so important to me. We both believe that our common religious belief will further unite us.

The wedding ceremony, which was conducted by Rabbi Ron Shulman, the chief rabbi of Chizuk Amuno, was both beautiful and quite spiritual. The cantor, Manny Perlman, sang "Because," at Paula's request, as she entered the Hoffberger chapel and also chanted the seven blessings that are recited in a traditional marriage ceremony.

> Our bond continued to deepen, and marriage became a possibility.

Paula looked stunning in an outfit that she had fortuitously found in London on our June 2012 trip to Europe. Although I say "fortuitous," her finding this perfectly fitting brocade dress and coat was more like *beshert* (which in Yiddish means "destined" or "meant to be").

Along with the coat and dress, Paula selected a pale gold silk jacket that complemented her dress to wear later at our wedding reception. She found her wedding clothes in one of the small boutiques in the Piccadilly Arcade where I often shop and had gone to find a new bathrobe. Not only did she find the outfit of a lifetime, but then she went across to the other side of the arcade to an Italian shop that handles shoes and bags and again, as if ordained, purchased the perfect pair of pale gold "Court" shoes (on sale) to go with her new attire. The only jewelry Paula wore during our wedding ceremony was a pair of deco-style pearl drop earrings, a gift from her mother and father, Elizabeth Anne and Herman George Tillman (of blessed memory).

An elegant reception and dinner followed the ceremony with, of course, the cake cutting. Paula has been *qvelling* (enjoying) ever since and the wonderful comments of our friends about the affair have put her on cloud nine. I am right there with her.

Paula and me at the home of Dr. Terry Pritt, Baltimore, 2013. There is an upside to my illness – my tux fits again after forty years in my closet.

ANNUAL TRIPS TO EUROPE MAINTAIN TIES WITH OLD FRIENDS

The Beauty of the Swiss Alps and the Discovery of the Jewish Museum In Hohenems, Austria, Bring New Significance to My Journeys

One of the highlights of our years together, since Paula became my significant other and then my wife, has been our annual trip to Europe. While I have maintained my love for London, where Paula and I spend a few days with our friends Naomi and Victor Stone (about whom I have written elsewhere in these memoirs), most of our time in Europe is spent in Switzerland and Liechtenstein. Here we visit with an old friend, Dirk Warren, whom Irv Tarlow introduced me to over fifty years ago, when Dirk was residing in Frankfurt.

Dirk, an American veteran, had returned to Germany after WWII, where he was quite successful distributing Japanese electronic products and then "45 rpm" records to the Army stores on the U.S. bases in Germany and elsewhere.

About five years ago, I told Paula that, in addition to stopping in London, I wanted to go to Zurich which was the first city I visited on my initial trip with George Englar to establish Grecian Formula distributorships in Europe. These desires led to my calling Dirk in Vaduz, Liechtenstein, to see if we could get together. Dirk was delighted to hear from me and sent his driver to pick us up at the Hotel Bauer au Lac, where Paula and I were staying, and drive us to his flat in Vaduz about an hour and a half away.

Dirk then took us to a charming, family-owned, small, forty-room hotel where we were to stay. The room he obtained for us had a balcony that overlooked the Alps and the valley below which was dotted with small farms and little white stucco farmhouses. The sight was overwhelming in its beauty. Moreover, the restaurant in the hotel was superb.

I had brought my Siddur (prayer book) with me and being accustomed to reciting the morning prayers, I would sit in a lounge chair on the balcony and pray, looking up at the mountains from time to time. After several days of this routine, I had formed a strong bond with the particular range of somewhat symmetrical mountain peaks that I faced each morning. They were the most vivid example of G-d's handiwork that I had ever seen, and looking at them gave me both a feeling of peace and of the nearness of G-d.

> One of the highlights of our years together, since Paula became my significant other and then my wife, has been our annual trip to Europe.

On most of our annual trips to visit Dirk, his wife, Elz, would come from Luxembourg to be with us, and on several occasions their daughter, Beryl, also joined us. On our honeymoon in 2012, Beryl drove all of us on a three-day trip to Munich through the Swiss and Austrian Alps and their famous ski resorts. One of the resorts we visited was St. Moritz, where I had not been since my bachelor days at least fifty years ago. We stopped for lunch at the famous Palace Hotel and, being off season, it appeared to be empty except for the five of us. Since this was our honeymoon, I volunteered to pick up the check. While the food, champagne and wine were all excellent, and the Old European ambiance with a waiter behind each chair was most elegant, the $900 bill presented to me was still a shocker.

One of the most enjoyable, purely coincidental, discoveries while visiting Dirk was learning of the Jewish Museum in Hohenems, Austria. The Prince of Hohenems invited the Jews to settle in this small community back in the 17th century, believing that the taxes collected from the Jews, who were known to be superb merchants, would help resolve his financial problems. And that is what happened (at least for a while) when a number of Jewish families became quite successful, particularly in the textile and clothing businesses.

I have made a number of very enjoyable visits to the Jewish Museum in Hohenems and have gotten to know its curator, Hano Loewey (Levi). When returning from my very first trip to Hohenems, I told my shul buddies about the museum. As soon as the business manager of the synagogue, who is part of my Shabbos morning schmoozers, heard the word "Hohenems," he said, "Roy, that's interesting, since I had a Hebrew teacher in Providence, Rhode Island, whose name was Jacob Hohenemser. He was the cantor at my synagogue and I always wondered where he got his name, but never asked him; I just called him 'Hoey.'"

Toasting with the Warrens on our honeymoon, St. Moritz, 2012

Praying on the balcony in Vaduz, Liechtenstein, 2012. Photograph by Paula Gately Tillman

My sketch of the Swiss Alps as they appeared to me from the balcony of the Park Hotel Sonnenhof, 2012

Also listening to my discovery of the Jewish Museum was the cantor of my shul, who then piped up and said, "Roy, you're not going to believe this, but when Cantor Hohenemser, who was a baritone, died unexpectedly, on a trip to California, his Rhode Island synagogue immediately began to search for a baritone cantor to replace him for the High Holidays. My father is a baritone cantor, so he applied for the job, got it, and held it for many years."

I thought this was unbelievably coincidental, much like the coincidences (or were they?) that occur in the Book of Esther. It so fascinated me that I wrote to Hano and asked him to trace the lineage of the Cantor Jacob Hohenemser who, it turned out, had been born in a small village in Germany where his family and ancestors had lived for many years. He agreed to do this for me and after about six months he had traced the cantor to a family, whose name was originally Wolf, that had lived in Hohenems in about 1750. I wrote an article about this coincidence to the editor, Judge Susan R. Shimer, of the semi-annual publication *The American Friends of the Jewish Museum, Hohenems,* which is sent to all of its members, and it was published in a special issue.

As if the business manager and cantor's father's relationship to this story of the Cantor Hohenemser weren't coincidental enough, I happened to tell the Rabbi Emeritus of my synagogue this story. As soon as he heard the name Hohenemser, he said, "Roy, you probably didn't know that I was the rabbi at Temple Emanuel in Providence before I came to Chizuk Amuno and that Cantor Hohenemser was the cantor there when I was the rabbi. As a matter of fact, I lived across the street from him." Well, that was the last bit of news I needed to give me the feeling that this entire episode was too coincidental; it felt more like it was destined.

THOUGHTS ON THE JOURNEY OF MY SOUL

As previously expressed in these memoirs, I believe that everyone is put on earth to serve a purpose and when that purpose is fulfilled G-d will end one's existence on earth. In reflecting on my own life I have mentioned several occasions on which I narrowly escaped death, not because of anything I did but because of external circumstances over which I had no influence or control. Had those circumstances been different, I might not be here, causing me to believe that it was just "…not my time to go."

If the director's meeting of DNYVF, which was to take place in the South Tower of the Twin Towers in New York City on the 94th floor of the offices of Fiduciary Trust Company on September 11, 2001, had not been moved to Chicago at the last minute, I would have been at that meeting. It is my understanding that the terrorist-controlled airplane struck the 94th floor of the South Tower around 9 AM, at which time I would have been either entering the building or on the 94th floor. I had nothing to do with the changing of the venue of the meeting to Chicago, so I have concluded that it was just "not my time to go."

In June 2011, while attending theater in London, I passed out due to the failure of my heart to cause blood to reach my brain. I was immediately hospitalized, diagnosed as needing a pacemaker and taken the next day to the Royal Brampton Hospital where the procedure was performed by an excellent surgeon. Needless to say, it was quite fortuitous that Paula and I were not on our way by plane and ship to the island of Paros in Greece which we were slated to do the very next day. There was nothing that I did to cause this occurrence when it took place. Suffice it to say, I believe it was just "…not my time to go," which most likely would have been the case had the event taken place while we were en route to Paros.

When I had to return to the Hopkins critical care unit at Bayview Hospital in June 2013 for the insertion of stents in my heart (a very risky procedure due to the possibility of it resulting in renal failure), I had agreed that the catheterizing procedure be done by its resident surgeon. On the morning the procedure was to be done, I had the premonition that I should postpone the surgery, since being allergic to the contrast dye (iodine) that had to be used to locate where the stents were to be inserted, I was at great risk of having my one remaining kidney shut down. However, before notifying anyone of my decision, the doctors on grand rounds entered my room, led by a Dr. David Meyerson whom I did not know. Dr. Meyerson told me that his team had been discussing my case and had concluded that the only doctor with the skills and experience that would significantly increase the likelihood of this delicate procedure succeeding without renal failure, and the only place having the state-of-the-art camera required to quickly locate where the stents should be placed (thereby reducing the time and amount of exposure of my kidney to the dye), was at the downtown campus of Hopkins Hospital. Thus, I was immediately transferred by ambulance to the CCU on the downtown campus to be catheterized by Dr. Jeffrey Brinker, who had been at Hopkins for thirty years. Some might say that it was a coincidence that I had a premonition and Dr. Meyerson rethought my situation, but I believe perhaps a fatal error was avoided because my purpose on earth had not been completed.

Notwithstanding, there will be a time when G-d feels that I have fulfilled the purpose for which he put me on earth and it will be "my time to go." Being in my 88th year and not in good health (but feeling relatively good), my lifespan on average would be five years. Although the chart says that someone of my age has a longevity of five years, I have pretty well gotten my "house in order" and, with the wonderful care being given me by Paula, I am confident that I will see these memoirs published. Understandably, this has reawakened some thoughts that I have previously had about the destiny of my soul.

Religious Jews believe that, according to the Bible, upon death the body returns to the earth from which it came and the soul returns to G-d, who breathed it into Adam's nostrils to give him life. However, for some time I have thought, like some Kabbalists (mystic Jews), in the reincarnation of the soul during its journey toward perfection (i.e., fulfillment of the 613 *mitzvot).* I like the concept because it encourages the performance of the positive deeds that you are commanded to do and likewise encourages fulfillment of the negative *mitzvot* that you are commanded not to do.

I believe that the many acts of service that I have performed, and my sincere efforts to avoid doing many of the *mitzvot* the Torah forbids, have had a positive effect on the way I have lived my life. By no means has my soul been perfected, nor will it be before I die. But, I would like to believe that I have made a good start and that, whatever level of perfection I will achieve, my soul will be reincarnated in someone who will continue to observe G-d's commandments and thereby further contribute to the perfection of my soul. This philosophy, that my soul will be on a journey toward perfection, makes me, a perfectionist, feel proud that I have played a significant role in the achieving of that objective.

> Notwithstanding, there will be a time when G-d feels that I have fulfilled the purpose for which he put me on earth and it will be "my time to go."

EPILOGUE

I have now told the story of my life up to the present, as well as I can recollect it. All of it I have typed myself and edited several times. While I have engaged a professional editor who, I believe, has improved it, I am satisfied that it is my best effort at recalling and reflecting on persons and events in my life that have played an important role in the development of my character and the shaping of my soul.

However, as I stated in the Prologue to these memoirs, my initial reason for writing my memoirs was to test my long-term memory in view of the fact that my short-term memory seemed to be deteriorating. As the reader has by now discerned, my recall was not complete. In some instances, I had to give up trying to remember a name or a place or date when some event of significance occurred. Yet, having admitted that, I am more than satisfied that I have been able to remember most of the events that defined how I grew up, how I was educated and how I, thereafter, spent my professional/business, communal and personal life.[63]

When recalling events in my life involving other people, the reader must have also noted that in some instances the words or expressions used by these persons were evidently imprinted on my mind so that I believe I was able to repeat them verbatim. Needless to say, most of these indelible words were those uttered by my father and, as I have pointed out, had a major impact on how I lived my life. The other instances in which conversations came back to me, almost literally, were situations where the utterance was either outrageously humorous or tragically sad or disappointing. I suppose the part of the brain that stores the long-term memory knows what is significant and what is not.

Having satisfied myself that much of my long-term memory is still intact, I now wish to deal with the other significant reasons (indicated in the Prologue) that motivated me to spend many hundreds of hours analyzing events in my life. The compelling question I asked myself was whether what I recalled shed light on why I believe G-d put me on earth. And if I discerned a common thread inherent in much of what I have done, how well did I pursue it, how well did I play the cards that G-d dealt me?

My older brother, Bert (of blessed memory), once told me that I had an "overactive sense of responsibility." While I smiled because it was a funny comment, I also felt good that it appeared to him that I was not only looking out for everyone in our Family, but also for just about everyone else. It was long ago that he made that remark and I accepted it as a compliment. Early on in my career, he had observed that I was doing not only what he thought I was supposed to be doing

> The compelling question I asked myself was whether what I recalled shed light on why I believe G-d put me on earth.

as the Family's lawyer, but for some reason, far more. As these memoirs indicate, I have gone on to do many things for the Hoffberger Family in carrying out what I considered to be my professional and business responsibilities and for the Baltimore community, in fulfillment of what I deemed my philanthropic obligations.

These memoirs have enabled me to look back and see a pattern in my behavior which, I believe, is a clue as to why G-d put me on earth. I believe "service to others" has been my calling. Whether out of a sense of perceived obligation, which I feel motivated me in my dedication to the Hoffberger Family, or out of a feeling of compassion, which I believe motivated me in my service to the community, I chose to travel a path that made "service to others" not only possible, but foremost in my thinking.

In the section of these memoirs dealing with my professional and business life, I believe I have shown that it was the Hoffberger Family that benefited from what I was able to successfully achieve. I could have pursued business opportunities on my own or, as is quite normal, taken a larger share of what I created, but I chose not to. Having observed as a youth that my father had assumed the obligation of keeping the brothers together (no doubt heeding the words of Grandmother Hoffberger to her sons that my father and his brothers should stick together to achieve success), I have chosen to follow in his footsteps by including the Family in whatever I did. Serving the Family's best interests became my mantra and hopefully, will be my legacy.

In the section on my communal activities, which included many different undertakings, I likewise sought to serve those in need, be it medical, educational, cultural, financial or social in nature. In some instances I did so through existing mechanisms, and in some I created my own solution to an unmet communal need. In all of these situations, I believe my basic motivation was that of compassion, even though, in the act of serving, my mind was not focused on so lofty a purpose.

I have also recited instances in my personal life where I chose to serve the psychological needs of others. Athena and Belina needed a father image when I married their mother. As I have previously explained, neither had a satisfactory relationship with her biological father. I, therefore, had the opportunity to step in and fill that need. Even after Rebecca and I divorced, the bond between Athena and Belina and me remained intact and has enabled me to continue to serve as their surrogate father.

> I likewise sought to serve those in need, be it medical, educational, cultural, financial or social in nature.

Thus, I believe that there was a G-d-given purpose to my journey through life – serving the needs, interests and aspirations of others. I believe that while traveling that path, I learned that performing "acts of loving-kindness" is far more rewarding than amassing wealth, seeking fame or obtaining power.

Having satisfied myself that serving my fellow man was my "raison d'être," I now wish to wrestle with the question of how well I fulfilled that mission. As I set forth in the Prologue, I like the way Rabbi Fohrman likens one's G-d-given capabilities and limitations to being dealt a hand of cards – some good, some problematic.

Some of us are born with better than average intelligence, some with great beauty, some with exceptional athletic ability, and some with serious disabilities that limit their ability to function physically as well as mentally. There is not much that can be done about what attributes and limitations G-d bestows upon each of us. So, when one is pondering the question, "Well, how did I do?" he must also qualify it by asking "…with what I was given?"

As I set forth in the Prologue, I thought "…I was dealt a pretty good hand…" It was not a "straight flush," but neither was it one which caused me to "fold." I don't think that I was capable of discovering penicillin or of setting an Olympic record, but with my G-d-given intelligence, I was able to accomplish a great deal.

Yet, as these memoirs also reveal, there was one "bad" card in my hand (probably genetic), and that was my "Black Dog." While it was a card that I could not "dispose of," it was also one that did not cause me to "fold." With help, not only did I not give up, but I played out my hand with courage. Moreover, I believe it also took courage to force myself to overcome the fears and anxieties that accompany depression so that I could pursue my life's purpose. Had I not had that card, I could have, perhaps, accomplished even more, but even with it, I did not "drop out of the game."

So, my conclusion about how "I played my cards" is: "pretty well." Although I would not say that my life was "filled with happiness," it has been filled with "purpose" and, as a result, has been fulfilling. Since I like how I have "played my cards," I can say that I like who I am today. While far from perfect, I am content with the way in which I have lived my life. I have done what was in my heart, and I believe that I have made a difference and have helped to "repair the world."

I am comforted by yet another thought that I believe is true. There is a theory (I think in mathematics) that "The whole can be greater than the sum of its parts." In googling this proposition, I discovered that "greater than" should really, in many instances, be interpreted as "more than" or, even better, "different than." I don't think that adding up my accomplishments fully reveals who I am. While it is reasonable to conclude that I have done many different things, I hope it is equally evident that I have tried throughout my life to act "beyond self." The "me" that I like is the "me" that I think others see when they tell me that I am "a good person." In that context, I hope that I have fulfilled G-d's commandment to "Love Thy Neighbor as Thyself."

At my desk, editing my memoirs in Liechtenstein, 2012. Photograph by Paula Gately Tillman

END NOTES

CHILDHOOD AND FORMATIVE YEARS

1 This and all subsequent unattributed photographs are from the Hoffberger Family archives. (page 2)

2 Women's Hospital (The Hospital for Women of Maryland) was close to the Maryland Institute College of Art (MICA). Some years after its closing, it was purchased by MICA and converted into the Robert and Jane Meyerhoff Dormitory. (page 2)

3 Having forgotten what my real Hebrew name was, on the occasion of Douglas' bar mitzvah, at the suggestion of a noted Hebrew scholar, Dr. Louis Caplan, I took the Hebrew name "Melech" (the king). This was based on my first name, LeRoy, which means "the king" in French. (page 2)

4 Each firstborn son of my father's generation was named after his deceased grandfather, Charles. My brother, who was the youngest of the firstborn grandsons, was Charles V. (page 2)

5 Her unusual name gradually came to me while I was driving in my car, and it came sequentially over a period of several days but in reverse order: first her last name, then her middle name and then her first name. Together, her names seemed to have a melodic sound, and I was always amused that when asked what her name was, she replied using all three. Once I remembered her last name (Scott), I kept repeating "dadada dada" Scott in a rhythmic way that sounded like her three names until I recalled her second name (Gloster) and finally her first name (Lillabelle). I loved Lilla, as we called her, and I can remember often hugging her and her hugging me. (page 4)

6 In contrast to these pleasing memories, I remember that one thing I could not stand was eating oatmeal. I did not mind its taste, but could not ingest it because of the lumps in it. Cream of Wheat was okay because it felt smooth in my mouth, but to this day, I do not eat oatmeal. (page 5)

7 Jacob worked for my parents for about thirty years, coming with us when we moved to Bancroft Road. There he lived on the third floor of our house and worked on the grounds until his death. I can still remember the morning my father found him dying on the floor of his bedroom. Every one of us was deeply saddened when he passed shortly thereafter. Jacob was as decent, kind, spiritual and loyal a human being as I have ever known and I had a great affection for him. While both Carey and Lilla worked for my parents for many years on Springdale Avenue, they opted not to do so when we moved out to 3404 Bancroft Road in the Park Heights area since that location was too far from where they lived. I never forgot them and recall attending their funerals, much later, when I was in my thirties or early forties. (page 6)

8 When I was about to enter the third or fourth grade, Dad contracted double pneumonia, from which he almost died. Antibiotics were unknown at that

"Tree of Life," working drawing by Gustav Klimt for the mosaic of the Palais Stoclet Frieze in Brussels.

© MAK-Austrian Museum of Applied Arts/ Contemporary Art

time, so when he survived the acute stage, his doctors prescribed that he spend six months in the mountain air, which was believed to be the best way to recover. So, off to Asheville, North Carolina, the entire family went for Dad to rest. Bert and I, of course, had to leave Public School #64, and instead attend a small school with multiple classes in one room. As I recall, I was the only kid in my class with shoes as it was then that the United States was in the worst of the Depression. I returned to #64 late in the school year, where my old classmates greeted me warmly. (page 16)

9 When I was about six or seven years old, my parents sent me off to summer camp with Bert, who had gone the summer before. This turned out to be a humiliating experience since, on occasion, I wet the bed and my counselor ridiculed me in front of my bunkmates. Needless to say, I never returned to camp and neither did Bert. It was after this that we began our summers at Bush River. (page 23)

10 Since I began writing these memoirs, Sylvan has died. Although we did not often see each other later in life, when we did we would always reminisce about our youth. (page 25)

WORLD WAR II

11 The Peddie School for Boys changed its name to "The Peddie School" when it became coeducational. (page 31)

12 After graduating from Peddie, Bill served in the Army during World War II at a supply depot in the U.S. and, after discharge, remained with the government in a high-level civilian position related to the military. He and his wife, Gertrude, live in Connecticut in an historic house. While I have only visited him once, and he and Gertrude came to Baltimore once, I have periodically stayed in touch with them with occasional phone calls and an annual exchange of Christmas cards. I have a real fondness for both Bill and Gertrude and hope I will have the opportunity to see them again. (page 32)

13 On June 18, 2012, Paula and I attended the burial of her father, Colonel Herman G. "Hank" Tillman, (Ret.) U.S.A.F., at Arlington National Cemetery. Colonel Tillman, who was one of Maryland's most highly decorated pilots, had served in the Air Force for thirty-one years until his retirement. He was buried with full military honors for his distinguished service and acts of heroism. When the band started to play "Abide with Me," I began singing the words: *"Abide with me, fast falls the eventide. When darkness deepens, Lord with me abide."* A tear came to my eye, not only because of how moving the ceremony was, but because it was the one song we all sang at Vespers at Peddie. The headmaster at Peddie had been right in his prediction that Vespers would one day outrank all other school experiences. (page 35)

14 I was retired from the Navy Reserve as a Lieutenant JG about 15 years after being discharged in August 1945. (page 40)

15 Today, I understand that "Woodie" (the more recent name by which the SPIA is affectionately called) receives hundreds of applications a year for ninety

places. It is the most prestigious school of its kind in the world and has many famous and infamous graduates. As President Wilson had hoped, many of our recent Secretaries of State and Defense, as well as senators and congressmen, have been graduates of the school. So have some good lawyers interested in politics, if I may say so. (page 42)

16   Pete, who also became a lawyer, was appointed by Republican Governor Cahill of New Jersey to be the Chief Justice of the Supreme Court of New Jersey. Tragically, Pete died, after having served for only 47 days. Between my junior and senior years, Pete and I took a trip out west to Nevada. We particularly made a stop in Reno since, as I recall, Pete had told me his father had been the mayor there. However, in googling Pete, I found out that his father had twice served as mayor of Bayonne, New Jersey. This strange inconsistency I must chalk up to my not-perfect memory! (page 45)

17   Because I have cherished my Princeton experience so much, I had the desire to thank Charlie Fredericks for the two times when his words influenced me to go there. At several reunions – both of Peddie and Princeton – I had thought I would have a chance to express my appreciation to him. However, I never managed to do so. When Charlie died, I wrote his wife, Stephanie, and told her in the letter how Charlie's hilarious but poignant remarks had helped to shape my higher educational life and how much I regretted that I had never told him. (page 46)

18   There was also a "night school" for students who had daytime jobs. That class was as large as ours, but I did not know any of the students. (page 50)

PROFESSIONAL AND BUSINESS LIFE

19   In her fifth term as a U.S. senator, Senator Mikulski was appointed chairperson of the Senate Appropriations Committee, the first woman ever to head the constitutionally mandated committee. (page 58)

20   A class system exists to categorize the age, amenities, aesthetics and general infrastructure of buildings. Class A is the most modern and sought after by investors – generally newly constructed and equipped with top-of-the-line fixtures, amenities and systems; Class B spaces are not so modern and not in the best commercial areas; Class C are the poorest quality structures on the market, located in the least desirable districts, and usually in need of major renovations, often due to their age. (page 59)

21   "Black Dog," the colloquial term used by Winston Churchill to describe his depression and wrongly attributed to him as its author, has its origin in ancient Greek and Roman times. It first appeared in Dr. Samuel Johnson's dictionary in the 18th century to describe his melancholia, as clinical depression was then called. (page 66)

22   In the article I googled on "The Origin of the Term 'Black Dog,'" the author's conclusion expresses how I have learned to regard my own situation:

"Depression is a constant dark companion that hopefully can be controlled and eventually mastered." (page 68)

23 Sir Lacey was the 2nd Baronet of Walton and the son of a former lord mayor of London. Lady Helen was the daughter of Field Marshal Sir William Robertson, the only soldier in the British Army ever to rise from private to field marshal. (page 74)

24 Hyman had been closely involved with Jacob Blaustein in the drafting of the accords with Ben Gurion concerning the dual relationship of diaspora Jewry with their country of origin and with the newly created state of Israel. (page 74)

25 Granada today is a multibillion-pound corporation with extensive entertainment and communication subsidiaries. I recall that the Bernsteins did not speak the "King's English" and had the demeanor of having fought their way up the ladder of success. In googling "Sidney Bernstein," I discovered that he was awarded a life peerage and died in 1993. I also learned that Granada still had its interest in bowling. (page 84)

26 Although the dollars Fair Lanes received for its pioneering effort were relatively modest, its return on investment was quite good. In light of what happened to bowling in England between the time we sold out and 1980, it was clear we had made a sound decision to sell. During this period, nearly two-thirds of all bowling centers in the U.K. closed. However, in the 1980s, bowling took off again with a mad frenzy. In fact, according to an article that I just googled, this is attributed to the film *Grease 2*, which must have hyped bowling as the thing for young Brits to do. (page 85)

27 This plan was considered sufficiently unique to be the "centerfold" of an extensive article on U.S. New Towns in *Life* magazine around 1968. While the final plan was prepared by the MNCPPC, it bore the unmistakable hand of Ed Echeverria. (page 95)

28 I began buying farmland in 1962 at about four to five cents per square foot and sold the last 107-acre parcel zoned for commercial use at $4 per square foot in 1989. (page 102)

29 Through my contacts over the years with several Montgomery County executives, I have discovered that the history of the founding of the New Town of Germantown, now a thriving community with a significant tax base, is not generally known. Although I have offered to give the Community College of Montgomery County, located in Germantown, all of my hundreds of files that tell in detail what I have related here, no one has expressed interest. Nevertheless, I will keep trying to get someone to undertake memorializing this story. Not that the decision of Fairchild to move to Montgomery Country and the subsequent birth of the New Town of Germantown is like a nebula to the birth of a star, but it is exciting that out of the coming together of entrepreneurial forces, a flourishing community took root. (page 102)

30 The sketches are hung in the corridor leading to my office and are a constant reminder of my early days in my Uncle Sam's firm. I view them with mixed emotions. While one sketch depicts me at my desk in what was formerly my uncle's office, meaning I was then the "boss," the other is of a loved one no longer alive. (page 107)

31 In 1989, Mr. Merrick and John Luetkemeyer sold their families' 27% controlling interest in the Bank to Alfred Lerner of Cleveland. Not very long thereafter, Grant Hathaway was made chairman and CEO of Equitable Bancorporation where he remained until it merged with MNC Financial (owner of the Maryland National Bank, Maryland's leading bank) in 1990. Al continued to rely on Grant's banking and lending expertise in the expansion of his financial empire. (page 108)

32 The truth of the matter is that the story really did not end with the purchase of the building by Maryland National. CPC opted to do a like-kind exchange that, under the Internal Revenue Code, postponed the capital gains taxes on the sale. It involved purchasing a residential apartment development in Richmond, Virginia, which unfortunately did not turn out to be particularly successful. After owning the apartment project for five or six years, I did another like-kind exchange with a REIT called Equity Residential, which is the largest owner and operator of apartments in the U.S. CPC ultimately came to own about 24,000 certificates, which Douglas wisely converted into shares and sold at a substantial profit. (page 110)

33 Just one further thought about my days practicing law at 215 North Calvert Street. Beginning with Beulah Saltz, who was originally my Uncle Sam's secretary and who worked for the Family for seventy years, I had a succession of talented and very likeable secretaries who, I think, despite my unpredictable moods, learned to like and appreciate me. I believe that a bond existed between each of them and me that transcended mutual respect and truly amounted to fondness. Although I was extremely demanding and had such high expectations of them that I even made some of them cry (for which I sincerely apologized), most of them have thanked me for not only having improved their skills, but for having taken a sincere interest in them as human beings. (page 117)

34 Dawson and his wife, Pattie, left Baltimore late in life to be with their children, most of whom lived on the Cape. Before leaving, he stopped by to say goodbye. It was a very sad parting for both of us. He has since died, but not in my memory. (page 127)

35 Recently, I picked up the *The Wall Street Journal* (4/19/12) to read an article titled: "Old Brands Get a Second Shot." The story indicated that the trademark for National Premium Beer – our premier brand, tasting much like a European Pilsner – was sold at auction to a Marylander in 2010 for $1,200. These new efforts to commercialize on what were cherished beers at a time when the Baltimore Orioles were the world champions and the mood of Marylanders was exuberant, are witness to the fact that National, under Jerry's leadership, left an indelible imprint on the minds of Marylanders. (page 130)

36 In March 1995, Merchants Terminal Corporation redeemed all of the preferred and common stocks owned by the Hoffberger Family Fund at their appraised value, totaling $9.2 million. This not only gave the Fund the opportunity to diversify its holdings and increase its income without additional investment risk but it removed a shareholder of Merchants (i.e., the Family Fund) that would not have been a "qualified shareholder" under the proposed provisions of S Corporation Act. My son Douglas became the new president of the Hoffberger Foundation in 2012. I have had the good fortune to observe him in action, and it is clear that he has acquired the skills and experience to lead the Foundation in a meaningful way. (page 152)

37 During the Industrial Revolution in England, factory workers were plied with gin to keep them from complaining about the abominable conditions to which they were subjected. Social reformers of the day coined the phrase, "Drink is the curse of the working class." My comment was intended to be a parody of that saying. (page 156)

COMMUNAL AND PHILANTHROPIC LIFE

38 After about thirty years of successful operation, the building needed renovating, which required the infusion of equity funds. These were provided by the Harry and Jeanette Weinberg Foundation, and the building is now known as "Weinberg House." (page 163)

39 CHAI is the acronym for Comprehensive Housing Assistance Inc. In Hebrew, "chai" means "life." Moreover, each letter in the Hebrew alphabet has a numerical value. The numerical value of the letter "chai" is 18. Therefore, when one sends a contribution to someone on a special occasion like a birthday, he may choose to send $18 (or a multiple thereof). Also, in a toast, one often lifts a glass and says, "L'Chaim!" – "To Life!" (page 163)

40 After the failure of my efforts in the 1980s to gain support for the day school system, the Weinberg Foundation, in response to the 2008 stock market crash that badly affected day school income from tuition and created a crisis in the Orthodox community, pledged to put up $15 million over five years to offset the lost revenue and encourage others to give. The terms of the Weinberg grant required that the community match it with $5 million. The campaign to raise the $5 million has just been concluded, so it appears that this time the campaign has been successful and will be repeated. (page 169)

41 The opening of the Owings Mills Campus resulted in the use of the athletic facilities, as anticipated. However, programming with Jewish content (that both the JCC and the Orthodox community have tried to initiate on the Sabbath) has not, to my knowledge, met with nearly the same degree of enthusiasm. I don't think that anyone ever thought that it would. (page 172)

42 In 2011, at the invitation of David Hoffberger, who has been the Foundation's liaison on the board of the Center, I had the pleasure of attending a session of the two-day event. Hundreds of students from 14 universities debated 15 different cases involving complex moral and ethical questions. Each

team was given three cases on the day of the event and assigned one side of the issue to advocate or defend. I was truly thrilled to see how well the students handled their side of the issue and how serious they were about the moral and ethical issues being debated. Hopefully, the Hoffberger Center is preparing a generation of business and professional persons who will know "right from wrong" when it comes to making meaningful choices in their careers. (page 178)

43 Even after City Hospital's ownership was transferred to Hopkins in the 1980s, Chesapeake Physicians continued to function as the employer of many of the hospital's doctors. (page 186)

44 Long after my chairmanship of City Hospital, in September of 2011, I received a long distance call from a man who introduced himself as Peter Whalen. Peter went on to say that he had created a foundation in his home city of Seattle, Washington called "Invictus," whose purpose was to provide psychiatric help for veterans returning from Iraq and Afghanistan who suffer from post-traumatic stress syndrome. He stated that he was calling to get my advice on fundraising for his cause. I asked how he knew me, and he said that he remembered me from his having served with me in 1980 on the mayor's transition committee that arranged for the transfer of City Hospital to Johns Hopkins. He added that he so admired my thinking and leadership on that occasion that he had held me as a model of what a community leader should be and that he had tried to emulate me in his communal career. Needless to say, I was quite moved by his kind words. (page 188)

45 Seen at this conferring of Honorary Doctorates at MICA on May 11, 2012 are (left to right): Fred Lazarus IV, president of MICA; Sheila Levrant de Bretteville, 2012 Honorary Doctorate; LeRoy E. Hoffberger, 2012 Honorary Doctorate; Joan Waltemath, Director of the LeRoy E. Hoffberger School of Painting, MICA; Ray Allen, Provost, MICA; and Michele Modell, 2010 graduate of the Hoffberger School of Painting and member of the MICA board of trustees. (page 193)

46 Recently, I attended a luncheon at the Hoffberger Graduate School of Painting and was overwhelmed by the imaginative paintings done by the 18 students now attending the school on Hoffberger fellowships. I am told that the eight annual openings per year are applied for by over 240 students worldwide. The school now competes with Yale, Columbia and Chicago for the best young artists who desire graduate degrees. The day was quite an emotional one for me and, I think, for the students who attentively listened to how the school was founded and to my stories about being a collector of German Expressionist art. (page 194)

47 Both of these works I gave to AVAM for its permanent collection. (page 198)

48 The congressional resolution also made AVAM qualified to apply for federal funds, and the museum subsequently received a grant which provided for the training of at-risk students from the nearby Southern High School by master ceramicists. They taught the students to make and install the mosaic tiles now on the outside concrete surfaces of the museum. (page 210)

49 I have now eaten many times in the new restaurant called Mr. Rain's Funhouse, which has fabulous food and a delightful ambiance. (page 212)

50 *The Queen You Thought You Knew* has been published by OU (Orthodox Union). Having read it, I now clearly understand how the two stories tie together in a fascinating way that only David could discover. While, as previously mentioned, some of the material for the book evolved while David was an employee of the Foundation, most of its content was written after he left. Nevertheless, feeling that the Foundation enabled him to develop both his teaching and writing skills, David has written a lovely acknowledgment in the book of my role and that of HFFTS in supporting his work. (page 225)

51 According to Rabbi Fohrman, there are (as of April 2014) about 165 Jewish Day Schools, around the world, using his methodology to teach Torah (the Pentateuch). Of these, two-thirds are Orthodox/Modern Orthodox and one-third non-Orthodox having a total of more than 25,000 students. Rabbi Fohrman teaches, primarily, via his website (alephbeta.org) on which, using audio and animated video formats, he gives lectures on the weekly portion of the Torah being read in synagogue as well as on various Biblical stories. His lectures provide an interpretation of otherwise obscure text, giving it a deeper level of meaning and relate one Biblical story to another revealing their hidden significance to the reader. (page 226)

MY PERSONAL LIFE

52 I owned this boat with Ed Hanrahan, and we kept it at the Gibson Island Club, where he was a member. Since Jews were not accepted as members, I could not use the club's facilities. I used to joke about this, saying, "I have a boat that's a member of the Gibson Island Club, but they won't take me!" (page 243)

53 In about 2007, I learned that Riva's husband, Buddy Robinson, whom I knew, had died several years previously. To my great surprise, one day I received a telephone call from her. Interestingly, I immediately recognized her voice, so it was as if I were picking up where I had left off so many years ago. I actually went to see her in Philadelphia on several occasions and enjoyed being with her. As a very rich widow, she had all the accoutrements that go with wealth – a beautiful estate home, a chauffeur-driven car, an apartment in New York, etc. More interestingly, she had had two children – a son, who is now a lawyer, and a daughter, whose name is Tory Burch. The name "Tory Burch" did not have any meaning to me until Riva told me that her daughter is a highly successful designer of shoes and women's accessories. Although I have never met Tory, I have since read several articles about her and have also noticed her shoes being worn by my granddaughters and daughter-in-law. Riva relished her daughter's success, as she should, and began spending much of her time in New York, hanging out with her daughter and her Hamptons crowd. While I was tempted to accept her many invitations to join in the fun, I decided against it. Not only was her lifestyle too different from what I am now comfortable with, but

having become seriously involved with my now wife, Paula Gately Tillman, I was quite content to live a much more quiet life. (page 243)

54 Douglas has continued his interest in sports and, as a member of the Maryland Club, has become an avid squash player. He has won numerous singles and doubles championships over many years and is admired by his fellow club members. Recently, he and his partner were runners-up in the national men's over-40 squash championship. As for Jack, when playing "war games" over the Internet was a rage throughout the country, he (at age 35) organized a team of fellow enthusiasts of all ages and from various parts of the country. His team, captained by him, competed against over one hundred other teams nationwide for about a year in strategizing "battle tactics" to defeat the enemy. Jack's team won the entire contest, and the team received $50,000 from the sponsors of the competition. (page 266)

55 Actually, Bert's given name was Charles Bertram Hoffberger V. As mentioned earlier, in the greater Hoffberger Family, it was traditional for each firstborn son to be named "Charles," after my grandfather. My older brother, being the fifth of firstborn sons, was therefore named Charles V. Later in life, when all of the firstborn male Hoffberger cousins were in our Family businesses, persons doing business with the Family became confused as to which Charles Hoffberger they were trying to identify. Thus, Bert decided to use his middle name and others either did likewise or acquired nicknames such as Chick, "Reds" Charlie and "Hollywood" Charlie. In these memoirs, I have therefore referred to my older brother as Bert and to the other Charles Hoffbergers by their acquired rather than their given names. (page 269)

56 Stan told me later that "home" was not their old condo but a new one that he had been remodeling to make getting around easier for Judy. She had designed their new bedroom, so Stan (instead of moving her from the hospital to the old condo) moved her into her new bedroom, where she died peacefully. (page 274)

57 Athena feels she has found her niche as the manager of a consignment store in Hampden (a working class neighborhood, now upward bound). Her ambition is to own the store or a similar store, as she delights in the histories and craftsmanship of previously owned furniture and objects. (page 279)

58 The new rabbi's name was Rex Perlmeter. He had interviewed very well, and I was most vocal in expressing my belief that he was the right rabbi to replace a rather uninspiring rabbi who was retiring. Besides, Rex was not only a Princeton graduate, but a member of the same eating club, Tower Club, as I. Notwithstanding any bias that may have created, I truly thought he would inspire a congregation that had in its long history some of the most inspiring spiritual leaders in America. Unfortunately, that did not happen and Rex's tenure was not a long one. (page 280)

59 Bernie Manekin died in 2010 after suffering from dementia. I missed his sitting next to me each Shabbos. One Saturday, I asked Richard Manekin how his father was doing, and he said, "Not well; we don't expect him to live much longer." My response was, "Can I come over and see him?" Richard

replied that I could, but that his father, while not comatose, had not been communicative for several days. I said, "I'm not coming as much to have a conversation with your dad as for my sake." We agreed that I should come at two o'clock that Shabbos afternoon, which I did. I entered Bernie's condo and was greeted by Richard and other members of the family. Bernie was in a hospital bed in the living room and was being attended by a hospice nurse who invited me to his bedside. As I reached Bernie, I bent over and gave him a kiss on his forehead and said, "Hello, Bernie. It's Roy, your old friend." I then sat down in a chair next to the bed which placed my head at the same level as Bernie's. Bernie slowly opened his eyes and without looking over at me, he said, "Roy." Knowing that Bernie had not spoken for several days, the nurse and his family were really startled. I sat there for a few more minutes and then I got up and said goodbye. When I got home, Richard called me to tell me that after I had left, Bernie once again pronounced my name. He died several days later. (page 281)

60 I actually did make the change on the occasion of one of my brother Stanley's visits. He and I went to Levinson's Funeral Home to pick out our and Paula's gravesites in the section reserved for my family at the Baltimore Hebrew Friendship Cemetery. We did so, and upon receiving a written form setting forth the burial details, I said to my brother: "Now Stan, we're good to go." (page 283)

61 A selection of Paula's black and white photographs and archives from Atlanta's late eighties club scene has recently been acquired by the Manuscripts, Archives and Rare Books Library at the Robert Woodruff Library at Emory University in Atlanta. One of Paula's black and white photographs from the late eighties New York downtown club scene has been acquired by the Fales Library, New York University Libraries, New York. In 2012, Paula was invited to serve as a member of the Contemporary Art Accessions Committee of the Baltimore Museum of Art. (page 288)

62 Susan is the editor of the semi-annual publication of *The American Friends of the Jewish Museum, Hohenems*. Paula and I have become friends with her and her retired husband, Zack. (page 291)

63 In fact, I recalled a great deal more than I have chosen to include in these memoirs. (page 298)

INDEX

Note to Readers: Italicized page numbers in the index refer to photographs and other graphic material. Page numbers with an "n" refer to footnotes that appear at the end of the book.